Doctrine

e King James Version of the

may be reproduced, stored in
or by any means, electronic,
without the prior permission
ed in literary reviews.

blication Data

K. Bernard.

dex.

h history. 3. Oneness

95-35396
CIP

M000207648

A
HISTORY of
Christian Doctrine

The Twentieth Century
A.D. 1900 - 2000

Volume 3

A History of Christian
Volume Three

The Twentieth Century
A.D. **1900 – 2000**

by David K. Bernard

©1999 David K. Bernard
Hazelwood, MO 63042-2299
Printing History: 2003, 2007, 2010

All Scripture quotations in this book are from th
Bible unless otherwise identified.

Printed in United States of America

Printed by

WORD AFLAME PRESS
8855 Dunn Road, Hazelwood, MO 63042
www.pentecostalpublishing.com

Library of Congress Cataloging-in-Pu

Bernard, David K., 1956–
    A history of Christian doctrine / by David
       p.   cm.
    Includes bibliographical references and in
    Contents: v. 3. The Twentieth Century,
A.D. 1900–2000.
    ISBN 1-56722-221-8 (pbk.)
    1. Theology, Doctrinal—History. 2. Chur
doctrine (Pentecostalism)—History. I. Title
BT 21.2.B425   1995
230'.09—dc20

Contents

Preface

This book surveys the history of Christian doctrine from A.D. 1900 to 2000. It generally follows chronological order and identifies the most significant events in church history, but the emphasis is on tracing doctrinal developments and controversies. To further this purpose, it discusses some events thematically rather than in strict chronological sequence.

We will use the words *church* and *Christian* in the most general sense, recognizing that the visible church structure is not necessarily the New Testament church as defined by message and experience. We will discuss the major groups of people who have identified themselves as Christian, providing an overview of Christendom in the twentieth century and discussing various doctrines and movements.

We devote special attention to the Pentecostal movement for three reasons: (1) Numerically and theologically, it is the single most important development within twentieth-century Christianity. (2) It contains the most authentic expressions of apostolic Christianity today. (3) Volumes 1 and 2 of this series have examined the basic doctrines of other major groups.

Occasionally material in this book may seem complex and foreign, but some treatment of details is necessary to provide background and to impart a feel for significant issues and problems. The main objective is to introduce the leading historical figures and movements and to convey a basic understanding of their doctrines.

This information will provide various perspectives on biblical issues and will aid in dialogue with people of different backgrounds. The reader will see how God has worked to restore and revive fundamental truths that were largely forgotten.

This book arose out of teaching church history for five years at Jackson College of Ministries in Jackson, Mississippi, and lecturing for the extension program of Kent Christian College in Dover, Delaware. Special thanks goes to Claire Borne for transcribing the taped material, which served as an outline and a partial rough draft.

It is important to remember that only the Bible is our authority for doctrine. We cannot establish spiritual truth by history, tradition, majority opinion, great leaders, or personal experiences, but only by the Word of God.

1

The Pentecostal Movement

The first day of the twentieth century marked the beginning of a new movement in Christianity that would sweep the world in the next hundred years. By century's end, more people would identify with this Pentecostal movement than any other label in Christendom, except for the Roman Catholic Church.

Although the modern Pentecostal movement was a new historical development, spiritually it was not new at all, but it sought to restore the doctrine and experience of the apostles and the first-century church. While in many ways it succeeded, in many ways the majority of adherents have not fulfilled its original promise. But the end is not yet.

The story begins with Charles F. Parham, an independent Holiness preacher and founder of a small Bible school.

He and his students began to study the baptism of the Holy Ghost in the New Testament. To understand their motivation, we must first understand the Holiness movement. Chapter 13 of *A History of Christian Doctrine, Volume 2* discusses the Holiness people and how they set the stage for the Pentecostals; we briefly summarize this information below.

Roots in the Holiness Movement

The Holiness movement arose within conservative Protestantism in America in the latter half of the nineteenth century. It was a revival of the founding principles of Methodism, which developed from the ministry of John Wesley, an eighteenth-century preacher in the Church of England.

The distinctive doctrine of the Holiness movement was Wesley's teaching of entire sanctification, which the Methodists had largely abandoned by this time. According to this doctrine, when a sinner first believes on Jesus, he is converted and justified and receives forgiveness of all sins. He still is dominated by his sinful nature, however, until he receives entire sanctification or Christian perfection. This divine work purifies his motives, desires, and thoughts. He still has the ability to sin, but his inward nature (the sinful nature inherited from Adam) is no longer a source of temptation. Wesley emphasized an ongoing process of sanctification with the goal of Christian perfection, but the later Holiness movement emphasized sanctification as a crisis experience. In essence, the Holiness groups taught that everyone should seek two distinct experiences with God, or works of grace: conversion and sanctification.

As people in the Holiness movement studied the Scriptures, particularly the Book of Acts, they noticed that the disciples were "baptized with the Holy Ghost," and they began to equate entire sanctification with the baptism of the Holy Ghost. They did not necessarily associate this experience with speaking in tongues, although there were some instances of speaking in tongues among them, as among the Methodists earlier.

A number of holiness-minded people in the late nineteenth century began to proclaim an alternate view of holiness. The practical effect was much the same, but the approach was somewhat different. They denied that the inward nature of sin is eradicated in this life, but they proclaimed that by His Spirit God gives Christians power to overcome and suppress the influence of the sinful nature. This view is sometimes called Keswick holiness, after a parish in England where meetings were held to promote the teaching.

Adherents of this position exhorted all Christians to seek a distinct encounter with God's Spirit in which they would receive power for Christian service and power to bear spiritual fruit. It could happen at conversion or afterward. Subsequently, they should live in the "fullness of the Spirit" and participate in the "higher Christian life." These teachers also began to use the scriptural terminology of being "baptized with the Holy Ghost" for this crisis experience.

An American group that was aligned with Keswick thinking was the Christian and Missionary Alliance, an evangelistic organization founded in 1887 by Presbyterian minister A. B. Simpson. He proclaimed a fourfold gospel of Jesus as Savior, sanctifier, healer, and coming

Lord. Many ministers in his organization would enter the Pentecostal movement.

In sum, adherents of both Wesleyan perfectionism and Keswick holiness advocated the life of holiness, but the former stressed the eradication of the sinful nature while the latter stressed the endowment of power to subdue the sinful nature. Both groups used much the same terminology, encouraging people who had repented to seek for a subsequent baptism of the Holy Spirit to give them victory over sin and enable them to do the will of God.

There was a strong call to go back to the doctrines and practices of the apostles in the New Testament church. In describing this desire, the adjective "Pentecostal" became common, and a rallying cry was, "Back to Pentecost." Some leaders began to press for the restoration of spiritual gifts, including prophecy, healing, and miracles. A minority of Holiness people, including the Fire-Baptized Holiness Church, began to seek for the "baptism of the Holy Ghost and fire" as a third crisis experience, but again not associating it with tongues.

Charles Parham and the Topeka Outpouring

In this atmosphere, Charles Fox Parham (1873-1929) opened Bethel Bible College in Topeka, Kansas, on October 15, 1900, at age twenty-seven. At the end of the first term, Parham asked his students to find the biblical evidence for the baptism of the Holy Ghost. Together they concluded that the initial evidence is speaking in tongues (foreign languages unknown to the speakers) as the Spirit gives utterance. (See Acts 2:4; 10:45-46; 19:6.)

Parham conducted prayer meetings with his students as the twentieth century dawned. On the evening of January

1, 1901, Agnes Ozman (1870-1937), a "city missionary" in Topeka and a student at the Bible school, asked Parham to lay hands on her that she might receive the Holy Spirit. When he did, she began to speak in tongues. On January 3, Parham, his wife, and twelve ministerial students also received the Holy Spirit with the sign of tongues.

The new Pentecostals concluded that the experience they had received was something more than what the Holiness movement had taught. Parham thought of it as a third crisis experience, as expressed in the common testimony of early Pentecostals: "Thank God, I am saved, sanctified, and filled with the Holy Ghost." He believed it was an endowment of power for service, and at first he thought that speaking in tongues would assist in foreign missions efforts.

Parham called his new group the Apostolic Faith movement, and he published a periodical called *The Apostolic Faith*. The group conducted meetings in Kansas and Missouri but did not grow rapidly at first. A significant breakthrough came in the fall of 1903 in Galena, Kansas. A woman from the town was almost completely blind from an eye disease. After she was instantly healed in one of Parham's services in Eldorado Springs, Missouri, she invited him to conduct meetings in Galena. There, more than eight hundred people were baptized in water, many hundreds received the Holy Ghost, and at least one thousand people testified that they were healed.

A convert in this revival was Howard Goss (1883-1964), who would become one of the founders of the Assemblies of God and later the first general superintendent of the United Pentecostal Church. He was an "infidel" (atheist) when he visited Parham's meeting. He testified, "This was my first contact . . . with Christianity of any sort. . . . I feel that I owe my conversion to Christianity to hearing people speak in other tongues."[1]

In the aftermath of this revival, Parham started several churches in Kansas, Missouri, and Oklahoma. He established headquarters for his movement in Baxter Springs, Kansas, a small town near Galena.

In 1905 Parham received an invitation to hold services in Orchard, Texas, about forty miles west of Houston. Many people were converted. Revival spread throughout the countryside and to Houston, where Parham conducted services in a downtown auditorium. The movement enjoyed great success there after a well-known woman was healed and raised from a wheelchair. Due to the tremendous response, Parham soon opened a short-term Bible school in Houston.

Goss came to Houston as a student worker, although he had not yet received the Holy Ghost. In April 1906, he and sixteen others received the Holy Ghost as they rode a train from Orchard to Alvin, Texas. Goss spoke in tongues for one week; it was two weeks before he could preach in English. Revival continued to spread throughout the Houston area and elsewhere in the state. Parham soon appointed Goss as field supervisor of the work in Texas.

In 1907 a controversy arose among some of the newer workers in Texas as to whether speaking in tongues was invariably the initial evidence of the Spirit baptism or simply one of the nine gifts of the Spirit. After a debate in Waco, the group was convinced that tongues was the initial evidence. Some of them, however, decided to seek confirmation at a revival in San Antonio. Pentecost had not yet come to that city; no one there had preached on tongues as the initial evidence. The group conducted their revival by preaching the baptism of the Holy Ghost but never mentioning tongues or any other "evidence." Goss reported the outcome: "No seeker was expecting any unusual manifestation. But, it made no difference. They all likewise spoke in tongues as the Spirit gave utterance when they received the Holy Ghost. This satisfied even the most skeptical among us."[2]

In 1906 Parham brought the Pentecostal message to Zion City, Illinois. This town was a religious community near Chicago founded by John Alexander Dowie, a prominent healing evangelist and the organizer of a Holiness group he called the Christian Catholic Church. Dowie had recently been discredited because of gross financial mismanagement, authoritarianism, and increasingly eccentric behavior, and he had lost control of his movement. Parham converted many of his followers to the Pentecostal message, including many ministers. The new leaders, however, resisted him vigorously.

From Parham's revivals in Kansas and Texas, the Apostolic Faith movement grew to about 13,000 people in 1906.[3] By 1908, there were about 25,000 adherents under Parham's leadership.[4]

Parham's Doctrine

Charles Parham upheld most of the doctrines of conservative Protestantism, including the inspiration and infallibility of Scripture, the trinity, the existence of angels and demons, the creation and fall of humanity, the Incarnation and Atonement, salvation by grace through faith in Jesus Christ, and the Second Coming. He took

the Wesleyan, Arminian view of grace, rejecting unconditional election and unconditional eternal security.

Like the Holiness movement, he proclaimed sanctification as a second work of grace and emphasized the
need for a holy life. As part of his teaching on holiness,
he advocated pacifism, holding that it was wrong to kill
another human being, even in war.

Like the Fundamentalists, Parham believed strongly
in the soon return of Jesus Christ to earth before the
Millennium. In his understanding, the end-time events
would occur in the following order: the Tribulation, the
Rapture, the Second Coming, the Millennium, and the
White Throne Judgment. He practiced a literal interpretation of Scripture.

In addition to the baptism of the Holy Ghost with the
initial sign of tongues, Parham also believed in the supernatural gifts of the Spirit. As a young preacher, he had
received a dramatic healing, and he believed so strongly
in divine healing that he did not use medicine. Even on
his deathbed, he refused a nurse's offer to give him pain
medication.

In a few areas, Parham embraced doctrines that
were not generally accepted in Protestantism or in
the Pentecostal movement. He taught British-Israelism:
the British and their descendants were the lost tribes
of Israel and would literally inherit God's promises to
Israel. He also taught annihilation: the lost would not
exist eternally in the lake of fire but would be completely destroyed. When accused of not believing in hell,
he replied that he believed in hell more than his critics;
he believed in a hell so hot it would completely burn up
those who went there. He also thought that some pagans

could inherit life on the new earth rather than destruction in the lake of fire if they lived a good life according to the knowledge they had.

Parham attached tremendous significance to the baptism of the Holy Spirit. He held it to be the fulfillment of Joel's prophecy of the latter rain, a sign of the soon coming of the Lord, the baptism that gives people full entrance into the church, a vital endowment of power that will enable the church to evangelize the world before the Lord's return, and the seal of protection during the Tribulation. It is the "full gospel" and "full salvation."[5]

Twenty-one days after the Holy Ghost outpouring, Parham preached a message in Kansas City, Missouri, that explained his views:[6]

> When the power of Pentecost came, we found the real, and everyone who has received the Baptism of the Holy Spirit has again spoken in tongues. . . .
>
> Thousands of Christians profess . . . the Baptism of the Holy Ghost, yet the Bible evidence is lacking in their lives. . . .
>
> If you desire a personal Baptism of the Holy Ghost, the sealing power, escaping plagues, and putting you in the position to become a part of the Body, the Bride or the Man-Child, seek the Holy Ghost.
>
> It is the Baptism of the Holy Spirit of promise, that seals the Bride and the same Baptism that puts us in one Body, (the Church). . . .
>
> Speaking in other tongues is an inseparable part of the Baptism of the Holy Spirit distinguishing it from all previous works; and . . . no one has received

Baptism of the Holy Spirit who has not a Bible evidence to show for it. . . .

Speaking with new tongues . . . [is] the only Bible sign given as the evidence of the Baptism of the Holy Ghost.

Parham equated "the sealing of the Holy Spirit of promise (which is evidenced by the speaking tongues)" with being "baptized by the Holy Ghost into one Body, the gloriously redeemed Church."[7] People who believe on Jesus can be saved in a lesser sense without this experience, but they will endure the rigors of the Tribulation. If they receive "the seal of the Holy Ghost," they will "escape the power of the Anti-Christ as well as the plagues and wraths." But "should you fail in the reception of a personal Pentecost you will be compelled to either accept the mark of the Beast or suffer martyrdom."[8]

Moreover, in eternity believers who do not receive the Spirit will inhabit the new earth rather than the new heavens. "Jesus [will] take out a people for His name, through sanctification, being born of the water and the Spirit, they see the Kingdom of God; Christ having given Himself for the Church." The church will receive "eternal spiritual life and immortality" in the "new heavens." By contrast, Christians who are "unsanctified" as well as "many heathens" will merely receive "everlasting human life" on "the new earth."[9]

In 1902, Parham published the foregoing message and teachings in a book entitled *A Voice Crying in the Wilderness*. In the same book, Parham also wrote that years earlier God had impressed upon him the importance of water baptism. Under the influence of Quaker teaching he had not practiced baptism, but one day God spoke to him about obeying all His commands. Parham specifically thought of the command to be baptized in Acts 2:38, and he was baptized the next day. Sometime later, however, he was persuaded that "triune immersion"—triple immersion with the trinitarian formula—was correct.

After opening his Bible school but apparently before the outpouring of the Holy Spirit, Parham realized that triune immersion was not scriptural. Thus, he began baptizing converts by single immersion in the name of Jesus Christ, and he associated this practice with confessing the deity of Christ, in contrast to liberal theology. Here is Parham's account:[10]

> For years after entering the ministry, we taught no special baptism of water, believing the Baptism of the Holy Spirit the only essential one; having been marvelously anointed from time to time and received the anointing that abideth, we put the question of water baptism aside.
>
> One day, meditating alone in the woods, the Spirit said:—Have you obeyed every command you believe to be in the Word of God?
>
> We answered, yes; the question repeated, the same answer given. The third time the question was asked, we answered, no,—for like a flood the convincing evidence of the necessity of obedience rushed in upon us, how Peter said, Repent, and be baptized every one of you in the name of Jesus Christ [Acts 2:38]. Was not this one baptism?
>
> Then came the second; and ye shall receive the gift of the Holy Ghost. Again Peter proceeded at

once to baptize Cornelius and all his house, who had received the Baptism of the Holy Spirit, with the Bible evidence of speaking in tongues. Thrusting aside all arguments, he said:

Can any man forbid water, that these should be baptized, which have received the Holy Ghost as well as we. (Acts 10:47.)

Paul did not recognize the baptism of John to repentance as sufficient, but baptized them in the name of the Lord Jesus Christ before he would lay hands upon them that they might receive the baptism of the Holy Spirit.

These and other Scriptures were so convincing that the next day we were baptized by single immersion.

Years afterward, through reading many arguments and discussions on triune immersion, [we] were intellectually persuaded that it was right, and persuaded many of God's children to be baptized by this mode, although we were never baptized by triune immersion.

About two years ago [1900], however, we found that for which we had searched . . . the cleansing of all unscriptural teachings. . . . We can well remember when we sought God in this cleansing, how some of the teachings we had believed to be so Scriptural and some we had loved so dearly and been the most preserving in propagating, were wiped from our minds.

Among them was triune immersion; though we had been able to discuss this question for an hour, we could not afterward find a single argument in its favor. Indeed, for months nothing, pro or con came upon the subject; until one day at the Bible School, we were waiting upon God that we might know the Scriptural teaching of water baptism. Finally the Spirit of God said: "We are buried by baptism into His death." We had known that for years; again the Spirit said: "God the Father, and God the Holy Ghost never died."

Then how quickly we recognized the fact that we could not be buried by baptism in the name of the Father, and in the name of the Holy Ghost, because it stood for nothing as they never died or were resurrected. . . .

So if you desire to witness a public confession of a clean conscience toward God and man, faith in the divinity of Jesus Christ, you will be baptized by single immersion, signifying the death, burial and resurrection; being baptized in the name of Jesus, into the name of the Father, Son and Holy Ghost; they are one when in Christ you become one with all.

Howard Goss testified that Parham baptized him in the name of Jesus Christ in 1903.[11] Parham published the foregoing account again in 1910, indicating that perhaps he was still baptizing in Jesus' name at that time. As many ministers entered the growing movement, however, for the sake of unity Parham reverted to the traditional trinitarian formula. When the Jesus Name controversy erupted, Parham affirmed trinitarian theology and denounced the Oneness movement.

William Seymour and the Azusa Street Revival

One of Parham's students in Houston was William Joseph Seymour (1870-1922), a black Holiness minister who was blind in one eye. Born in Louisiana, he now lived in Houston. In early 1906, Seymour traveled to Los Angeles in response to an invitation from a small Holiness church there.

Seymour preached the Pentecostal message in Los Angeles, even though he had not yet received the Holy Ghost. The leader of the church rejected this doctrine and locked Seymour out of the building. (She later joined the movement, however.) He continued services in the homes of two sympathetic families: first in the home of Edward Lee, where he stayed, and then in the Asberry home on Bonnie Brae Street.

On April 9, Lee received the Holy Spirit at his home while praying with Seymour and Lucy Farrow. Farrow was a black Holiness pastor in Houston who had entered the Pentecostal movement through Parham, and she had introduced Seymour to Parham. She was very effective in laying hands on people and praying for them to receive the Holy Ghost, and she had come to Los Angeles to help Seymour achieve a breakthrough.

That night, at the service on Bonnie Brae, when Seymour related what had just happened to Lee, the Holy Ghost fell. Jennie Moore, who later married Seymour, and several others received the Holy Ghost. Three days later, Seymour and others also received the Spirit.

The small group rented an old, two-story building on Azusa Street in downtown Los Angeles and began services on April 15. The Azusa Street Mission held services daily for three years, from 1906 to 1909. Many miracles, healings, and baptisms of the Holy Spirit occurred. There were documented accounts of the dead being raised.[12] The meetings were characterized by spontaneous, demonstrative worship and strong moves of the Spirit. They were racially integrated, an amazing development in that segregated, prejudiced time. Frank Bartleman (1871-1936), a Holiness evangelist and the foremost chronicler of the revival, wrote, "The 'color line' was washed away in the blood."[13] Blacks and whites, men and women, served in public leadership and ministry roles.

While Parham and his students initiated the twentieth-century Pentecostal movement, it was the Azusa Street revival that spread the Pentecostal message throughout the world. In September 1906, Seymour began publishing the news of the revival in a paper called *The Apostolic Faith*, which was widely disseminated in the Holiness movement and elsewhere. Missionaries, ministers, and lay members from across the United States and around the world flocked to Los Angeles, received the Holy Spirit, and carried the message everywhere. Many who could not attend nevertheless read the news of the revival and sought and received the same experience for themselves.

On April 18, 1906, *The Los Angeles Times* published its first report of the revival.[14] The article was entitled "Weird Babel of Tongues," with these subtitles: "New Sect of Fanatics Is Breaking Loose. Wild Scene Last Night on Azusa Street. Gurgle of Wordless Talk by a Sister." The first paragraph stated:

> Breathing strange utterances and mouthing a creed which it would seem no sane mortal could understand, the newest religious sect has started in Los Angeles. Meetings are held in a tumble-down shack on Azusa street, near San Pedro street, and the devotees of the weird doctrine practice the most fanatical rites,

preach the wildest theories and work themselves into a state of mad excitement in their peculiar zeal.

Later in the day, a special edition of the newspaper featured the great San Francisco earthquake, in which it reported that 452 lives were lost. It included the following article on the front page:

Much strange phenomena was witnessed by this reporter at the Azusa Street Mission yesterday, as I was there for the Sunday morning worship service.

The sight that greeted my eyes as I entered into the small building seemed to be commonplace enough. The old wood-slatted pews seated about twenty people, mostly from the lower scale of the social ladder. There were a couple of the parishioners that seemed to be of the wealthier class, however.

All of these faced the black man standing behind the slender wooden pulpit.

The "worship" began with prayer; prayer that was conducted in a manner totally strange to me. All hands were uplifted and the parishioners began to audibly speak the requests, interspersing them, with much cries of "Amen," "hallelujah," and "praise the Lord."

The singing was also different, as loud, boisterous numbers were sung in place of the conventional hymns. I was shocked to my Sunday School roots as the people left their seats and began jumping up and down, and running around the church building.

At one point during the sermon, a hush fell over the congregation and an elderly man began to utter strange guttural sounds. This, of course, was the much discussed "glossolalia," the supposed speaking in tongues as evidence of the Holy Spirit.

Surprisingly enough, after the sermon, the people seemed normal enough, socializing and speaking of everyday life. I found the pastor, Brother Seymour, to be a very affable fellow.

What is my conclusion?

Well, the worship was shockingly different, unlike anything I had ever seen before. It would be easy to say that it is conceived of by Satan himself. However, since the reports of happenings at the Azusa Street Mission are spreading like wildfire all over southern California, we shall let time be the judge.

Frank Bartleman, who had also attended meetings in the Lee home and in the Asberry home on Bonnie Brae Street, wrote vivid accounts of the Azusa Street Mission. He later described the worship as follows:[15]

> The Spirit dropped the "heavenly chorus" into my soul. I found myself suddenly joining the rest who had received this supernatural "gift." It was a spontaneous manifestation and rapture no earthly tongue can describe. . . . It was indeed a "new song," in the Spirit. . . . It was sometimes without words, other times in "tongues." The effect was wonderful on the people. It brought a heavenly atmosphere. . . .
>
> In the beginning in "Azusa" we had no musical instruments. In fact we felt no need of them. . . . All was spontaneous. . . . All the old well-known hymns were sung from memory, quickened by the Spirit of

God. "The Comforter Has Come" was possibly the one most sung. We sang it from fresh, powerful heart experience. Oh, how the power of God filled and thrilled us. Then the "blood" songs were very popular. . . . The "new song" was altogether different, not of human composition.

Brother Seymour generally sat behind two empty shoe boxes, one on top of the other. He usually kept his head inside the top one during the meeting, in prayer. There was no pride there. The services ran almost continuously. Seeking souls could be found under the power almost any hour, night and day. The place was never closed nor empty. The people came to meet God. . . .

No subjects or sermons were announced ahead of time, and no special speakers for such an hour. No one knew what might be coming, what God would do. All was spontaneous, ordered of the Spirit. . . .

When we first reached the meeting we avoided as much as possible human contact and greeting. We wanted to meet God first. We got our head under some bench in the corner in prayer, and met men only in the Spirit, knowing them "after the flesh" no more. The meetings started themselves, spontaneously, in testimony, praise and worship. . . .

Someone might be speaking. Suddenly the Spirit would fall upon the congregation. God himself would give the altar call. Men would fall all over the house, like the slain in battle, or rush for the altar en masse, to seek God.

The Apostolic Faith contained the following description in the November 1906 issue:[16]

Here you find a mighty pentecostal revival going on from ten o'clock in the morning till about twelve at night. . . .

There is such power in the preaching of the Word in the Spirit that people are shaken on the benches. Coming to the altar, many fall prostrate under the power of God, and often come out speaking in tongues. Sometimes the power falls on people and they are wrought upon by the Spirit during testimony or preaching and receive Bible experiences. . . .

The demonstrations are not the shouting, clapping or jumping so often seen in camp meetings. There is a shaking such as the early Quakers had and which the old Methodists called the "jerks." It is while under the power of the Spirit you see the hands raised and hear speaking in tongues. While one sings a song learned from heaven with a shining face, the tears will be trickling down other faces. Many receive the Spirit through the laying on of hands. . . .

Little children from eight years to twelve stand upon the altar bench and testify to the baptism with the Holy Ghost and speak in tongues. In the children's meetings little tots get down and seek the Lord.

It is noticeable how free all nationalities feel. . . . No instrument that God can use is rejected on account of color or dress or lack of education. . . .

The singing is characterized by freedom. . . . Often one will rise and sing a familiar song in a new tongue.

Doctrine of the
Azusa Street Mission

The October 1907 to January 1908 issue of *The*

Apostolic Faith identified the following seven teachings as "the principles of the doctrine of Christ":[17]

1. Repentance.
2. Faith in our Lord and Saviour Jesus Christ.
3. Water baptism.
4. Sanctification.
5. The baptism with the Holy Spirit.
6. Second coming of our Lord Jesus Christ.
7. Final white throne judgment.

The original statement of faith published by the mission listed and discussed six topics: repentance, faith, justification, sanctification, the baptism with the Holy Ghost, and healing. Three of them were distinct crisis experiences with God and part of full salvation:[18]

First Work.—Justification is that act of God's free grace by which we receive remission of sins. Acts 10:42, 43. Rom. 3:25.

Second Work.—Sanctification is the second work of grace and the last work of grace. Sanctification is that act of God's free grace by which He makes us holy. . . . Sanctification is cleansing to make holy. . . .

The Baptism with the Holy Ghost is a gift of power upon the sanctified life; so when we get it we have the same evidence as the Disciples received on the Day of Pentecost (Acts 2:3, 4), in speaking in new tongues.

While the Azusa Street participants considered that a person was "saved" by the "first work" of grace, before sanctification and the baptism of the Holy Ghost, they spoke of all three experiences as part of "Bible salvation." The headline and subheading at the top of the first issue of *The Apostolic Faith* reads: "Pentecost Has Come: Los Angeles Being Visited by a Revival of Bible Salvation and Pentecost as Recorded in the Book of Acts."[19] The November 1906 edition of *The Apostolic Faith* describes the baptism of the Holy Ghost as "the real Bible salvation," "the mark of the prize of the high calling in Christ Jesus," and "heaven in our souls."[20] In 1908, William Seymour wrote, "If you are sanctified and baptized with the Holy Ghost and fire, you are married to Him already. God has a people to measure up to the Bible standard in this great salvation. Bless His holy name. Amen!"[21]

Following Parham, Seymour frequently cited the parable of the ten virgins to emphasize the importance of the baptism of the Holy Ghost. In his application, the oil of the five wise virgins is the Holy Ghost. Thus, only people who have been baptized with the Holy Ghost will go up in the Rapture and enjoy the marriage supper of the Lamb. Christians who have not received the Holy Ghost will have to endure the Tribulation and be martyred. He explained:[22]

> Those that will be permitted to enter in [the marriage supper of the Lamb] are those who are justified, sanctified, and baptized with the Holy Ghost—sealed unto the day of redemption. . . . Above all, we want to get the oil, the Holy Ghost. Every Christian must be baptized with the Holy Ghost for himself. . . . Now is the time to buy the oil; that is, by tarrying at the feet of the Lord Jesus and receiving the baptism with the Holy Spirit. . . .

Those that get left in the rapture and still prove faithful to God and do not receive the mark of the beast, though they will have to suffer martyrdom, will be raised to reign with Christ. . . . By proving faithful to death, they will be raised during the millennium and reign with Christ. But we that are caught up to the marriage supper of the Lamb will escape the plagues that are coming on the earth. . . .

Dearly beloved, the only people that will meet our Lord and Savior Jesus Christ and go with Him into the marriage supper of the Lamb, are the wise virgins— not only saved and sanctified, with pure and clean hearts, but having the baptism with the Holy Ghost.

Articles in *The Apostolic Faith* affirmed that people who continued to walk with God would receive the message and experience of the Holy Ghost and warned that those who rejected this message and experience could be lost:[23]

- Friends, if you profess to know the Spirit of God and do not recognize Him when He comes, there is cause for you to be anxious about your own spiritual condition.
- Men and women that are walking in the light can quickly see that this is of God.
- Many church members are paying their way to hell. They are paying preachers to preach against the baptism with the Holy Ghost. They are getting poisoned against the truth and it is damning their souls. People need the baptism with the Holy Ghost that they may know God.

- After the white throne judgment, we are going to see men and women who have scorned this holiness and baptism, and they will be cast down into the burning hell. . . . O, accept this salvation.
- How will you miss hell if you stumble over this precious Gospel, if you ignore this Gospel which God has granted signs and wonders to follow?

Azusa Street participants spoke of the baptism of the Holy Ghost as the decisive turning point in their lives. Although they identified previous experiences of conversion and sanctification, their testimonies typically described the baptism of the Holy Ghost as the time they experienced the full saving power of Jesus Christ:[24]

- Adolph Rosa (Portugese Methodist minister from Cape Verde Islands): "All pride, and self, and conceit disappeared, and I was really dead to the world, for I had Christ within in His fullness."
- William Durham (prominent pastor in Chicago): "Then I had such power on me and in me as I never had before. And last but not least, I had a depth of love and sweetness in my soul that I had never even dreamed of before, and a holy calm possessed me, and a holy joy and peace, that is deep and sweet beyond anything I ever experienced before, even in the sanctified life. And O! such victory as He gives me all the time."
- Maggie Geddis: "O the love, joy, and peace that flooded my being as I arose from the floor. I was indeed a new creature."
- C. H. Mason (founder of the Church of God in

Christ): "This was wedlock to Christ. . . . He had complete charge of me. . . . It was a complete death to me. . . . The glory of God filled the temple."

When Mason attended Azusa Street, he went to the altar in response to a call for sinners to be justified, even though he was a leader in his Holiness denomination. He explained his thought at the time: "It may be that I am not converted, and if not, God knows and can convert me."[25]

The Azusa Street Mission affirmed that the "Bible evidence" of baptism with the Holy Ghost is speaking in tongues. Seymour wrote in 1907, "Beloved, when we receive the baptism with the Holy Ghost and fire, we surely will speak in tongues as the Spirit gives utterance. We are not seeking for tongues, but we are seeking the baptism with the Holy Ghost and fire."[26] There were many reports of people from other countries coming to Azusa Street and hearing their native languages spoken by people who received the Holy Ghost. There were also reports of people seeing flames of fire and clouds of glory.

The Azusa Street Mission did not believe in baptismal regeneration, but it emphasized the necessity of practicing water baptism as a commandment of the Lord, and it considered water baptism to be part of the "full Gospel":[27]

Baptism is not a saving ordinance, but it is essential because it is a command of our Lord. Mark 16:16, and Acts 2:38. . . . It is obedience to the command of Jesus, following saving faith. We believe every true believer will practice it. . . .

It should be administered by a disciple who is baptized with the Holy Ghost and fire, in the name of the Father, Son, and Holy Ghost. Matt. 28:19-20. . . .

We believe that we should teach God's people to observe all things whatsoever He has commanded us [Matthew 28:20], practicing every command and living by every word that proceedeth out of the mouth of God. This is a full Gospel.

The foregoing statement reflects the use of the trinitarian baptismal formula. However, at least some converts from Azusa Street were baptized in the name of Jesus. By March 1907 a minister named Joshua Sykes founded a Pentecostal church in Los Angeles that required baptism in the name of Christ rather than the trinitarian formula.[28] The official history of the Apostolic Assembly of the Faith in Christ Jesus, a Mexican-American Oneness Pentecostal organization, states that a man named Luis Lopez received the Holy Spirit at Azusa Street and was baptized in the name of Jesus in 1909.[29] When controversy later arose over the baptismal formula, however, Seymour affirmed trinitarianism and the trinitarian baptismal formula, but he continued to have some fellowship with Jesus Name believers.[30]

True to their Holiness heritage, the new Pentecostals emphasized a life of holiness both inwardly and outwardly. One article said, "[Jesus] saves you from telling stories, from gambling, playing cards, going to horse races, drinking whiskey or beer, cheating, and everything that is sinful or devilish. The Lord Jesus Christ will cleanse you and make you every whit whole."[31] Another article testified of two women who discarded their jewelry after being convicted by the Spirit, and it concluded, "So the Spirit has been working in harmony with the Word, teaching His people how to dress according to the Bible. Gold watches, rings, etc. have disappeared, and gone into sending the Gospel."[32] Seymour admonished, "O beloved, after you have received the light, it is holiness or hell. God is calling for men and women in these days that will live a holy life free from sin."[33]

The Decline of Parham and Seymour

After ministering in Zion City, Parham visited the Azusa Street Mission in late 1906 at the invitation of Seymour, who initially acknowledged him as originator of the movement.[34] Parham felt that the worship manifestations were excessive, however, and overly influenced by blacks. While he acknowledged that many people were genuinely receiving the Holy Spirit at Azusa, he denounced the mission for "extremes, wild-fire, fanaticism," and false manifestations.[35] Apparently, he was affected by racial prejudice and also resented that the revival was not under his direction. At this point, Seymour rejected Parham's leadership completely.

The next year, in July 1907, Parham was arrested in San Antonio, Texas, on a moral charge.[36] Although the charge was soon dropped, his enemies publicized the incident, particularly the leadership in Zion. Parham soon lost most of his following and influence. He continued his evangelistic ministry from his home base in Baxter Springs, Kansas. To his death in 1929, Parham was sidelined from the leadership of the movement he had initiated. A small group remained faithful to him and exists today as the Apostolic Faith, centered around a Bible college in Baxter Springs.

Perhaps in an effort to distance themselves from

Parham, other leaders began to describe themselves as Pentecostal more than Apostolic. Eventually, the term "Apostolic" came to be used primarily for Oneness Pentecostals. In particular, it is the preferred term among Oneness groups that are predominately black or Hispanic.

Florence Crawford (1872-1936), an Azusa Street member in 1906, started the Apostolic Faith Mission in Portland, Oregon, in 1908 as a rival organization to Seymour's. She disapproved of Seymour's marriage to Jennie Moore and felt that Seymour was not emphasizing the doctrine of sanctification as he should. She took Seymour's mailing list, thereby shutting down his paper, and she started her own paper, also called *The Apostolic Faith*. Her group exists today as a small organization. Following her teaching, it has been known over the years for advocating strict holiness of conduct and dress and separation from those who do not.

Seymour's struggles with Parham, Crawford, and William Durham (discussed in chapter 2) eroded his leadership role. The revival at Azusa Street dwindled in 1909, picked up again in 1911 with the preaching of Durham, and then diminished again in 1912. Most of the whites left the mission, and in 1915 Seymour changed the constitution of the church to specify that a "person of color" must always be the leader. He also moved away from the doctrine of tongues as the initial evidence of the Holy Spirit, holding that tongues did not always come immediately, although it was still expected as a sign that would follow Holy Spirit baptism. After Seymour's death in 1922, his wife carried on as pastor until her health failed. The building was demolished in 1931.

Opposition and Persecution

The early Pentecostals encountered all kinds of opposition and persecution. The existing denominations—especially Holiness groups and Fundamentalists—typically forced them out, denounced them, ridiculed them as "Holy Rollers," and said they were of the devil. Prominent Holiness leaders said the Pentecostal movement was "the last vomit of Satan," "emphatically not of God," "wicked and adulterous," "anti-Christian," "sensual and devilish."[37] Others called the movement "heresy" and a "cult."[38] Pentecostal workers were threatened, beaten, shot at, tarred and feathered. They were pelted with rocks and with rotten fruit, vegetables, and eggs. Tents ropes were slashed; tents and buildings were set afire. Howard Goss explained:[39]

> We could never be sure we were not going to be injured. Some workers were attacked, some were beaten, some had bones broken, some were jailed, some were made to leave town, some were rotten egged, and some were shot at. We were stoned, but at least we were never "sawn asunder."
>
> Church services were disturbed by roughnecks for many years. Tents, buildings, and sometimes residences were burned; drinking water was poisoned, and windows were broken. We were sometimes threatened by angry mobs or by raging individuals when some member of their family had been converted. Often, we had no protection; there were times when the police chose to close their eyes because we were the strangers, while the city paid them a salary.

Many of the early Pentecostal preachers sacrificed

greatly to spread the gospel. They lived by faith and started churches in tents, brush arbors, storefronts, and rented halls. Non-Pentecostal historian Robert Mapes Anderson described their hardships:[40]

> These lived often in extreme poverty, going out with little or no money, seldom knowing where they would spend the night, or how they would get their next meal, sleeping in barns, tents and parks, or on the wooden benches of mission halls, and sometimes in jail. Bands of workers would pool their funds, buy a tent or rent a hall, and live communally in the meeting place, subsisting at times on flour and water, or rice, or sardines and sausages. . . . The Pentecostals found their chief asset in the spirit of sacrifice and the enormous drive of their leaders.

Conclusions

The ministry and teaching of Charles Parham was the immediate cause of the Pentecostal movement. The distinctive message that he and his students introduced was *the baptism of the Holy Ghost with the initial evidence of speaking in tongues.*

As volumes 1 and 2 of this series document, this occasion was by no means the first time since Bible days that someone had received the Holy Spirit with the evidence of speaking in tongues. But it was the first recorded time in modern church history when people sought for and received the Holy Spirit with the *expectation* of speaking in tongues. The biblical knowledge and expectation of the evidentiary role of tongues is what set this movement apart from earlier outpourings of the Spirit and led directly to

Pentecostalism as a distinct movement. The Pentecostals also differed from recipients in earlier times by proclaiming this experience as the *norm* and urging everyone to receive it. Without this doctrine of tongues as the initial evidence of receiving the Holy Ghost, the modern Pentecostal movement would not have begun.

William Seymour is equally significant for the history of the movement. The Azusa Street revival that he led became the impetus for *the worldwide spread of Pentecostalism*. Although Seymour's influence rapidly diminished after 1911, almost every Pentecostal organization in the world owes its existence, directly or indirectly, to Seymour's Azusa Street Mission in Los Angeles.

The Pentecostal movement was a logical, scriptural extension of the ideas of the Protestant Reformation of the 1500s, the Methodist revival of the 1700s, and the Holiness movement of the 1800s. It was the next step in the restoration of apostolic doctrine and experience to professing Christendom.

Modern Pentecostalism did not originate solely with one person, and it quickly grew beyond any one person's leadership. Parham and then Seymour played vital roles in the formative years, but the restoration of biblical doctrine and experience occurred in a group setting. Interestingly, neither Parham nor Seymour was the first in his own group to receive the Holy Spirit. Many leaders quickly emerged, the movement proliferated by a spiritual spontaneous combustion, and no central human authority was able to shape, direct, or control it. It was not the creation of an individual, but it was the sovereign move of God in response to the spiritual hunger and quest of thousands of sincere believers.

2

The Finished Work Controversy

The first doctrinal division in the Pentecostal movement came over sanctification. Both Parham and Seymour embraced the Wesleyan-Holiness position that sanctification was a second work of grace, and they added the baptism of the Holy Spirit as a third experience. They taught that a person first had to be converted, or justified. Then he needed to be sanctified, at which time he was instantly purified from inward sin. Then and only then, he could be baptized with the Holy Spirit. Before we discuss the doctrinal division, let us trace the formation of several other important Pentecostal groups that advocated this teaching.

G. B. Cashwell, Revival in the South, and the Pentecostal Holiness Church

One of the most notable examples of the spread of Pentecostalism from the Azusa Street revival is the story of Gaston Barnabas Cashwell (1862-1916), a prominent minister of the Holiness Church of North Carolina, which later became known as the Pentecostal Holiness Church. After receiving the Holy Spirit at Azusa Street in late 1906, Cashwell returned to North Carolina and began to preach the Pentecostal message in Dunn, his hometown.

A great revival took place, attended by many ministers, and it lasted for the month of January 1907. Many ministers, denominational leaders, and lay members received the Holy Ghost. As a result, four small Holiness organizations in the South became Pentecostal: the Pentecostal Holiness Church, the Fire-Baptized Holiness Church, the Tabernacle Pentecostal Church, and the Free Will Baptist Church. The first three soon merged, and the resulting organization is now called the International Pentecostal Holiness Church. The fourth group became known as the Pentecostal Free Will Baptist Church.

One of the men who received the Holy Spirit under Cashwell was Joseph H. King (1869-1946), general overseer of the Fire-Baptized Holiness Church (beginning in 1900) and later bishop of the Pentecostal Holiness Church until his death. Previously, the Fire-Baptized Holiness Church, founded by Benjamin Irwin in 1895, had taught a "third blessing" beyond justification and sanctification called the "baptism of fire." Now it identified the baptism of the Holy Ghost with tongues as the third blessing.

Future founders of the Assemblies of God, M. M.

Pinson and H. G. Rodgers, also received the Holy Ghost under Cashwell's ministry. Because of his widespread impact, Cashwell became known as the apostle of Pentecost to the South. He later left the Pentecostal Holiness Church due to political conflict, however, and continued his ministry in his previous organization, the Methodist Church.

A. J. Tomlinson and the Church of God

In January 1908, Ambrose Jessup Tomlinson (1865-1943), the general overseer of the Church of God, invited Cashwell to speak to the leaders of the organization in Cleveland, Tennessee. While Cashwell was preaching, Tomlinson received the Holy Spirit, falling to the floor and speaking in tongues. Thereafter, this group also became Pentecostal.

The Church of God had been founded in 1886 by R. G. Spurling as a Holiness organization originally called the Christian Union and later the Holiness Church. In 1896, a great revival took place in the Shearer Schoolhouse in Cherokee County, North Carolina. About 130 persons received the Holy Spirit with tongues, and many healings took place. However, this experience did not become a doctrine, nor did the group as a whole seek it. When the Pentecostal movement became widely known in 1906, many people in the Church of God began to seek the baptism of the Holy Spirit with tongues and to preach it.

In 1907 the organization became officially known as the Church of God, a name already in use by another Holiness organization that never adopted the Pentecostal message. To avoid confusion, the two groups are identified by their headquarters. The Pentecostal group is the Church of God (Cleveland, Tennessee), while the non-Pentecostal group is the Church of God (Anderson, Indiana).

In 1914 Tomlinson was elected general overseer for life, but due to dissatisfaction with his authoritarian leadership, he was replaced in 1923. He refused to accept his removal and led a split, which he regarded as the true church. Ultimately, it became known as the Church of God of Prophecy, which also has headquarters in Cleveland, Tennessee.

C. H. Mason and the Church of God in Christ

Charles Harrison Mason (1866-1961) founded the Church of God in Christ in 1897 as a Holiness organization, along with his friend, C. P. Jones. Both were black Baptist pastors who embraced the doctrine of entire sanctification. In 1907 Mason visited Azusa Street and received the Holy Spirit. While Mason was away from his home church in Memphis, Glenn Cook, the business manager of the Azusa Street Mission, preached at Mason's church and won many people in his organization to the Pentecostal message.

Jones and a majority of leaders rejected the Pentecostal doctrine, however, and expelled Mason and his followers. The non-Pentecostals reorganized as the Churches of Christ (Holiness), which remains today as a small group. The Pentecostals reorganized in 1907 as the Church of God in Christ with Mason as general overseer and chief apostle, an office he held until his death in 1961. The Church of God in Christ is the largest Pentecostal body— and one of the largest black Protestant bodies—in North America.

Due to the Holiness roots of most black trinitarian Pentecostal groups, they are commonly known in the black community as "sanctified" churches.

William Durham and the Finished Work Doctrine

Shortly after the great Azusa Street revival, a prominent minister named William H. Durham (1873-1912) began to question whether sanctification was actually a separate experience. Durham was a Baptist who had a conversion experience in 1898. Under the influence of Holiness teaching, for three years he sought for a definite experience of sanctification. Finally, in 1901, he had an experience that he identified as sanctification, and he began to teach sanctification as a second work of grace.

Durham soon started a ministry in Chicago called the North Avenue Mission. Influenced by Charles Parham, who was preaching in nearby Zion, Illinois, many of the members of Durham's mission received the Holy Ghost. Durham became convinced that this experience was genuine. In early 1907 he visited the Azusa Street revival in Los Angeles and received the Holy Ghost on March 2.

By his own testimony, Durham came to three important conclusions during this time.[41] First, the baptism of the Holy Ghost was different from the experiences that he had identified as conversion and sanctification. "I saw clearly, for the first time, the difference between having the influence and presence of the Spirit with us, and having Him dwell within us in person."

Second, he realized that he could not simply "claim" the baptism of the Holy Ghost as did the Holiness people who equated it with entire sanctification. "I could not kneel at the altar, and claim the Holy Ghost and go away.

This was a real experience. I must wait until He came."

Third, speaking in tongues was invariably the initial evidence of this experience. "Dear reader, the Spirit may not deal with you just as He did with me; but when He comes within you, to take up His abode, He will speak in tongues and magnify God."

Durham's baptism in the Holy Spirit was glorious. He fell prostrate on the floor for three hours, his whole body shook one section at a time, and finally he spoke in tongues for a long time. This experience completely overshadowed his 1901 blessing. He concluded that sanctification was not a separate work of grace subsequent to conversion but that the baptism of the Holy Ghost with the sign of tongues was the true experience that a converted person should seek. He reinterpreted his 1901 experience as a renewal of his conversion in 1898.

From the time he received the Holy Ghost, Durham could never again preach on sanctification as a separate work of grace. Instead, "the Spirit began to reveal in my heart the finished work of Christ on the Cross of Calvary. . . . The Spirit kept revealing in my heart the precious Gospel as preached by the Apostles: identification with Jesus Christ in His death, burial and resurrection."[42]

In 1910, Durham began to preach what he called "the finished work of Calvary." He taught that there was no second work known as sanctification. Instead, sanctification is an integral part of conversion and an ongoing process. To be holy, we do not need to seek a second work of grace, but we simply need to appropriate the benefits of the finished work of Calvary. We can begin living the sanctified life immediately by realizing that with His blood Jesus purchased everything we need. He explained, "The living faith that justifies a man, brings him into Christ, the Sanctifier, in Whom he is complete, not with regard to sanctification only, but everything else that pertains to his salvation."[43]

Durham objected that the "second work of grace theory has done more to blind the eyes of people to the simple truth of the Gospel than any other one theory," because it had led many "truly saved people" to believe they were not saved until they received the second work. "They are told that when God pardoned them He left them full of sin and corruption, and that it requires a second work of grace to save them from hell." In reality, when a person repents and believes, he "is saved from sin, death, and hell, is a real child of God, possesses eternal life, does not need another work of grace, but needs to abide in Christ, receive and walk in the Spirit, hold fast the faith, grow in grace and in the knowledge of God and of Christ."[44]

At conversion, the believer not only receives justification (forgiveness of sins) but also sanctification (purity of heart). "God in conversion brings a man into Christ and makes him holy by washing away all his sins, inward and outward, and giving him a new, clean heart, thus making a new creature out of him."[45]

To Durham, the doctrine of a second work of grace detracted from the gospel and the Atonement by implying that Christ's atoning sacrifice was not powerful enough to deal completely with a person's sin when he repented and believed. Thus he insisted, "The Finished Work is by far the most important teaching in the Bible."[46]

The Controversy Erupts

Durham first proclaimed the Finished Work message

at a Pentecostal convention in Chicago in 1910. Also in 1910, he conducted a camp meeting in Malvern, Arkansas, where Howard Goss was pastor at the time. He convinced Goss and many of Parham's former followers of the truth of his message. Controversy erupted immediately.

In 1911, Durham went back to Los Angeles. The focus of revival there had shifted from the Azusa Street Mission to Elmer Fisher's Upper Room Mission. Durham sought to preach there, but because of the controversy, Fisher refused to let him. Durham then went to the Azusa Street Mission. Seymour was away on an extended trip, and Durham was allowed to preach.

A great revival broke out, reminding the participants of Azusa Street in its heyday in 1906-09. Many called it the second Azusa outpouring. Frank Bartleman wrote that it was the second shower of the latter rain. In less than three months, over 150 received the Spirit, many backsliders were renewed, and notable healings took place. Durham attributed the success to his emphasis on tongues as the initial evidence of the Holy Ghost (which Seymour was no longer stressing) and on the Finished Work message.[47]

When Seymour returned, however, he objected to Durham's doctrine and, taking a cue from his own experience, padlocked the door of the mission so that Durham could not continue services there. Durham responded just as Seymour had five years earlier. He started his own services at Seventh and Los Angeles Streets, and the revival continued. His assistants at this time were Harry Van Loon and Frank J. Ewart. After a few months, Durham returned to Chicago, leaving his new Los Angeles mission in their hands.

The Finished Work message spread rapidly through revival services and also through a periodical that Durham published called the *Pentecostal Testimony*. Durham's preaching was powerful, and his message inspired great faith. Four hundred people received the Holy Spirit under his personal ministry in 1911 and two hundred in the first three months of 1912.[48]

The major leaders of the Pentecostal movement at the time all opposed Durham, however, including Parham, Seymour, Cashwell, Mason, and Tomlinson. They held that the Spirit could not come upon an unsanctified life, meaning that a person first had to receive sanctification as a definite, instantaneous, second work of grace. It was commonly stated that the Holy Ghost would not fill an unclean vessel (which many have erroneously thought to be a biblical quotation), referring not to repentance but to entire sanctification.

Florence Crawford labeled Durham's teaching as "a devilish theory from the pit of hell." Parham accused Durham of "counting the blood of the covenant an unholy thing" and having "committed the sin unto death." He prophesied Durham's destruction within six months, saying that whichever one of them taught false doctrine, God would kill him.[49]

Durham vigorously defended his message, preaching everywhere, taking little rest, and damaging his health in the process. At age thirty-nine, he contracted pneumonia and died in Los Angeles on July 7, 1912, within the six months proclaimed by Parham. When he heard that Durham had died, Parham commented, "How signally God has answered."

Opponents typically accused Durham of abandoning

the message of holiness, but E. N. Bell, later the first chairman of the Assemblies of God, wrote in his defense shortly after his death, "He was much misunderstood. No one among us believed more firmly than he in Bible holiness, nor insisted more strongly that without holiness no man could see the Lord, holding it as God's only standard for all believers."[50]

Durham himself asserted that "God's one standard is entire sanctification." He affirmed the importance of "growth after conversion" and living "a holy, separate life." He taught that God expects Spirit-filled believers "to live a clean, holy, separate life, to crucify the flesh, and walk in the Spirit."[51]

Durham's Doctrine of Full Salvation

The Finished Work doctrine had implications for the baptism of the Holy Spirit as well as for sanctification. If sanctification was not a second work of grace but began at conversion as the believer appropriated the benefits of the Cross, then what about the baptism of the Holy Spirit? Was it a second work of grace, or was it too associated with conversion?

Durham continued to regard the baptism of the Holy Spirit as a second crisis experience following conversion. Since sanctification had no initial objective sign, it was easy for him to collapse it back into his previous encounter with God at repentance. But the baptism of the Spirit was an overwhelming emotional and spiritual experience, and it came with the initial sign of speaking in tongues. Durham knew it was more than what he had received previously, which he had already identified as conversion, so he did not equate the two.

Nevertheless, Durham did begin to speak of the baptism of the Holy Ghost as an integral part of God's plan of salvation that should immediately follow repentance and faith. Since all that believers needed to do was to appropriate the finished work of Calvary, they could receive the Spirit without delay.

Durham's personal testimony revealed that he considered people to be saved from hell at the initial moment of faith, yet God's plan was for them to complete their salvation experience with water baptism and the baptism of the Holy Spirit:[52]

> Faith instantly sprang up in my heart to accept Him as my full Savior, and the moment I did so, I felt the quickening power of the Spirit, was made a new creature in Christ, and unutterable joy filled my soul. . . .
>
> I had no one to tell me that the next step was to be buried with Him, in Whom I had died and had been made alive. Had I been taught the truth, as the Apostles taught it, had I been baptized and had hands laid on me, I would have at once received the Holy Ghost. . . .
>
> My greatest difficulty was in harmonizing my experience with that in the Acts of the Apostles. My difficulty was, that I mistook soul rest and peace, and the sweet holy joy of salvation, and the witness, and influence of the Spirit, for the gift of the Spirit. . . .

For Durham, "God's glorious message of full salvation," the "Full Gospel," and God's "plan of salvation" included the baptism of the Holy Ghost.[53] Indeed,

Durham insisted quite strongly that to belong to the New Testament church, a person had to be baptized with the Holy Spirit with the evidence of speaking in tongues:[54]

> The baptism in the Holy Spirit is the seal of a finished salvation in Jesus Christ. . . .
>
> God's standard of the baptism in the Holy Spirit is found in Acts 2:4, and He has only one standard.
>
> The Church of Jesus Christ is composed of Pentecostal people. . . .
>
> We have an abnormal Christianity in the world today (that is, those we must recognize as Christians, but who are not filled with the Holy Spirit) for which it is impossible to find any Scriptural provision. In other words, only Spirit-filled people are recognized as being in a place that they are pleasing to God. Wherever we find converts in the New Testament who are not filled with the Holy Spirit, we find the Apostles dealing with them to lead them into the experience.
>
> We conclude, therefore, that a Church, from a Scriptural standpoint, is a company of people who are called out of the world, made new creatures in Christ Jesus, buried with Him by baptism into death, and filled with the Holy Spirit. . . .
>
> The denominational churches of today are of purely human origin. Not one of them has any Scriptural authority for its existence. . . . As said above, people become members of Christ's true, holy, spiritual Church when they are born of the Spirit and filled with the Spirit, as this is the only normal Scriptural experience.

Durham saw Acts 2:38 as the paradigm for New Testament salvation. He quoted this verse on the masthead of his *Pentecostal Testimony*. In a widely distributed tract entitled *Salvation in Christ for All*, he wrote:

> If the Bible teaches anything it is that salvation is by grace through faith. . . .
> The question then is: How may a man receive this great blessing of full deliverance through Christ? Acts 2:38-39 tells us: [quotation]. . . . This is a wonderful truth! Men do not have to join any particular church, nor subscribe to any creed of man, but can be saved eternally by simply repenting and believing on the Lord Jesus Christ; and then they can receive the gift of the Holy Ghost with signs following, as in the days of the Apostles.

He said the three steps of Acts 2:38—repentance, water baptism, and the baptism of the Holy Ghost—were God's standard of salvation. By these steps a person identified with the death, burial, and resurrection of Jesus Christ:[55]

> When we appeal the case to the Scriptures, we see that They teach to repent and be baptized and receive the gift of the Holy Spirit. Acts 2:38-39. All through the Acts and the Epistles of Paul, we see this order of teaching. Not one single Scripture ever mentions any second work of grace. But the rule laid down by Peter on the day of Pentecost is continually followed, both in teaching and practice. . . .
> The Epistles were written for the instruction of

those who had received the Holy Spirit according to the standard of God lifted up in Acts 2:4. . . .

Peter's answer [in Acts 2:38] forever settles the question as to what the standard of God is. . . .

We are identified with Him by faith in His death on the Cross, and in His burial, by our immersion in water; and in His glorious resurrection life by the blessed Holy Spirit, Who is supposed to come upon us when we come up out of the water. And, thank God, we have lived to see the blessed day that He has restored the Scriptural order of things, and the Spirit is falling on thousands and they are speaking in tongues as at the beginning.

A prominent Fundamentalist preacher, A. C. Dixon, once met with Durham and asked what his distinctive doctrine was. Durham told him it was speaking in tongues as the initial evidence of the Holy Ghost. Dixon exclaimed that by this doctrine he indicted all Christendom, whereupon Durham solemnly replied, "Sir, they deserve to be indicted."[56]

Durham died before the Oneness movement began, but Ewart believed he would have received the Jesus Name message had he lived. He was a trinitarian, but according to one report he performed at least one baptism in Jesus' name.[57] He placed great emphasis on the name, person, and work of Jesus Christ:[58]

- Christ is all and in all. As we yield to the Holy Ghost, we will see more in Him and less in everything else. If there is no other name under Heaven, whereby men can be saved, we ought to constantly proclaim that blessed name in all the earth.

- Not in even one place in the New Testament is it ever taught that there is any other way of salvation except through Jesus Christ. Over and over again it is declared that there is no other way, no name except His great name that has salvation in it.

The Outcome of the Controversy

The Finished Work doctrine split the emerging Pentecostal movement in half. In general, the organizations that had already formed by 1910 rejected Durham's message, while the organizations that formed after 1910 embraced his message.

The groups who rejected the Finished Work message and continued to teach three crisis experiences included the Apostolic Faith groups of Charles Parham, William Seymour, and Florence Crawford; the Pentecostal Holiness Church; the Church of God (Cleveland, Tennessee) and its later offshoot, the Church of God of Prophecy; and the Church of God in Christ.

The Pentecostal groups that accepted the Finished Work view included the Assemblies of God and the International Church of the Foursquare Gospel. The Oneness groups, including the United Pentecostal Church International and the Pentecostal Assemblies of the World, also accepted the Finished Work. Indeed, as we shall see in chapter 4, their doctrine of the new birth appears to be a logical development from the premises that Durham championed.

A few small Oneness groups, offshoots of the Holiness movement or of the Church of God in Christ, teach sanctification as a second work of grace. The largest Oneness organization to do so is the Apostolic Overcoming Holy Church of God, which was founded in 1917 by William T. Phillips (1893-1974), a black Holiness minister in Alabama.

Among trinitarians, a significant practical difference emerged around mid-century between the Second Work and Finished Work churches. Originally, all Pentecostals emphasized holiness of life, including standards of conduct and dress. In the 1940s through 1960s, however, the Assemblies of God began to relax its stand in these areas, but the Second Work groups were much slower to abandon them. It was not until 1988, for example, that the Church of God (Cleveland, Tennessee) officially deleted its rules against makeup, jewelry, movies, and women cutting their hair.

In the United States, about half of Pentecostals today belong to Finished Work groups. In the rest of the world, the vast majority of Pentecostals hold to the Finished Work doctrine. Even among the Second Work groups, the doctrine of sanctification as a second work of grace is rarely emphasized today, being mostly overshadowed by the baptism of the Holy Ghost.[59] To a great extent, then, Durham's views have prevailed everywhere.

Why did the Finished Work message gain such widespread acceptance? Why did it become the wave of the future? We can identify three major reasons.

First, as the Pentecostal revival exploded, many converts came directly from a life of sin without claiming a prior experience of sanctification. While people such as Parham and Seymour had sought and received definite experiences with God years before the outpouring of the Holy Ghost, many new believers had not. At Azusa Street, for example, sinners often repented and then immediately received the Holy Ghost. Some were filled with the Spirit immediately after having demons cast out of them. *The Apostolic Faith* published accounts of people who were saved, sanctified, and filled with the Holy Ghost all in one service. For more and more people, the theory of three crisis experiences did not fit the reality of what happened to them.

Second, many of the men who became leaders in the Pentecostal movement after 1910 did not come from a Wesleyan-Holiness background. For instance, Durham, Ewart, and Bell were former Baptists. They had been taught the standard Protestant view of sanctification as a progressive, ongoing work throughout a Christian's life.

Third, the Finished Work position has the stronger biblical support. Holiness people had equated entire sanctification with the baptism of the Holy Spirit, but when early Pentecostals differentiated the two, there were no clear examples in the New Testament of people receiving sanctification as a distinct, instantaneous work. Moreover, the Epistles present sanctification as beginning at conversion (the new birth) and continuing throughout the Christian's life.

For instance, Paul wrote that at our conversion we were washed, sanctified, and justified in the name of the Lord Jesus and by the Spirit of God (I Corinthians 6:11). Everyone in the church is already "sanctified in Christ Jesus," yet we are all "called to be saints," that is, sanctified ones (I Corinthians 1:2). The implication is that sanctification is our lifelong identity, calling, and pursuit as Christians.

Sanctification is instantaneous at the new birth in

that we are immediately cleansed and set apart from sin and given a holy nature. The old nature still resides within us, however. Therefore, sanctification must also be progressive. We must continue to pursue holiness (sanctification) unto the coming of the Lord (Hebrews 12:14). As we walk in the Spirit, we become more and more like Christ and less and less like the world. "But we all, with unveiled face, beholding as in a mirror the glory of the Lord, are being transformed into the same image from glory to glory, just as by the Spirit of the Lord" (II Corinthians 3:18, NKJV). The ultimate goal of this process of sanctification is perfection at the coming of the Lord: "Now may the God of peace Himself sanctify you completely; and may your whole spirit, soul, and body be preserved blameless at the coming of our Lord Jesus Christ" (I Thessalonians 5:23, NKJV).

Conclusions

Despite his short Pentecostal ministry of five years, William Durham was a powerful, unusually anointed preacher who exerted tremendous and lasting influence within the developing Pentecostal movement. The Finished Work doctrine was not unique to him, of course. In a general sense it was characteristic of mainline Protestant theology. A century before, most Methodists had abandoned the idea of sanctification as a second work of grace, and some non-Pentecostal contemporaries of Durham in the Holiness movement had formulated essentially the same doctrine in their own context. Nevertheless, Durham almost single-handedly introduced this message to Pentecostals, redirected the course of the movement, and broadened its theological appeal. As a result, the majority of Pentecostals adopted basically the Keswick position of two experiences—conversion and baptism of the Holy Spirit as an endowment of power—yet with the important distinction of tongues as the initial evidence of the Spirit.

Of equal importance is the contribution that Durham made toward the development of the Jesus Name movement. Although he died a little over one year before its emergence, he set the stage for Oneness Pentecostal theology in several important ways:

1. He taught that we can receive all the benefits of the Atonement by repentance and faith, without waiting for a subsequent experience. While he retained the idea of two experiences (conversion and Spirit baptism), he acknowledged that when there is full scriptural understanding and faith we can expect the baptism of the Spirit to come immediately.

2. While some Pentecostals during and after his day sought to modify the distinctive doctrine of the Holy Ghost baptism, Durham staunchly affirmed the original teaching of Parham and Seymour that receiving the Holy Ghost is necessary to enter into the New Testament church and that speaking in tongues is the initial evidence.

3. He established Acts 2:38 as the paradigm for New Testament salvation, and he equated the three steps of repentance, water baptism, and the baptism of the Holy Ghost with the death, burial, and resurrection of Jesus Christ.

4. He stressed the importance of water baptism, and he exalted the name of Jesus.

5. He had a major influence on future leaders of the

Oneness movement. Many of his ministerial colleagues were soon baptized in Jesus' name, including Harry Van Loon, R. E. McAlister, and A. H. Argue. As chapter 3 discusses, the most prominent early proponent of the Oneness message was Durham's associate and successor, Frank J. Ewart.

3

The Jesus Name Controversy

The second doctrinal division in the Pentecostal movement came over water baptism in the name of Jesus Christ and the oneness of God. The Oneness doctrine affirms that God is one personal being, not a trinity of persons, and that Jesus Christ is the manifestation of the fullness of God, not just one of three persons. (See Deuteronomy 6:4; Colossians 2:9; I Timothy 3:16.)

Trinitarians called this belief "the New Issue" and "Jesus Only," the latter because proponents baptized in the name of Jesus only instead of using the traditional trinitarian formula. Some trinitarians, however, began to use this label to accuse Oneness believers of denying the Father and the Holy Spirit. For this reason, most Oneness believers eventually rejected the designation "Jesus Only,"

and today they generally regard it as an unfair mischarac-
terization. Instead, they call themselves Apostolic, Jesus
Name, or Oneness Pentecostals.

Historical Roots

The Oneness doctrine did not arise in a vacuum. As
volumes 1 and 2 of *A History of Christian Doctrine* discuss, throughout history many Christians have baptized
in the name of Jesus, and many have promoted a concept
of God that is essentially the same as the Oneness view.
There is no historical link between these earlier groups
and Oneness Pentecostals, however.

We do find roots of Oneness thinking in American
revivalism of the eighteenth century and in the Holiness
movement of the nineteenth century. These movements
were characterized by a strong devotion to Jesus Christ
and frequent use of the name of Jesus in prayer, praise,
testimony, and song. In a way, as Episcopalian priest
David Reed has argued, the Oneness doctrine was a
theological expression of the practical piety of American
revivalism, Holiness groups, and the earliest Pentecostals.[60]

In these movements, there was also a strong impulse
toward restorationism, that is, restoring the message and
experience of the apostles and the first-century church.
Indeed the entire Pentecostal movement was based on
restorationist thinking. Given this focus, it was only a
matter of time until people began to realize that the apostles always baptized in Jesus' name and never spoke of
God in the terms of fourth-century trinitarian orthodoxy,
and further to see these points as doctrinally significant.

In this regard, Edith Blumhofer, an Assemblies of God

scholar, wrote in an official history of her church:[61]

> The doctrinal departure aside, if one admits the strong restorationist component at the heart of the definition of Pentecostalism, Oneness proponents were more zealously restorationist, more doggedly congregational, and more Christocentrically spiritual—in short, in some important ways more essentially Pentecostal than the mainstream.

Walter Hollenweger, secretary of evangelism for the World Council of Churches, similarly commented that the Oneness doctrine "is more in accordance with religious feeling and practice of Pentecostalism than a doctrine of the Trinity taken over without understanding from the traditional churches."[62]

Another important factor was the baptism of the Holy Spirit. When the early Pentecostals were baptized with the Holy Ghost, they no longer had a theoretical concept of God but a direct, personal experience. They did not receive three divine spirits, but one Spirit. They did not encounter various divine persons or have multiple relationships with the Godhead, but they had an intensely personal relationship with one God.

Moreover, the Holy Spirit came upon them as they exalted Jesus Christ and the Atonement. For example, in the Azusa Street revival, some of the most popular hymns were "There Is Power in the Blood" and "Under the Blood." Participants were challenged not merely to preach "the baptism with the Holy Spirit" but "Christ in the power of the baptism."[63] The baptism of the Holy Spirit actually intensified their focus on Jesus Christ.

Finally, they received illumination from the Holy Spirit. Jesus promised, "But the Comforter, which is the Holy Ghost, whom the Father will send in my name, he shall teach you all things, and bring all things to your remembrance, whatsoever I have said unto you. . . . When he, the Spirit of truth, is come, he will guide you into all truth . . . He shall glorify me: for he shall receive of mine, and shall show it unto you" (John 14:26; 16:13-14). The indwelling Spirit played a vital role in helping them to understand and rediscover biblical truth, including truth about the oneness of God and the full deity of Jesus Christ.

Thus, it is no surprise that Charles Parham, the catalyst for the entire Pentecostal movement, began to baptize in Jesus' name after the pattern of the Book of Acts. We have also seen that some people in Los Angeles were baptized in Jesus' name during the Azusa Street revival, and perhaps some people under Durham's ministry in Chicago were also. Gary McGee, an Assemblies of God scholar, discovered that a missionary in Latin America baptized in Jesus' name in 1904.[64]

Another early example was Andrew D. Urshan (1884-1967), an immigrant from Persia (Iran) who received the Holy Ghost in Chicago in 1908. He established a Persian mission there and was ordained by William Durham in 1910. That same year, he came to a new understanding of truth as he pondered the question: Why did the apostles always baptize in the name of Jesus in the Book of Acts when Jesus Himself had instructed them to baptize in the name of the Father, Son, and Holy Ghost in Matthew 28:19? As he meditated on this matter, Acts 4:12 came to his attention, and he concluded that the Lord Jesus Christ was "the one name of the Father, Son, and Holy Ghost":

> The blessed Lord showed me then and there, that "The Lord Jesus Christ" is the ONE PROPER NAME of God for this gospel dispensation; because in Him, Jesus Christ, Our Lord, all the fullness of the Godhead dwelt; and to Him, all power in heaven and earth, was given; that repentance and remission of sins should be preached everywhere in Jesus' Name ONLY. [See Colossians 2:9; Matthew 28:18; Luke 24:47.]

He called this new understanding "a wonderful revelation of the Triunity in Christ" and "a blessed revelation of Christ's absolute deity." He did not mean an extrabiblical revelation, however, but as he explained when he first received the Holy Ghost, "The scriptures were illuminated to my soul as never before, by the Blessed Holy Spirit, who faithfully brought to my remembrance, with new meaning, that which I had read years ago and made it fresh as the morning dew." As a result of his study, in 1910 Urshan printed Acts 2:38 on the side of his baptismal tank and began to baptize all new converts "into the name of the Lord Jesus Christ."[65]

The Worldwide Camp Meeting, Arroyo Seco, 1913

These early examples of baptism in Jesus' name did not lead to the formation of the Oneness movement, however. The events that ultimately resulted in controversy and division began with the Worldwide Apostolic Faith Camp Meeting organized by R. J. Scott and George Studd and held at Arroyo Seco near Los Angeles, on a campground used by the Azusa Street Mission. The month-long meeting began on April 15, 1913, and perhaps two thousand people attended.

The main speaker was Maria Woodworth-Etter (1844-1924), a well-known Holiness evangelist who had embraced the Pentecostal message. Expectations were high, and they were fulfilled, for 364 people received the Holy Spirit. Many miracles of healing took place as Woodworth-Etter prayed "in the name of Jesus."

Of particular significance to the future of Oneness Pentecostalism was the message of Robert E. McAlister (1880-1953), a Canadian preacher who had received the Holy Spirit at Azusa Street in 1906. Speaking at a baptismal service, he explained that single immersion was the proper mode for baptism, not triple immersion as some people practiced. As proof he cited the baptismal accounts in the Book of Acts. The apostles baptized in the name of the Lord Jesus Christ; they never baptized using the words "Father, Son, and Holy Ghost," as triple immersion requires.

At this, "an inaudible shudder" swept over the congregation, and McAlister fell momentarily silent.[66] A missionary to China named Frank Denny leaped to the platform, pulled McAlister aside and asked him not to teach this doctrine, because it would associate him with a certain minister named Sykes who was currently baptizing in that manner. (See chapter 1.) McAlister then explained that it was not wrong to baptize using the words of Matthew 28:19.

McAlister's observation that the apostles always baptized in Jesus' name planted a seed in the minds of several people that day. A man named John Schaepe (1870-1939) was so inspired by this thought that he spent the night in prayer. Early the next morning he began running through the camp shouting that he had received a revelation of the power of the name of Jesus. Quite a few of the campers were greatly stirred as Schaepe fervently explained his newfound understanding.

Detractors sometimes say that Schaepe founded the Oneness movement and that he did so by an extrabiblical revelation. Actually, little is known of Schaepe (pronounced "Sheppy" and sometimes misspelled "Scheppe"). In 1919 he was listed as a minister with the Pentecostal Assemblies of the World, a Oneness organization, but he did not play a significant role in the movement after 1913.

As the quotations in this chapter from Andrew Urshan, Frank Ewart, and Frank Small show, early Pentecostals used the term "revelation" to refer to the illumination of Scripture by the Holy Spirit. David Reed has accurately noted, "'Revelation' was primarily a term used by Oneness exponents to describe the subjective confirmation of the objectively stated truth in the Bible."[67] From the beginning, Oneness believers appealed to Scripture as the authority for their doctrine and rejected the idea of extrabiblical revelation. They believed that the Holy Spirit had helped them rediscover and understand biblical truths that had long been neglected.

Frank Ewart and the Oneness of God

Another man who was deeply impressed by McAlister's message was Frank J. Ewart (pronounced "You-ert") (1876-1947). A Baptist bush missionary in Australia, he immigrated to Canada in 1903 and became a pastor there. The Baptists dismissed him when he received the Holy Spirit in 1908 under Florence Crawford in Portland, Oregon. In 1911 he became the assistant pastor to William Durham's mission in Los Angeles, and when Durham died in 1912, Ewart became the pastor.

Ewart had been studying the name and oneness of God for some time, so McAlister's comments were especially intriguing to him. Ewart invited him to his home, and they began to discuss the implications of using the name of Jesus in water baptism. McAlister suggested that the words "Lord" (meaning master), "Jesus," and "Christ" (meaning "Anointed One") represented "Father, Son, Holy Ghost" respectively. Therefore, when the apostles baptized in the name of the Lord Jesus Christ, they fulfilled Matthew 28:19.

After the camp meeting, Ewart left the pastorate of his church and began a new work in Los Angeles with McAlister and Glenn Cook (1867-1948). Cook had been the full-time business manager of the Azusa Street Mission under Seymour. By this time, he was a noted evangelist, having brought the Pentecostal message to Indianapolis and to the Church of God in Christ in Memphis. He had also conducted successful campaigns in Oklahoma, Missouri, and Arkansas.

Ewart and McAlister continued their study of the name of Jesus and the doctrine of God, and they included Cook in their discussions. After several months McAlister returned to Canada and shared his thinking with ministers there, particularly Franklin Small (1873-1961). Small was one of the first people in Winnipeg, Manitoba, Canada, to receive the Holy Spirit in 1907. He became an assistant pastor in Winnipeg to A. H. Argue, who had received the Holy Spirit under Durham.

In Los Angeles, Ewart merged his work with that of Elmer Fisher and continued working with Fisher and his associate, A. G. Garr. (Garr was the first white pastor to receive the Holy Ghost at Azusa Street and the first Pentecostal missionary to India and Hong Kong.) Ewart occasionally preached on the power of the name of Jesus and was astonished by the tremendous results in healings and Spirit baptisms. Fisher and Garr urged Ewart to continue preaching on the name of Jesus, but they were opposed to baptizing in Jesus' name.

In November 1913, at the eighth annual Pentecostal convention in Winnipeg, McAlister preached the first sermon on the exclusive use of the name of Jesus in water baptism. Frank Small was asked to take charge of the baptismal service, and he baptized thirty new converts in the name of Jesus Christ. These were the first Jesus Name baptisms to result from the Arroyo Seco camp meeting.

Ewart eventually decided that he needed to take a clear stand for water baptism in the name of Jesus Christ. He concluded that the essential name to use in baptism was Jesus and that the titles of Lord and Christ could be added.[68] Moreover, he concluded that this practice had great significance regarding the doctrine of God. The apostles baptized in Jesus' name because the Father, Son, and Holy Ghost are not three distinct persons but three manifestations of one God, and Jesus is the revelation of the Father, Son, and Holy Ghost. The reason why there is such power when believers preach, pray, and baptize in Jesus' name, is that the fullness of the Godhead dwells in Jesus.

Because of his new convictions, Ewart parted company with Fisher and Garr. He pitched a tent (which Fisher helped him obtain) and began meetings in Belvedere, California, just outside Los Angeles. Glenn Cook agreed with Ewart's message, and they decided to work together. On April 15, 1914—exactly one year after the Arroyo Seco camp meeting began—Ewart preached his first sermon on Acts 2:38. He proclaimed that the full message of salvation consists of repentance, water baptism in Jesus' name, and the baptism of the Holy Ghost, and he associated baptism in Jesus' name with the oneness of God in Christ. Then Ewart baptized Cook in the name of Jesus Christ, and Cook baptized Ewart. This action—the first rebaptisms in the name of Jesus Christ—was the decisive step in starting Oneness Pentecostalism as a distinct movement.

Frank Small, quoted with approval by Ewart, later explained the doctrinal significance of rebaptism in Jesus' name:[69]

Through the illumination of Scripture, the new message had resolved itself into the fullness of God in Christ (II Corinthians 5:19; I Thessalonians 5:18; I Timothy 3:16). This teaching developed in Los Angeles. It might be stated that until this time, the message of water baptism in the Name of Jesus had been based on record only. We knew beyond a shadow of a doubt that the apostles had baptized in the Name of Jesus, but we still did not fully understand *why*. But, in due time when complete scriptural revelation came, the absolute fullness of God in Christ was proven. Out of the development of this truth came the act of re-baptizing converts who had previously been baptized using the titles Father, Son, and Holy Ghost.

The Spread of the Jesus Name Message
A great revival broke out under Ewart and Cook in the Los Angeles area. Ewart reported:[70]

> All kinds of incurable diseases were healed in the Name of Jesus, and people were filled with the Holy Ghost, speaking in other tongues.
>
> One of the greatest, most startling characteristics of that great revival was that the vast majority of the new converts were filled with the Holy Ghost after coming up out of the water. They would leave the tank speaking in other tongues. Many were healed when they were baptized.

Many missionaries and preachers came to the meetings and were rebaptized in Jesus' name. Even more significantly, Ewart's periodical, *Meat in Due Season*, carried the Jesus Name message and reports of the revival far and wide. Many more people were touched and converted by the paper than by the revival itself. Missionaries to China, Japan, and India were soon baptized in Jesus' name.

During this revival, Ewart endured much opposition from local church people as well as from a gang of hoodlums. The latter threatened him and his wife on numerous occasions, planted "stink bombs" in the services, and even burned down the tent. The town constable did nothing to protect them, but the persecution ended when the gang leader was converted. Ewart had to go to court several times on charges of disturbing the peace, as the Baptists complained against his meetings.

In 1919, when Ewart established a permanent church in the Los Angeles area, he would sometimes baptize as many as fifty people in one service. He recorded two thousand names on the baptismal roll before he stopped counting for fear that God would not be pleased.[71]

Cook embarked upon an evangelistic campaign in 1914 to bring the Jesus Name message to the Midwest, where he had earlier brought the Pentecostal message. In St. Louis, he baptized "Mother" Mary Moise, who administrated a home for the downtrodden; her associate, "Mother" Barnes; and Ben Pemberton, a young minister under her. In Indianapolis, Cook baptized two influential pastors, L. V. Roberts and Garfield T. Haywood, and they baptized their congregations. A total of 465 people were baptized in Jesus' name in Indianapolis, in the first such event east of the Mississippi River.

The baptism of Haywood (1880-1931) was particularly significant. He was the black pastor of a large interracial congregation, an extremely influential teacher, and the publisher of a widely read periodical, *Voice in the Wilderness*. He was undoubtedly the most prominent black leader of the Finished Work camp, but his gifts as teacher, preacher, author, and songwriter were recognized by blacks and whites alike.

In 1911 Haywood had obtained ministerial credentials with a small, obscure organization called the Pentecostal Assemblies of the World that began in 1906 or 1907 in Los Angeles. At this time its general superintendent was J. J. Frazee of Portland, Oregon, who had come out of Florence Crawford's ministry there. By 1913 Haywood had influenced Ewart, Cook, and McAlister to associate with this group.[72] However, at the time of his rebaptism, he was in close fellowship with the Assemblies of God.

The Assemblies of God

The Assemblies of God was organized at a convention on April 2-12, 1914, in Hot Springs, Arkansas. (The conference ended three days before Ewart and Cook rebaptized each other.) The prime movers were Howard Goss and Eudorus N. Bell. The need for this organization arose from two major factors: the demise of Parham's organization, particularly in the South, and the lack of an organization that embraced the Finished Work doctrine.

It appears that the primary catalyst for the formation of the new organization was Howard Goss, pastor in Hot Springs at that time. He had previously been Parham's field director for Texas, but he and most workers in Texas and Arkansas had broken with Parham over the allegations of Parham's misconduct, and they had accepted Durham's Finished Work teaching.

In 1910, Goss had received permission from C. H. Mason to use the name of his organization—Church of God in Christ—to issue credentials to white ministers and to obtain clergy railroad discounts. Mason exercised no authority over them, and they did not adhere to his doctrine of sanctification as a second work of grace. Moreover, they apparently conducted little or no business among themselves.

Another loose ministerial association had formed in 1909 in Dothan, Alabama, under H. G. Rodgers. They chose the name Church of God, not realizing that a preexisting Pentecostal organization was using the same name.

They joined Goss's group in 1913. The combined list of ministers numbered 352, but the group did not function as a true organization.

Goss began to see the need for an active organization that would examine ministerial qualifications, protect churches from charlatans and troublemakers, and promote missionary efforts. He approached E. N. Bell (1866-1923) with his thoughts. Bell was an older minister who had been to seminary and who had pastored Baptist churches for seventeen years before coming into the Pentecostal movement under Durham. He was a pastor in Malvern, Arkansas, and editor of an influential monthly paper, the *Word and Witness*. Most of the workers in the South who had left Parham were still quite young— Goss himself was only about thirty—and had accepted Durham's doctrine, so they naturally looked to Bell for leadership.

Bell likewise saw the need for organization, and he used his paper to announce a "general council" to promote five stated purposes: unity, stabilization, missions outreach, legal identity, and schools and publications. Bell and Goss signed the initial call for organization. Soon they were joined by Daniel C. O. Opperman (1872-1926), Mack M. Pinson, and Arch P. Collins. Opperman had been the superintendent of the high school system at Zion. After receiving the Holy Ghost in Parham's work, he became a leading Pentecostal educator, conducting short-term Bible schools for workers. All five of the men who issued the call for a new organization were associated with the autonomous white wing of the Church of God in Christ.

Over 300 people attended this first meeting, with 128 registering as ministers and missionaries. They voted to form an organization and chose as their official name The General Council of the Assemblies of God. Bell was elected as general chairman, a title later renamed general superintendent. J. Roswell Flower (1888-1970) became the first secretary-treasurer. Born in Canada, he was a convert from the Christian and Missionary Alliance who pastored a small church in Indianapolis and published a weekly, *The Christian Evangel*. The two papers of Bell and Flower became the official organs, with Bell as the editor.

The first executive presbyters—some elected and some later appointed by those elected—were Bell, Collins, R. L. Erickson, Flower, Cyrus B. Fockler, Goss, Daniel W. Kerr, Thomas K. Leonard, Opperman, Pinson, John C. Sinclair, and John W. Welch. The assembled ministers agreed not to have any creed but the Bible, but their purpose was to create an organization for Finished Work Pentecostals.

In the fall of 1914, the new organization conducted its first regular meeting, which was its second general council. Collins replaced Bell as chairman, Opperman became the first assistant chairman, and Bennett F. Lawrence (1890-?) became the first assistant secretary.

Rebaptism of Leaders

Almost immediately, the new organization faced the issue of water baptism in the name of Jesus Christ. Many prominent ministers were being baptized in Jesus' name. At first, the leaders of the Assemblies of God opposed this teaching, notably Bell, Goss, and Flower.

In July 1915, a dramatic event occurred at the third interstate encampment of the Assemblies of God in Jackson, Tennessee. The host pastor was H. G. Rodgers, and Bell conducted the camp. They chose L. V. Roberts of Indianapolis as the main speaker. After he preached his first sermon, which was on Acts 2:38, both Rodgers and Bell were baptized in Jesus' name.

In August 1915, L. C. Hall (1867-?) preached a camp meeting in Little Rock, Arkansas. A convert from Dowie's Zion City, Hall had recently been baptized in Jesus' name, and he preached this message. Bell performed the baptisms and baptized Goss. Although Parham had baptized Goss in Jesus' name twelve years earlier, neither man had attached doctrinal significance to the formula, and Goss wanted to identify clearly with the Jesus Name doctrine. Hall also brought Jesus Name baptism to eastern Texas, baptizing Harvey Shearer and others.

About this time, two other Assemblies of God officials, Lawrence and Opperman, were baptized in Jesus' name. Opperman began advocating the message in his periodical, *The Blessed Truth*.

Hall then conducted a campaign in Ontario, Canada, in November 1915 with George Chambers that resulted in hundreds being rebaptized in Jesus' name. About the same time, G. T. Haywood preached for R. E. McAlister in Ottawa and rebaptized him along with many others. Almost all the Canadian Pentecostal leaders accepted the Jesus Name message, including A. H. Argue, George Chambers, R. E. McAlister, and Frank Small.

At a thirty-day Bible conference in Elton, Louisiana, beginning December 15, 1915, Harvey Shearer (the conference chairman) and Howard Goss proclaimed the Oneness teaching in that state. All but one minister in attendance accepted Jesus Name baptism, including Robert LaFleur and Oliver Fauss. According to notes that

Fauss took, the conference leaders taught "the oneness of God in Christ" instead of "three persons in the Godhead" and taught that "Acts 2:38 is God's plan" of salvation.[73] All twelve ministers of the Assemblies of God in Louisiana embraced the Jesus Name message.

In short, within two years after Ewart and Cook rebaptized each other, many early Pentecostal leaders were baptized in Jesus' name. Some simply acted in obedience to the apostolic pattern but did not fully embrace the Oneness doctrine, or else did so for only a short time. Many, however, accepted both Jesus Name baptism and the associated Oneness doctrine. In addition to Argue, Mother Barnes, Bell, Chambers, Cook, Ewart, Goss, Hall, Haywood, Lawrence, McAlister, Mother Moise, Opperman, Roberts, Rodgers, Shearer, and Small, early Pentecostal leaders who accepted Jesus Name baptism include Frank Bartleman, William Booth-Clibborn (grandson of the founder of the Salvation Army), Frank and Elizabeth Gray (missionaries to Japan), Elmer K. Fisher, Thoro Harris (songwriter), S. C. McClain, Aimee Semple McPherson, C. H. Mason (but not until 1930), Harry Morse, F. S. Ramsay (missionary to China), R. J. Scott, George B. Studd, Harry Van Loon.[74] (See Appendix B for a description of most of these leaders.) As trinitarian historians point out, the Jesus Name message came very close to sweeping the Assemblies of God.

The Controversy in the Assemblies of God

In the meantime, the third general council of the Assemblies of God convened in October 1915 in St. Louis. With the approval of some executive presbyters, J. R. Flower, the secretary-treasurer, convened the meeting specifically to suppress the so-called New Issue. Collins, the chairman, and Opperman, the assistant chairman, did not want to do so, and they arrived late. In their absence, Flower took charge and asked J. W. Welch (1858-1939) to chair the meeting.

About one hundred ministers were in attendance, and a debate was organized. E. N. Bell and G. T. Haywood presented the case for baptism in Jesus' name. Speaking for the traditional trinitarian formula were Collins and Jacob Miller. William Schell was originally scheduled instead of Miller, but he was prepared to speak on church history. When he learned that the debate was to be confined to Scripture, he withdrew.[75] The next day, however, he was allowed to speak for two hours on "the baptismal formula as given by the [Post-]Apostolic Fathers."[76]

The conference decided that either baptismal formula was acceptable but that more time was needed to pray and study the issue. It then recommended a compromise formula: "The substitution of the name of 'Jesus Christ' for the word 'Son' (Matt. 28:19) would better harmonize Matt. 28:19 with the book of Acts (Acts 2:38; 8:16; 10:48; 19:5) and, as a formula, would be preferable to the use of any one passage to the exclusion of the other."[77]

Despite the professed desire for further discussion and deliberation, the conference elected staunch trinitarians to every position and removed everyone who had accepted baptism in Jesus' name or who had a conciliatory attitude toward it. Bell, Collins, Goss, Lawrence, and Opperman all lost their positions. Welch replaced Collins as chairman.

During 1916, the leadership of the Assemblies of God fought strongly against the Oneness message. Flower's opposition was the most decisive of all. From a study of church history, he concluded that the Oneness teaching was essentially a revival of modalistic monarchianism or Sabellianism, which the mainstream church of the third and fourth centuries had deemed heresy. He argued that if the Assemblies of God adopted this position, it would break fellowship with historic and contemporary Christianity. Although both sides appealed to Scripture, for many people the ultimate test was the verdict of tradition.

One of Flower's most significant accomplishments was influencing Bell to switch sides and endorse trinitarian baptism again. Bell never denied Jesus Name baptism as such, but he suppressed his practice of baptizing in Jesus' name for the sake of unity and continued fellowship with the Assemblies of God. Eventually he denounced the Oneness doctrine.

Welch announced that the general council in 1916 would decide the issue. The fourth general council of the Assemblies of God convened October 1-7, 1916, in St. Louis. The leadership appointed a committee to write a doctrinal statement, even though the organizing conference two years earlier had voted not to adopt such a statement. The committee was composed of D. W. Kerr, T. K. Leonard, S. A. Jameson, Stanley H. Frodsham, and E. N. Bell. Bell was the only one who had been baptized in Jesus' name; the others were staunch trinitarians. Bell was apparently placed on the committee because of his great influence and also to reestablish him firmly in the trinitarian camp.

Kerr (1856-1927), a former minister with the Christian and Missionary Alliance, was the most prepared and had the most influence on the committee. He had studied the issue thoroughly and already had rebuttals for the Oneness position. He was the primary author of the document that the committee formulated, the "Statement of Fundamental Truths," which consisted of seventeen points. The statement strongly advocated trinitarianism—some would say almost tritheism—and expressly denounced the Oneness doctrine on a number of points. (See chapter 5.)

Vigorous debate ensued. In a personal interview, Carl M. O'Guin, the last surviving participant, gave the following description of the meeting. O'Guin was twenty years old at the time. He was living with Welch, and he supported the trinitarian position. He later became a district superintendent in the Assemblies of God.[78]

According to O'Guin, the most influential leaders in the Assemblies of God at the time were Bell, Goss, Kerr, Opperman, and Welch. Bell was by far the most respected. On the Jesus Name issue, his opinion was especially important, for the other four leaders mentioned were evenly split between strong trinitarians (Kerr, Welch) and strong Oneness believers (Goss, Opperman).

In the debate, the main advocates of trinitarianism were Kerr, Leonard, Pinson, and Welch, while the main advocates of Oneness were Ewart, Goss, and Haywood. Ewart and Haywood were not officially members of the Assemblies of God but were given the privilege to speak because of their close fellowship and significant influence. J. R. Flower's input was mostly behind the scene; he was only twenty-eight at the time.

O'Guin estimated that about eighty ministers were in attendance, about fifteen or twenty of whom had been rebaptized in Jesus' name.[79] With the exception of a few leaders, most of these men were quite young. Many of the preachers had not yet made up their minds on the issue, and the position of the leaders was the deciding factor for some. Most of them did not consider the Jesus Name message to be heresy.

In O'Guin's opinion, Kerr was "stern, strict, and intolerant," and Leonard was the most effective debater. Leonard (1861-1946) had been the man to suggest the name Assemblies of God in the beginning, and he was the primary author of the first constitution, which he considered to have been inspired of God. O'Guin said he was "a witty Irishman, a law unto himself," and no one could control him. He staked out a harsh position, not wanting to compromise on anything but issuing an ultimatum to the Jesus Name people to accept trinitarianism completely or leave. As O'Guin recalled, most of the ministers did not really agree with such a hard-line stance, but they did not have the courage to oppose Leonard. O'Guin concluded that the decision was too hasty. He said, "If we would have taken a humble attitude and waited on the Lord, I believe God would have solved the problem without division."

O'Guin remembered that Leonard especially did not like Haywood and was glad for the chance to "belittle" him. It is well documented that during the debate Leonard spoke of the Oneness people as "hay, wood, and stubble," obviously alluding to G. T. Haywood as well as I Corinthians 3:12. He also said they were in the wilderness and had "a voice in the wilderness," referring to Haywood's paper, *Voice in the Wilderness.*[80]

In the end, the conference adopted the trinitarian statement. It also voted to require that the words of

Matthew 28:19 be incorporated in the baptismal formula. The Oneness ministers had no alternative but to leave the organization. As they left the conference floor to discuss their options, they heard the assembly sing, "Holy, holy, holy, Lord God Almighty, blessed trinity."

As a result of this conference, 156 out of 585 ministers dropped out of the Assemblies of God—about one-fourth of the total. Presumably, almost all of them were Oneness, although a few left because they objected to the adoption of a statement of faith and felt that the handling of the controversy was too harsh.

Robert Mapes Anderson, a non-Pentecostal historian, concluded that doctrine was not the only factor in the dramatic shakeup of the young Assemblies of God in 1915-16, but a power struggle was also involved.[81] He noted that the six most influential men in the formation of the Assemblies of God in 1914 were Bell, Goss, Opperman, Collins, Pinson, and Rodgers. They were all from the South, and they had all been associated with the white wing of the Church of God in Christ. All of them lost their positions. The men who gained power during this time—Flower, Welch, Kerr, and Leonard—were from the upper Midwest and Northeast. Flower, Welch, and Kerr had formerly belonged to the Christian and Missionary Alliance (Welch and Kerr were former Alliance officials), and Leonard had belonged to the Christian Church.

Anderson also raised the question of whether racism played a role, particularly in light of Leonard's animosity toward Haywood. Practically all the blacks in the Finished Work camp looked to Haywood for leadership, so by the decision of 1916, the Assemblies of God became "an all but 'lily white' denomination," and Oneness Pentecostals became the most biracial wing of the entire Pentecostal movement.[82]

Those Who Stayed

A few of the ministers who were baptized in the name of Jesus simply acted in obedience to the apostolic pattern but never fully adopted the Oneness position. As indicated by Frank Small's remarks and by Oliver Fauss's notes from the Elton Bible Conference, however, most people did associate their rebaptism with a new understanding of the full deity of Jesus Christ and the oneness of God in contrast to traditional trinitarianism. Some of these people drew back from their new belief and practice when opposition came. Ministers who never completely left trinitarianism, or who ultimately endorsed it again, included A. H. Argue, E. N. Bell, George Chambers, Elmer Fisher, R. E. McAlister, Aimee Semple McPherson, L. V. Roberts, and Maria Woodworth-Etter.

Later such people tended to minimize the extent to which they had embraced the Oneness doctrine. Many of their testimonies at the time, however, reveal a profound spiritual and theological awakening when they were baptized in Jesus' name.

For example, R. E. McAlister later became a strong opponent of the Oneness message in Canada. When he was baptized, however, he wrote, "I have had a revelation to my soul of the one God in threefold manifestation. How my heart melted in His presence! I could only cry and weep."[83]

The most significant defection from Jesus Name baptism back to trinitarian baptism was E. N. Bell. Trinitarian historians have commonly stated that Bell never accepted the Oneness message but merely was baptized to follow the Book of Acts. Some have attributed his baptism in Jesus' name to psychological pressures, such as being tired, overworked, and afraid of failure. A careful study of his testimony, however, reveals that he emphasized classic Oneness themes, although he did retain some trinitarian terminology. Had he remained faithful to his new understanding, he would have undoubtedly attained a consistent Oneness perspective.

In 1915 Bell gave three reasons why he was baptized in Jesus' name.[84] First, he had entertained doubts about his previous water baptism ever since he had received the Holy Spirit, and he believed it would "please God for me now to be buried with Him in baptism." It was a matter of conscience, a matter about which God had been dealing with him for a long time.

Second, before the meeting in which he was baptized, God dealt specifically with him. He could not preach on any other topic: "God took away every other message until I would obey."

Third, he realized that the apostles taught and practiced baptism in the name of the Lord Jesus Christ. It was the apostolic pattern; thus he needed to follow it.

In his first article after being baptized in Jesus' name, published in August 1915, Bell described his new spiritual experience and theological understanding. The article, entitled "Who Is Jesus Christ?," begins as follows:[85]

> The lost Christ being re-discovered as the Jehovah of the Old Testament and the True God of the New. A realization of Christ as the Mighty God being received.

I want to thank God today for the discussion of water baptism in the name of Jesus Christ, because it has proven the means of discovering to me a mightier Christ than I ever realized before. The water baptism issue in the name of Christ, taken alone, would be comparatively a small and tame matter. Just so, it first seemed to me and to many others, and seems to some still, because they have not seen what is involved in it and do not have the full apostolic vision of Jesus Christ as Lord or Jehovah. The baptismal issue is only one cog in the wheel that will roll out and up to your bewildered and joyful vision the most glorious Christ you ever beheld, if you will let it, by beginning to walk in the light by obeying Him.

I can say today, before God and all men, that His joy is rolling in my soul now as never before. As I write, His glory convulses my whole physical frame, and I have to stop now and then and say, "Glory," or "Oh, glory," to let some of it escape. Night before last, as I lay on my bed, I heard in the Spirit the sweetest, most soul-thrilling song on the wonderful name of Jesus I ever heard since I was born. If people knew what God is putting in my soul, by a brand new vision of Jesus and the wonders hid in His mighty and glorious name, they would cease pitying me for being baptized in the name of the Lord Jesus Christ, and begin to shout and help me praise the Lamb that was slain, who is now beginning to receive some honor and praise, but who will eventually make the whole universe—sea, earth and sky, reverberate with universal praise and honor to His great name. Hallelujah to His name forever!

The section titles of the remainder of the article are as follows: "Jesus is Jehovah. He is Eternal God and Creator. He is the Mighty God. Jesus is the True God. He is Emmanuel—God With Us. He is Lord of Lords. He is One With the Father. Trinity or Godhead, all in Christ. Father's Name Given Jesus. The Real Vision of Jesus Lost."

In the article, Bell quoted and discussed Colossians 2:9, then dealt with the trinity, and concluded as follows:

Now, it is a wonder how He [Jesus] could be God, or God could dwell in Him. It is more a wonder that the whole "Godhead" dwells in him. It is still a greater wonder that the *fulness* of the Godhead dwells in him; and a wonder on wonders how *all* the fulness of the Godhead is in Jesus. But all this is declared of our glorious Christ.

Don't be afraid the Father and the Holy Ghost will be left out. We all believe in God the Father and in the blessed Holy Ghost. We can expect to continue to speak of both, just as the Apostles do in the New Testament, whenever occasion demands it and when that is our subject; but just now our subject is the *wonders in Christ*.

It is unreasonable, when magnifying Jesus as Lord, to expect us to stop and mystify our readers with the Greek mysteries about the Trinity. Anyway, few even after years of study on the Trinity, know much more about it than when they began. . . . So don't let anyone make you go into hysterics over the mysteries of the Trinity being neglected while we are exalting Jesus Christ. I never knew of any one being saved by a study of the Trinity, but exalting

Jesus the Christ as the mighty Lord, able to save unto the uttermost, will bring this great salvation to thousands on thousands. . . .

The whole Godhead, in all its fulness, is in Jesus.

Hence, baptism in the name of Jesus was the apostolic custom everywhere. . . .

All may baptize with the phrase in Matthew 28:19 who feel so led, and I will love and fellowship them just the same; but personally, with my present light, I could not conscientiously do so any more. I prefer to use the real name common to both Father and Son, as the Lord commanded me to baptize in "The Name," not in a relationship phrase which is no proper name at all. Lord, help the dear brethren to see that Father and Son are, by no means, proper names.

Recognizing that the whole Godhead was always present in Jesus, the Apostles baptized either in a part or all of His name; sometimes Jesus Christ; at other times, Lord, or Lord Jesus. (See Acts 2:38; 8:16; 10:44; 19:5.) But there was never a hint, from their first sermon at Pentecost to the death of the last Apostle, that they understood Jesus to mean to use the phrase as in Matthew 28:19, rather than the *name*. But when the church lost the secret of this *name*, it began to fall into liberalism and formalism, without understanding the true meaning and intent of the forms they were using. Now God is restoring the spiritual vision of the mighty Jehovah-Christ, the wonders in His name, and Christ is becoming daily larger and more glorious to our vision.

Oh, thank God forever for it. Well, we must stop,

but we have only just started into this great subject of *who Jesus Christ is.*

It is amazing that someone with this insight would suppress such a glorious message and experience for the sake of fellowship. Yet that is what Bell did. In 1920 he was elected a second time as general chairman of the Assemblies of God, a position he held until his death in 1923.

We should also note that some ministers eventually left Oneness circles in order to return to a broader base of fellowship and ministry. They maintained or renewed fellowship with trinitarians and conducted their later ministry primarily among them, but they never renounced their Oneness views. Examples were William Booth-Clibborn, L. C. Hall, and H. G. Rodgers.

Conclusions

The Oneness message was not an aberration but a logical, scriptural development among the earliest Pentecostals, given their restorationist impulse, emphasis on Scripture, and willingness to reevaluate and abandon doctrinal tradition. From the very start of the Pentecostal movement, some people were baptizing in Jesus' name, including Charles Parham himself. Very soon some, such as Andrew Urshan and Frank Ewart, were rethinking their understanding of the doctrine of God. The ministries of Parham, William Seymour, and especially William Durham prepared the way for the Jesus Name message, and this point will be even more apparent as we discuss the doctrine of salvation in chapter 4. As we shall see, in formulating and expounding their doctrine, the Oneness people employed key concepts, phrases, and passages of Scripture that were already in use. For example, early preachers such as Parham and Durham had already drawn attention to Acts 2:38, and the Oneness movement extended that emphasis.

As with the Pentecostal movement generally, it would be a mistake to identify one person as the founder of the Oneness movement. More than any other individual, Frank Ewart was responsible for the theological formulation of the Oneness view of the Godhead. We should not neglect, however, the significant roles that others played at the very outset. R. E. McAlister contributed the crucial insight that the apostles always baptized in Jesus' name, and he and Ewart discussed the related doctrinal issues for months. John Schaepe was a catalyst with his insight regarding the power of the name of Jesus. Frank Small was the first to act upon the new thinking by baptizing converts in Jesus' name. Glenn Cook was instrumental in discussing the doctrine with Ewart, in jointly taking the decisive step of rebaptism, and in bringing the message to other leaders. Several other key thinkers began contributing significant insights almost immediately, notably G. T. Haywood and in a few years Andrew Urshan.

Advocates of the Oneness message came from the front ranks of Pentecostal leaders, including one of Parham's earliest converts and closest associates (Howard Goss), one of Seymour's full-time coworkers at Azusa Street (Cook), and Durham's assistant pastor and successor (Ewart). Many of the founders of the Assemblies of God and the Pentecostal Assemblies of Canada accepted the Oneness message in whole or in part. Indeed, the first general superintendents (or equivalent) of four major trinitarian Pentecostal organizations were baptized in Jesus' name: the Assemblies of God (E. N. Bell), the Pentecostal Assemblies of Canada (George Chambers), the International Church of the Foursquare Gospel (Aimee Semple McPherson), and the Church of God in Christ (C. H. Mason). Clearly, Oneness Pentecostals were classical Pentecostals and not later offshoots.

As a result of the controversies over sanctification and the oneness of God, by the end of 1916 the Pentecostal movement was split three ways. In chapters 4 and 5, we will trace further expansion and organizational developments, examine doctrinal positions, and draw conclusions, giving particular attention to the Oneness Pentecostal movement in chapter 4.

Oneness Pentecostal Organizations

When the Assemblies of God adopted its trinitarian statement of faith in October 1916, the Oneness ministers were left without an organizational home. The other major Pentecostal organizations in existence were Second Work Pentecostals who had retained the doctrine of the trinity as part of their theological system. The Oneness message had arisen within the Finished Work wing of the Pentecostal movement, of which the Assemblies of God was the chief representative.

Most Oneness Pentecostal ministers had been forced to leave two organizations: first, when they received the Holy Spirit, and second, when they were baptized in Jesus' name. Many Pentecostals had long questioned the need and value of organization; indeed, Parham himself opposed organization by this time. Many Oneness Pentecostals understandably felt that organizations too often promoted the traditions of men and stifled the move of the Spirit. As a result, there are many independent Oneness Pentecostals even to this day.

The Pentecostal Assemblies of the World

Nevertheless, the majority saw the need to form a Oneness Pentecostal organization. To further this purpose, a large group of Oneness ministers met in Eureka Springs, Arkansas, in late December 1916 and organized in early January 1917. They elected D. C. O. Opperman as chairman, Lee Floyd as secretary, and Howard Goss as treasurer. Opperman, Goss, and H. G. Rodgers were appointed as a credential committee. The group named themselves the General Assembly of the Apostolic Assemblies (GAAA). Among the ministers who joined were Booth-Clibborn, Ewart, Fauss, Hall, LaFleur, Pemberton, and Schaepe.

This organization lasted only one year because of two factors. First, America entered World War I in April 1917, and since the organization was so new, its ministers could not obtain exemption from military service. Second, they could not obtain clergy discounts on the railroad, which was almost essential at a time when few ministers owned automobiles.

In the meantime, a small organization known as the Pentecostal Assemblies of the World (PAW), founded in 1906 or 1907 in Los Angeles, had become a Oneness organization under the influence of G. T. Haywood, a member since 1911. It was able to obtain noncombatant status for its ministers, so in late 1917 or early 1918, the

GAAA merged with the PAW.

This organization was interracial. E. W. Doak (white) was elected as general chairman, G. T. Haywood (black) as general secretary, and Opperman (white) as general elder. Most Oneness groups today have originated, directly or indirectly, from the PAW.

The earliest list of PAW ministers we have is for 1919-20.[86] On it were the following men whom we have already mentioned in this book: Booth-Clibborn, Chambers, Denny, Doak, Ewart, Fauss, Floyd, Goss, Gray, Hall, Haywood, LaFleur, Morse, Opperman, Pemberton, Ramsey, Schaepe, Shearer, Small, and Studd. Others on the list who would become key leaders in the future were S. N. Hancock, B. H. Hite, W. E. Kidson, R. C. Lawson, S. C. McClain, L. R. Ooton, G. B. Rowe, A. R. Schooler, Wesley Steelburg (son-in-law of Elmer Fisher and future general superintendent of the Assemblies of God), J. M. Turpin, S. L. Wise, and W. T. Witherspoon.

The total number of ministers was 704 (excluding two apparent duplicates). Of the total, 203 (29 percent) were women, many of whom were wives of ministers, such as Goss, Hall, and Lawson. The ministers lived in 36 of the 48 states, the District of Columbia, four provinces of Canada (17 ministers), and four other countries (at least 30 foreign missionaries or national workers in China, Japan, Persia, South Africa, and unspecified locations).[87] Over 80 percent of the ministers resided in three areas—the West Coast, the Midwest, and the South—with the top three states being California (15 percent), Indiana (14 percent), and Texas (8 percent). Many were based in three cities: Indianapolis, Los Angeles, and Oakland. Approximately 25 to 30 percent were black,[88] and three

Hispanic surnames appear on the list.

Organizational Efforts in Canada

In Canada, most of the early Pentecostal leaders had accepted the Jesus Name message. Some leaders—including R. E. McAlister, George A. Chambers, R. E. Sternall, Frank Small, and Howard Goss—began meeting in 1917 to plan a Canadian organization. (Goss was pastor in Picton, Ontario, at the time.) Their intention was to work closely with the Pentecostal Assemblies of the World, so they named their organization the Pentecostal Assemblies of Canada (PAOC).[89] Indeed, Chambers and Goss were listed as PAW ministers for 1919-20. The two most influential organizers were Chambers, the first general chairman (superintendent), and McAlister, the first secretary-treasurer. The group did not formally obtain a federal charter until 1919.

Much like the Assemblies of God in 1914, in the first meeting of the board of trustees the PAOC voted not to adopt a doctrinal statement as a basis of fellowship. Between 1917 and 1920, however, a shift took place away from the Oneness position, with both Chambers and McAlister repudiating the doctrine.

The first general assembly, held in November 1919 and attended by 31 ministers and lay delegates, issued the following statement: "We recognize a three-fold relationship of Father, Son, and Holy Ghost being clearly taught in the New Testament. . . . As to baptism, we feel like leaving the matter of formula with the individual."[90] In late 1919 some independent Pentecostal churches in western Canada joined the Assemblies of God. In 1920, the PAOC itself affiliated with the Assemblies of God. Although this formal association was short-lived (until 1925), it marked the transition to a definitely trinitarian organization.

Frank Small, one of the founders of the PAOC, felt betrayed by this change of doctrine and affiliation. In 1921, he led ten Oneness ministers out of the PAOC and founded the *Apostolic Church of Pentecost of Canada* (ACPC) as a Oneness organization. It is unique among historic Oneness organizations in that it teaches unconditional eternal security, which Small strongly advocated. In 1953, the ACPC was joined by the Evangelical Churches of Pentecost, a group that included many who taught "the triunity of the Godhead" (in distinction to the trinity). Consequently, there is considerable latitude on the doctrine of God, but the key points of identity are the Pentecostal experience, baptism in Jesus' name, and eternal security. In 1998, the reported constituency in Canada was 14,000 and worldwide was 42,000.

Almost all the Pentecostals in the Maritime Provinces embraced the Oneness message. Most of them joined the ACPC and then later went to the United Pentecostal Church, which is now the largest Oneness group in Canada. A number of Oneness ministers, particularly in Ontario, stayed in the PAOC until the leadership forced them out in 1940. Most of them also eventually joined the United Pentecostal Church.

Racial Division

Back in the United States, the segregation laws of the South put tremendous pressure on the PAW. Most of the black ministers resided in the North, and all conferences had to be held in the North due to segregated accommodations in the South. Most Southern ministers, however, could not afford the cost of travel to the North and so could not attend. In order to work effectively, they felt that they needed to participate in their organization and to have conferences in various parts of the country, including the South.

In 1922 a group of Southern ministers organized a fellowship conference in Little Rock, Arkansas, that was well attended. There was a great outpouring of the Spirit, with a communion service for ministers lasting until 3:00 A.M. This Southern Bible Conference impressed upon the white ministers how much they needed such meetings in their area, but it aroused concerns among black ministers that they were deliberately being excluded.

The result of these pressures was a division along racial lines in 1924. Most of the white ministers withdrew from the PAW, while a few stayed. Even though the PAW was now almost totally black for the first time, whites were still given some leadership positions in an effort to preserve the ideal of integration.

While some racial prejudice was undoubtedly involved in the split, it appears that most of the white ministers did not withdraw because of personal prejudice but because of the legal and social hindrances to organizational function and growth. S. C. McClain, a white minister from the South, explained how the church rejected prejudice yet struggled with societal obstacles:[91]

> I, being Southern born, thought it a miracle that I could sit in a service by a black saint of God and worship, or eat at a great camp table, and forget I was eating beside a black saint, but in spirit and truth God was worshipped in love and harmony. . . .

While all Spirit-filled ministers agreed that with God there is not a color line and in the hearts of the people of God there should be none, yet ministers laboring in the South had to conform to laws and customs.

James Tyson, a contemporary black historian with the PAW, offered the following analysis:[92]

Racial prejudice was a factor in the development of early Pentecostalism. . . . Barely two generations had passed since the eradication of slavery, and there still remained a mindset of white/black, superior/inferior attitudes. These deeply entrenched philosophies unfortunately carried over into many Pentecostal organizations, as is demonstrated by the fact that up until 1918 most groups were either all white or all black.

This attitude was not just relegated to the white brethren, for many blacks distrusted whites. . . . Much suspicion and reverse discrimination was expostulated by blacks against their white brethren. When doors were opened for blacks to join ranks with whites of like spiritual persuasion, many refused the invitation with the general feeling they would be cast in secondary roles. . . .

The merging of the General Assemblies of the Apostolic Assemblies and the Pentecostal Assemblies of the World was a bold and courageous move. The new group would be one of the first Pentecostal organizations to truly attempt to promote racial harmony, and initially this move was more than symbolic. Even though in 1918 seventy to seventy-five percent of the constituency was white, there seemed to be a determined effort to promote brotherly love and to exalt Christ as the Creator of all people.

Nevertheless it would not be long before this chivalrous effort would fail. Racial considerations would again surface in a few years. . . .

Perhaps if the P.A.W. had been conceived in the 1970s or 1980s, the forces of pride, tradition, and upbringing would not have been the same, and the history of the organization would have been drastically different. Undoubtedly, great outside pressure was put on the brethren, both whites and blacks, by the prevailing thinking of the country at that time.

In 1925, the white ministers who withdrew from the PAW formed three organizations primarily along regional lines: (1) the Pentecostal Ministerial Alliance, later renamed the Pentecostal Church Incorporated (PCI), in Jackson, Tennessee; (2) the Apostolic Churches of Jesus Christ, in St. Louis; and (3) Emmanuel's Church in Christ Jesus, in Houston. The latter two soon merged to become the Apostolic Church of Jesus Christ. The PAW, meanwhile, adopted a modified form of episcopal church government and elected G. T. Haywood as its first presiding bishop.

The desire for interracial unity was so strong, however, that in 1931 the Pentecostal Assemblies of the World and the Apostolic Church of Jesus Christ merged to form an integrated organization again, known as the Pentecostal Assemblies of Jesus Christ (PAJC). Although the ministerial membership was eighty percent white, it mandated that the board of presbyters be fifty percent black.[93] Some blacks did not believe this merger would be successful, so a leading black minister, Samuel Grimes, renewed the charter of the PAW before it expired. He and other ministers kept it alive as a separate organization with a small constituency.

Unfortunately, the same pressures as before continued to work against the integrated body. In 1936, the conference voted that the racial composition of the board of presbyters should be the same as that of the ministerial constituency and that conferences could be held anywhere in the U.S. At this point the PAW had 87 churches (black), as opposed to 126 ten years earlier (black and white). The PAJC had 245 churches (black and white), and the PCI had 168 (white).[94]

In 1937, the PAJC leadership finally acceded to the wishes of the Southern ministers for a conference closer to home by holding one in Tulsa, Oklahoma. Since Tulsa was segregated, the blacks did not attend. As a result, no significant business was conducted, and the conference voted to meet in the North the next year. But it was too late. By 1938, almost all the remaining black ministers had withdrawn from the PAJC and returned to the PAW.

As of 1998, the PAW reported 1,760 churches and 450,000 constituents in the U.S. with a total of 4,141 churches and 1,000,000 constituents worldwide.

Over the years, the resulting organizations grew further apart in structure and function, but many ministers maintained a degree of fellowship. Consequently, there has always been greater interracial interaction in Oneness ranks than in other branches of Pentecostalism and Protestantism.

In summary, the Oneness Pentecostals as a group denounced racial prejudice and tried harder and longer than any other group to overcome the social pressures of racism. The reasons for the whites leaving in 1924 and the blacks leaving in 1938 were not trivial and should not simply be dismissed as prejudice. Nevertheless, it is unfortunate that a better solution could not have been found—one that would have confronted the culture with the radical claims of the gospel. The PAW and later the PAJC were perhaps the most integrated bodies in America at the time, and perhaps American history itself could have been affected had the ministers been able to elevate their vision beyond the difficulties of the time to see the plan of God for racial reconciliation.

The United Pentecostal Church International

In short, by 1938 there were two sizeable white Oneness organizations that were almost identical in structure, doctrine, and practice: the Pentecostal Church Incorporated (PCI) and the Pentecostal Assemblies of Jesus Christ (PAJC). After some unsuccessful attempts, in 1945 they merged to form the United Pentecostal Church, which immediately became the largest Oneness Pentecostal organization in the world. The general superintendent of the PCI, Howard Goss, became the first general superintendent of the new organization. The general superintendent of the PAJC, W. T. Witherspoon, became the assistant general superintendent. At the time of the merger, there were 521 listed churches in the U.S. and Canada. (In their 1945 directories, the PCI listed 175 and the PAJC listed 346. The first UPC church directory, in 1947, listed 617 church.[95])

In 1946, the Full Gospel Pentecostal Church joined the new organization. It was composed of Oneness ministers in New Brunswick, Nova Scotia, and Prince Edward Island who had withdrawn from the Apostolic Church of Pentecost of Canada because they did not believe in unconditional eternal security.

In 1972 the organization officially became known as the United Pentecostal Church International (UPCI). In addition to Church Administration, the work of the organization is conducted by the following divisions: Editorial, Education, Foreign Missions, Harvestime (radio), Home Missions, Women's, Sunday School, and Youth.

The UPCI also operates the Pentecostal Publishing House. It publishes books and tracts under the name of Word Aflame Press, with about 150 books currently in print. Under the name of Word Aflame Publications, it also produces a multi-year curriculum for Sunday school (nursery through adult), including various undated adult electives, and a curriculum for children's church. The UPCI is the only Oneness organization to have its own publishing house and Sunday school curriculum; thus it plays an important role in supplying literature to the rest of the Oneness movement. Indeed, about one-half of its customers are outside the UPCI.

As of June 30, 1998, the UPCI reported 3,861 churches and 8,219 ministers in the United States and Canada, organized into 53 districts. Elsewhere in the world, it reported 21,407 churches and preaching points, 15,882 ministers, and almost 2,000,000 constituents in 136 nations.[96] Thus the total number of churches worldwide was 25,268.

As of February 1999 there were about 4,000 churches

in the U.S. and Canada, not counting daughter works.[97] The reported 1998 Easter Sunday attendance in the U.S. and Canada was 416,807 (almost 110 per church), but if we include estimates for nonreporting churches, the total is about 500,000 (about 130 per church).[98]

To compare these numbers with other denominations, we need to use an inclusive number for constituents, for mainline denominations report many more adherents than regular attendees. They typically count all those who have been baptized or all who claim identification. Even the Assemblies of God (AG) reports significantly more constituents than those in actual average attendance. For instance, in 1997 it reported an average Sunday morning worship attendance of 132 per church, but average number of constituents per church was 208, almost 60 percent more.[99] Using this type of estimate, the total UPCI constituency in the U.S. and Canada would be almost 800,000, and in the rest of the world it would be 3,200,000, for a total of 4,000,000.[100]

The best comparison is probably the number of churches. For example, in 1997 the UPCI reported 3,821 churches in the U.S. and Canada, while the AG reported 11,884 churches in the U.S. and Puerto Rico. This ratio is about one to three, roughly the same as the ratio in 1916 of ministers who left the AG (156) compared to those who stayed (429). Thus the growth of the UPCI has paralleled that of the AG. Indeed, a comparison of growth in number of churches from 1958 to 1992 showed that the UPCI grew by 123 percent, the AG grew by 40 percent, and the Church of God (Cleveland, TN) grew by 54 percent.[101] From 1988 to 1998, the UPCI in the U.S. and Canada grew 9 percent in the number of churches and 27 percent in reported Easter attendance.[102]

Elsewhere in the world, the UPCI has grown quite rapidly. From 1988 to 1998, it grew at a rate of 154 percent in total constituency, or about 10 percent per year. The increase in churches was 118 percent.[103]

The largest UPCI national church or mission field is the Apostolic Church of Ethiopia, started by UPCI missionaries. Despite having faced severe persecution from the Ethiopian Orthodox Church and repression from a communist regime, the church has grown rapidly and now reports over 1,000,000 constituents. An annual outdoor crusade in Wara regularly attracts hundreds of thousands of attendees. In the first such crusade, in 1992, an estimated 130,000 people attended, 20,000 claimed their healing, and 25,000 received the Holy Spirit.[104] In 1999 an estimated 700,000 attended and 50,000 received the Holy Spirit.[105] The leadership of the Ethiopian church holds the unusual view that Mary was not the biological mother of Jesus but that His humanity was a direct creation of God out of the substance of His Word.

In other mission fields—including the Philippines, El Salvador, and Papua New Guinea—thousands have received the Holy Spirit in one service or in one week of services. For example, in April 1999 in one service, 4,700 received the Holy Spirit in the Philippines.[106]

The UPCI is the only Oneness organization to have a large missions program in all areas of the world. For a listing of UPCI national churches and mission fields with over 10,000 constituents, see Appendix G.

Because of the historical events we have examined, the UPCI is typically classified as a white organization, but this designation is no longer true. If we consider the international constituency, the UPCI is about 75 percent nonwhite.

If we consider only the U.S. and Canada, the UPCI is approximately 20 percent nonwhite. In these two countries, the UPCI conducts services in 42 languages. It has approximately 300 Spanish-language churches, 200 additional Spanish-language daughter works, and a total Hispanic constituency (including those in English-speaking churches) of approximately 70,000. Total black constituency, in both majority black and majority white congregations, is estimated at 75,000.[107]

Blacks now hold district offices—district board member, departmental director, or departmental secretary—in eight districts (15 percent), including representation on five district boards. Hispanics hold district offices in seven districts (13 percent), including representation on three district boards. Two districts have Asian/Pacific Islander and Native American officials. A total of fourteen districts (26 percent) have at least one person from these minority groups holding a district office. These districts are in the West (six), the South (three), the North (two), and Canada (three).

Six general divisions have a national board composed of members from each district, and some of them also have regional directors. All six divisions have one or more minority representatives as board members or regional directors. The General Board also has had minority representation for some years, not by legislation but through elections. Much progress has been made in this area, but clearly much more is needed.

The highest concentrations of United Pentecostal believers are as follows:[108]

Country, State, Province	UPCI Constituency	General Population	UPCI %
Mizoram, India	65,000	730,000	8.9%
Ethiopia	1,000,000	55,000,000	1.8%
Louisiana, U.S.A.	68,000	4,500,000	1.5%
New Brunswick, Canada	8,000	725,000	1.1%

Other Oneness Organizations in America

A number of other Oneness organizations have originated in the United States. In this section we discuss those that have attained a worldwide constituency of 20,000 or more as reported by Talmadge French in 1998. (Reported worldwide constituency is given in parentheses following the name.)

In 1919, R. C. Lawson, a convert of Haywood's and an early black leader in the interracial PAW, founded Refuge Temple, a large and powerful church, in New York City. From this base, he formed his own organization, the *Church of Our Lord Jesus Christ of the Apostolic Faith* (COOLJC) (140,000). He disagreed with the PAW on two major issues: he opposed allowing women to be pastors, and he opposed remarriage after divorce for any reason. An all-black group, COOLJC has retained a relatively conservative stance on matters of lifestyle and dress, and it has had strong leadership. At century's end it was led by William Bonner, one of Lawson's sons in the gospel.

In 1930, Sherrod C. Johnson split from COOLJC and formed the *Church of The Lord Jesus Christ of the Apostolic Faith* (24,700). The main issues were personal leadership, Johnson's stricter views on modesty of dress, and his unusual belief that the Sonship ceased at the death of Jesus.

In 1933, Henry Brooks left COOLJC to form *The Way of the Cross Church of Christ International* (31,000 constituents). He founded a large church in Washington, D.C.

In 1957 another split from COOLJC took place, led by Smallwood Williams. Again, the main disagreement was over authoritarian leadership. The new group has also relaxed some of the standards of dress. It is known as the *Bible Way Church of Our Lord Jesus Christ Worldwide* (101,000). Williams founded a large, influential church in Washington, D.C. He became quite active in the Civil Rights movement of the 1960s, serving as president of the Southern Christian Leadership Council in the city. He worked closely with Martin Luther King and met various federal officials, including President Lyndon Johnson.

Also in 1957, S. N. Hancock split from the PAW, forming the *Pentecostal Churches of the Apostolic Faith Association* (25,000). Hancock was a convert of Haywood's who became a leading PAW bishop and who married Haywood's widow. The division was caused primarily by a leadership struggle. However, Hancock also began to deviate from the Oneness position, proclaiming an adoptionist Christology that seemed to make the Son less than the Father, less than the true God. The organization has since rejected this doctrine, however.

Another group with roots in the PAW is the *United Church of Jesus Christ (Apostolic)* (32,300).

There are many Hispanic Apostolics in America. The largest group is the *Apostolic Assembly of the Faith in Christ Jesus* (116,700); it is the largest Hispanic Pentecostal church of any kind in the U.S. Many Hispanic ministers were part of the early PAW, but when the split along racial lines occurred in 1924, most of the Hispanics left. In 1925 they formed their own association to focus on ministry in Spanish. In 1926 they chose their name and elected Antonio Nava as president. These Apostolics require women to wear head coverings in church and do not allow women to preach.

After the UPCI, the best-known predominately white group in the U.S. is the *Assemblies of the Lord Jesus Christ* (48,500). It was formed in 1952 as a merger of three small Oneness groups, which in turn had originated with the departure of whites from the PAW in 1924.

Another predominantly white group is the *Church of Jesus Christ* (37,000), a conservative, loose-knit fellowship of formerly independent ministers.

The *International Ministerial Association* (63,600) adopted the Latter Rain teaching of the 1950s and left the UPCI. (See chapter 9.) W. E. Kidson, a prominent United Pentecostal minister, led this split in 1954.

Over the years, there have been several other breakaways from the UPCI and its predecessor organizations. Some have sought to be more strict in the doctrine of salvation and holiness of dress than the main group, and some have sought to relax standards in these areas. None of them have attained the size of the groups identified here, however.

As we have seen, almost all Oneness groups are aligned with the Finished Work camp. Several in the black community, however, originated in the Holiness movement and teach sanctification as a second work of grace. The largest is the *Apostolic Overcoming Holy Church of God* (35,000), whose founder, William Phillips, also taught that blacks are descendants of the Jews.

The *Church of God (Apostolic)* (31,000) also teaches the second blessing. It began as a Holiness church in 1897 and adopted Oneness Pentecostal views around 1915.

Several other small Oneness bodies, mostly offshoots of the Church of God in Christ, also teach sanctification as a second work. The largest group that apparently has such roots is the *Original Glorious Churches of God in Christ Apostolic Faith* (30,000).

In addition to the larger Oneness organizations, there are hundreds of small groups and independent works. There are Oneness sabbatarian groups and sacred name (Yahweh) adherents.

Many of the smaller groups and independent ministers are part of the *Apostolic World Christian Fellowship* (AWCF), an umbrella association that offers recognition to everyone who identifies with the plan of salvation according to Acts 2:38. It does not screen candidates or discipline members, but its purpose is to provide identification and fellowship. Its founder, Worthy Rowe, is the son of a Oneness pioneer, G. B. Rowe, who left the UPCI over the "Adam doctrine." He held that as to His humanity, Jesus was the reincarnation of Adam. For this reason, the UPCI has not associated with the AWCF, but it has sought one-on-one fellowship with other major Oneness organizations.

Other Oneness Organizations
around the World

The Pentecostal movement came to Mexico from American Hispanic Pentecostals. The earliest known

Mexicans to receive the Holy Spirit did so in 1914, and they were baptized in Jesus' name. From the U.S. contacts, an indigenous Mexican church came into being, known today as the *Apostolic Church of the Faith in Christ Jesus* (302,200 constituents worldwide), one of the largest churches in the country outside the Roman Catholic Church.

From this church have come two personality-based groups, the *Christian Gospel Spiritual Church* (20,000) and the *Light of the World* (600,000). The latter group is also known as the Aaronistas, because its founder, Eusebio Joaquin, assumed the name of Aaron and announced that he was a special prophet. It is quite exclusive and authoritarian in its theology. The Lord's Supper is celebrated only at the headquarters church in Guadalajara (the largest Protestant building in Mexico), and the faithful take a pilgrimage there once a year for that purpose. This group is now the largest Jesus Name Pentecostal body in Mexico and Central America.

From the work of Canadian, British, and American missionaries of the UPCI came the *United Pentecostal Church of Colombia* (1,000,000). Begun in 1936, it endured much persecution, including martyrdom, from Roman Catholics. It became completely indigenous in 1967. Today, it is the largest Protestant church in Colombia, and it has been the subject of two published church growth studies.[109]

In Chile, the *Voice in the Desert Apostolic Church* (70,000) originated from missionary efforts of the Assemblies of the Lord Jesus Christ. It is affiliated with that American group.

One of the earliest Pentecostal missionaries in China,

F. S. Ramsey, accepted baptism in Jesus' name by 1915 under the influence of Ewart's *Meat in Due Season*. Great revival erupted from Ramsey's base in Ta Fung Fu, Shansi Province, northern China. By 1917, Paul Wei, a Chinese Pentecostal, had embraced the Oneness message, and he established the *True Jesus Church* in Tianjin and Beijing (his hometown). By 1918 he was joined by Chang Ling Sheng and Barnabas Chang. Sheng had been baptized in Jesus' name by Ramsey, and he assumed leadership of the True Jesus Church when Wei died in 1919. The True Jesus Church is now the largest church in China and one of the largest in Taiwan. It reports 12,000 churches and 3,300,000 constituents worldwide, with 3,000,000 in mainland China and 100,000 in Taiwan.[110]

As its name indicates, the True Jesus Church is a strong Oneness organization. It teaches baptism in Jesus' name and the baptism of the Holy Spirit as the new birth. It also advocates holiness in lifestyle and dress. It holds two doctrines unusual for Pentecostals, however: it strongly advocates worship on the Sabbath, and it allows infant baptism.[111] Moreover, "baptism must be full immersion in natural, living [flowing] water . . . with the candidate's head facing downward."[112]

The True Jesus Church is the second largest Oneness Pentecostal body in the world. When we consider the total number of churches and ministers, as well as our estimates of inclusive constituency, the UPCI is clearly the largest.

In the early years of the movement, there were more Oneness missionaries in China than any other country. All missionaries were expelled when the communists seized power in 1949. From these efforts over the years, as well as more recent works, Talmadge French estimated that there are perhaps 1,000,000 independent Jesus Name believers in China.[113]

In Japan, missionaries B. S. Moore and Frank and Elizabeth Gray accepted the Jesus Name message in 1915. Leonard Coote, a British businessman, received the Holy Spirit under the Grays and took over their work. Through contact with Coote and others, a Pentecostal pastor named Jun Murai accepted the Jesus Name message in the 1930s. He established the *Spirit of Jesus Church*, which is the largest Christian denomination in Japan today, with a reported 256 churches, 520 house churches, and 420,000 constituents. It is a remarkable success story in a land that has been very difficult for Christian missions.[114]

Perhaps under the influence of the True Jesus Church, the Spirit of Jesus Christ is also sabbatarian. Its most unusual doctrine is proxy baptism for the dead.

In Indonesia, there is a large "triunity" group that baptizes in Jesus' name, the *Pentecostal Church of Indonesia* (1,000,000). This church is an amalgamation with diverse views on the Godhead. It originated from missions efforts by Bethel Temple in Seattle, founded by W. H. Offiler. Glenn Cook baptized Offiler in Jesus' name in 1915. Offiler did not embrace the full Oneness position, however, but taught a modified "triunity" view.

In recent years, the Philippines has been a productive field for Oneness Pentecostal missions. A number of organizations have formed there, some breaking away from the UPCI. The group reporting the largest number other than the UPCI is the *Jesus Church*, which claims five churches and 40,000 constituents.

John G. Lake, a convert from Zion City, took the Pentecostal message to South Africa. One of Lake's converts, C. J. Beetge, accepted the Oneness position in 1944. He established the Assemblies of Christ, now known as the *Reformed Christian Church of South Africa*. This group has 200 churches; it claims 200,000 constituents, which seems high for the number of churches.

Shiloh United Church of Christ Apostolic (Worldwide), based in the United Kingdom, has 130 churches and claims a questionably high figure of 101,000 constituents, almost all in Africa.

Pentecostal missions came to Russia and the countries of the former Soviet Union in 1915-16 under the ministry of Andrew Urshan. He baptized converts in Jesus' name, and he himself was rebaptized in Jesus' name by one of them. Urshan established a strong Oneness church, led by N. P. Smorodin, which became known as the *Evangelical Christians in the Spirit of the Apostles*. These believers were persecuted severely, with Smorodin dying in prison in 1953. Today, most of these churches are independent. Some have formed an organization based in St. Petersburg, some are part of an organization in Kazakhstan, and some have joined the UPCI. The total constituency of all the known churches outside the UPCI is about 28,000.

For a listing of major Jesus Name Pentecostal organizations worldwide, with total churches and constituency, see Appendix F.

Summary of Oneness Pentecostal Beliefs

In our survey of major Oneness organizations worldwide, we have noted a diversity of beliefs and practices. All of them share key beliefs with conservative Protestantism, including the existence of one true God; the creation of the universe by God; the inspiration and authority of Scripture; the existence of angels, the devil, and demons; the fall and sinfulness of humanity; the Incarnation (Jesus Christ is God manifested in the flesh and the Son of God); the Atonement (the death, burial, and resurrection of Jesus Christ); salvation by grace through faith in Jesus Christ; water baptism; the New Testament church as the people of God; the priesthood of believers; the rapture of the church; the second coming of Jesus Christ to earth; the Millennium; the last judgment; eternal punishment for the unrighteous; and eternal life for the righteous. With the exception of a small American "spiritual communion" group called the Associated Brotherhood of Christians, they observe the Lord's Supper, and most practice foot washing as an ordinance.

Like other Pentecostal groups, they all teach the baptism of the Holy Spirit with the initial sign of tongues, spiritual gifts for today, and divine healing.

In addition, these groups share three major Oneness Pentecostal distinctives: (1) the Oneness view of the Godhead, (2) the plan of salvation according to Acts 2:38, and (3) holiness of lifestyle and dress (at least in some measure). We have already examined the doctrine of God in chapter 3, and we will examine the doctrine of salvation next. The teachings on holiness are not unique to Oneness Pentecostals, but they characterized the Holiness and Pentecostal movements generally, including Trinitarian Pentecostals until the latter half of the twentieth century. Thus we will discuss this point in chapter 5, even though Oneness Pentecostals are the main proponents of these teachings today.

The section titles of the Articles of Faith of the UPCI are as follows:

> Preamble [authority of the Bible], The One True God, The Son of God, The Name [Jesus], Creation of Man and His Fall, Repentance, Water Baptism, The Baptism of the Holy Spirit, Fundamental Doctrine [the plan of salvation according to Acts 2:38], Divine Healing [in the Atonement], Sacrament or Communion, Foot Washing, Holiness, The Grace of God [against unconditional eternal security], The Restitution of All Things [against universalism], Conscientious Scruples [pacifism and noncombatant military service], Secret Societies, Etc. [opposition], Translation of Saints [the Rapture], Marriage and Divorce [remarriage allowed for "innocent party" in cases of "fornication"], Tithing, Second Coming of Jesus, Millennium, Final Judgment, Public School Activities [opposition to secular mandates that contradict holiness principles], Religious Holiday [designation to assist people in attending the general conference].

The Doctrine of Salvation

One of the distinctive positions of Oneness Pentecostals is that God's standard of full salvation for the New Testament church is repentance, water baptism in the name of Jesus Christ, and the baptism of the Holy Spirit with the initial sign of speaking in tongues. The major Oneness groups hold that this experience is "the new birth," although there is some debate on this issue.

While there are differences between groups and even within groups on the proper theological characterization of these three steps of faith, there is agreement that God commands everyone to obey them. There is also agreement that these steps do not constitute salvation by works. Rather, they are applications of the grace of God, purchased by the blood of Jesus Christ, and they are expressions of faith in God.

This understanding of salvation did not suddenly spring into being with Oneness Pentecostals. Rather, the groundwork was laid in the teaching and terminology of John Wesley and other early Methodists and then by the earliest Pentecostals, including Charles Parham, William Seymour, and especially William Durham.

The concept of "full salvation" appears in the writings of John Wesley and other Wesleyan and Holiness authors.[115] As we saw in chapter 1, Wesley believed in two distinct works of grace: justification and entire sanctification (Christian perfection). Both John Wesley and his designated successor, John Fletcher, spoke of sanctification as being "baptized with the Holy Spirit."[116]

In an unpublished manuscript, Fletcher invoked Wesley's authority for equating the phrases "to be born again of water and of the Spirit" and "being baptized with water and with the Holy Ghost." He specifically linked John 3:3, 5 with Acts 2:38, citing them in the same paragraph. Fletcher further said of Wesley, "He explicitly rests the doctrine of full Christian regeneration on the full or Pentecostal dispensation of the Spirit." Fletcher allowed for the existence of "two sorts of children of God": "imperfect believers in Christ" and "those who are perfected by the full baptism of the Holy Ghost." He argued, however, that the Christian church began on the Day of Pentecost, that "the peculiar glory of the Christian Church consists in the Pentecostal fullness of the Spirit," and that "we must be baptized with [the Holy Ghost] baptism and refining fire, before we can be styled true (I would say complete or truly spiritual) 'members of Christ's mystical body.'"[117]

Early Pentecostals, including Parham, Seymour, and Durham, applied the terms "full salvation" and "full gospel" to the baptism of the Holy Spirit with the initial evidence of tongues. (See chapters 1 and 2.) Parham taught that one must be baptized with the Holy Spirit to be truly part of the church, to escape the wrath of the Tribulation, and to inherit the new heavens. In one place he even used the phrase "being born of the water and the Spirit" to refer to the complete experience of entering the church, as opposed to an initial confession of faith.

Seymour likewise spoke of the baptism of the Spirit as necessary to be part of the church and to escape Tribulation wrath. His *Apostolic Faith* paper emphasized the need of "walking in the light" and accepting this "Bible salvation." Those who rejected it were in danger of going to hell.

Durham explicitly identified repentance, water baptism, and the baptism of the Spirit as God's "plan of salvation," citing Acts 2:38. Being baptized with the Holy Spirit was necessary to be part of the church; people who did not receive this experience had at best an "abnormal Christianity."

Thus, when the early Oneness pioneers began proclaiming water baptism in the name of Jesus Christ, it was only a small advance for them to say that all three elements of Acts 2:38 were necessary for entrance into the New Testament church. For the earliest and most significant Oneness leaders, belief in Acts 2:38 as the "new birth" and "full salvation" came almost simultaneously with belief in the Oneness doctrine of God.

From the start, Frank Ewart equated being "born again" with baptism in Jesus' name and the baptism of the Holy Ghost.[118] He reported the following testimony, apparently from 1914 or 1915: "Brother E. D. Yeoman . . . declared that he never was saved until he surrendered to Christ, was baptized in Jesus' name, and received the gift of the Holy Ghost."[119]

George Farrow, who attended Ewart's church in Los Angeles and composed "All in Him," wrote in January 1915:[120]

> Many of the saints here are seeing it and walking in the light. This truth is water baptism in the name of Jesus Christ. . . . It may seem to be very nonessential at first thought. . . . But God has surely been blessing this truth and talking very definitely to many about its importance. . . . I also am coming to see that under the present light that we have, nothing short of the baptism in the Holy Ghost is really salvation in the highest sense of the word.

G. T. Haywood taught that the new birth is water baptism in the name of Jesus and the baptism of the Holy Spirit with tongues.[121] In 1913, even before his baptism in Jesus' name, he drew up a tract showing that water baptism and the baptism of the Holy Ghost were necessary to enter into the kingdom of God.[122] In 1914 he penned the hymn "Baptized into the Body":[123]

Verse 1: Have you been baptized into the Body? Baptized with the Holy Ghost; There is but one way to enter in it, Just as they did on Pentecost.

Chorus: Are you in the Church triumphant? Are you in the Savior's Bride? Come and be baptized into the Body, And forevermore abide.

Verse 2: There is but one Church, Bride or Body, And into it we're all baptized; By the one, true, promised Holy Spirit; Tho' by the world we're all despised.

Verse 3: Every creed has claimed to be the Body, But the "plumb-line" proved untrue, All their dreams; for God has so determined, To bring His Son's true Bride to view.

Verse 4: Many thought that they were in the Body, 'Til the Holy Ghost had come; When the Word of God was opened to them, They entered in, and yet there's room.

Verse 5: Those who died before the Holy Spirit/ Came upon us from on high/ May, by faith with Saints of old departed, Arise to meet Him in the sky.

Verse 6: When the Bridegroom comes, will you be ready; And your vessel all filled and bright? You will be among the foolish virgins, If you do not walk in the light.

Oliver Fauss took the following notes at the 1915 Elton Bible Conference:[124]

God is bringing us back to Acts 2:38, His plan. . . . God's pattern is Acts 2:38, this is plain. . . . We have no record of God being in these people until the Day of Pentecost (Colossians 1:27; John 3:3). Cornelius was a just man, but not saved (Acts 10:22; 11:14-18; Matthew 28:19; Mark 16:15; Luke 24:47; Acts 2:38).

Howard Goss contrasted "the Spirit-filled Christian and the nominal church attendant." He said, "These last are all alike without a Saviour, and thus have no scriptural promise of ever seeing heaven, because they have not actually been adopted into God's family, nor have they legally become His child, and thereby have no rightful claim on Him."[125]

During the struggles over Jesus Name baptism, the Assemblies of God, in its 1915 and 1916 general councils, censured the view that the baptism of the Holy Spirit is the new birth.[126] In 1917, E. N. Bell denounced the view that water baptism is part of salvation.[127] Clearly, they dealt with ministers who taught that the birth of water and Spirit was baptism of water and Spirit.

Andrew Urshan similarly taught that obeying Acts 2:38 constitutes being "born of water and of the Spirit." He proclaimed, "You must be born again or be lost!"[128]

The Articles of Faith of the GAAA (1917) stated that there was but one entrance into the true church, the body of Christ, namely, "a baptism of water and Spirit." Moreover, "God's standard of salvation" includes "a holy, Spirit-filled life with signs following."[129]

The PAW's original doctrinal statement as a Oneness body repeated the foregoing statements from the GAAA and also said, probably still quoting from the GAAA, "In order to escape the judgment of God and to have the hope of enjoying the glory of life eternal, one must be thoroughly saved from their sins, wholly sanctified unto God and filled with the Holy Ghost." The PAW's 1919 conference affirmed by majority vote, "The new birth (being 'born again') includes a genuine repentance, water baptism in Jesus' name, and the baptism of the Holy Ghost, evidenced by speaking in other tongues as the Spirit gives utterance."[130]

Let us turn to the two organizations that merged to form the UPCI: the PCI and the PAJC. The first doctrinal statement of the PMA, later renamed PCI, said, "The Bible way of salvation is repentance toward God, faith toward our Lord Jesus Christ, obedience to the Word of God by baptism in water (in Jesus' name), and receiving the gift of the Holy Ghost, as in Acts 2:4, 38."[131] In the September 1929 issue of the *Apostolic Herald*, the voice of the PMA, Goss stated that to be in the Christian church "one must be baptized in the Holy Spirit," but he felt that sins were remitted before water baptism.[132] In the August 1930 issue of the *Apostolic Herald*, Farrow wrote that Acts 2:38 is the new birth.[133]

In 1936, when discussing a possible merger with the PCI, the PAJC convention insisted that the basis of union be the following: "that baptism in water in Jesus' name, and the baptism of the Holy Ghost, with the initial evidence of speaking in other tongues, be recognized as constituting the new birth, and be accepted as one of our fundamental doctrines." A committee of PCI leaders responded, however, that "the matter of the new birth be left open to personal conviction."[134]

At the merger of these two groups in 1945, there were still some differences of opinion on the new birth, but a strong majority believed that the complete Acts 2:38 experience was necessary for salvation. S. W. Chambers, who was elected general secretary at the merger, said most ministers believed in the necessity of both water baptism and the baptism of the Holy Spirit. He regarded the differences as primarily of terminology, not so much of basic belief.[135] E. J. McClintock, PCI pastor in Idaho at the time of the merger and later director of the UPCI General Sunday School Division, gave the same explanation, independently using almost the same words. He said the ministers agreed on the necessity of the three steps of Acts 2:38 but did not all agree on terminology.[136] Nathaniel Urshan, son of Andrew Urshan and general superintendent of the UPCI for many years, agreed with the assessment of Chambers and McClintock and stated that the majority believed Acts 2:38 to be the new birth.[137] Indeed, an analysis reveals that about eighty-five to ninety percent of the merged body held that the full Acts 2:38 experience was essential to salvation.[138]

The two major histories of the UPCI, by Arthur Clanton and Fred Foster, state that the most significant difference of opinion was on the essentiality of water baptism.[139] Clanton explained that the PCI allowed greater latitude on the new-birth message than the PAJC. David Gray of the PCI, who became the first youth president of the UPC, confirmed this statement.[140] In short, not everyone agreed that Acts 2:38 was "the new birth," and in particular, a significant minority did not believe that "remission of sins" necessarily occurred at water baptism. What Chambers, McClintock, Urshan, and Gray have pointed out, however, is that despite the different interpretations, there was agreement that the Acts 2:38 experience is God's plan for New Testament salvation, whatever the precise theological terminology that one should attach to each step or to the experience as a whole.

J. L. Hall, editor in chief of the UPCI, chairman

of the UPCI's Historical Committee, and a leading Pentecostal historian, offered the following explanation of the Fundamental Doctrine:[141]

There does not appear to have been a doctrinal difference between the two groups, for most ministers in the PAJC and PCI held to the necessity of the Acts 2:38 experience. However, a few ministers in each group—more in the PCI than in the PAJC—held that a person may be saved at repentance. The merging agreement included the "Fundamental Doctrine" statement affirming that salvation includes water baptism and the gift of the Holy Ghost—something the overwhelming majority of both the PAJC and PCI believed. However, to show patience toward ministers who practiced Acts 2:38 but who held to the view that salvation—at least in part—occurred at faith and repentance, the "Fundamental Doctrine" also includes the second paragraph calling for unity in Spirit until all came to the same view. There was no tolerance on the salvation message of Acts 2:38, for this is clearly stated. It was only tolerance toward those who needed time to accept the view of salvation as stated in the first paragraph.

The Fundamental Doctrine of the UPCI states:[142]

The basic and fundamental doctrine of this organization shall be the Bible standard of full salvation, which is repentance, baptism in water by immersion in the name of the Lord Jesus Christ for the remission of sins, and the baptism of the Holy Ghost with the initial sign of speaking with other tongues as the Spirit gives utterance.

We shall endeavor to keep the unity of the Spirit until we all come into the unity of the faith, at the same time admonishing all brethren that they shall not contend for their different views to the disunity of the body.

The first paragraph relies on Acts 2:38. We have already discussed antecedents for the term "full salvation" and for the use of Acts 2:38 as a paradigm.

The second paragraph is based on Ephesians 4:3, 13. Many early Pentecostals made a similar appeal to maintain "the unity of the Spirit until we all come into the unity of the faith." In 1913 this phrase appeared in the writings of Frank Ewart, D. W. Kerr, and Andrew Urshan, and on the masthead of *The Christian Evangel* (J. R. Flower's paper that would later become an official organ of the Assemblies of God).[143] In 1914, the statement appeared in the original constitution of the Assemblies of God, and in 1919 it appeared in the original constitution of the Pentecostal Assemblies of Canada.[144]

In recent years, a number of trinitarian theologians have identified Acts 2:38 as the paradigm for New Testament salvation, including Frederick Bruner (Evangelical), James Dunn (Evangelical), Leighton Ford (Evangelical), David Pawson (Charismatic), and Kilian McDonnell and George Montague (Catholic Charismatics).[145] Gordon Fee, an Assemblies of God theologian, has similarly argued that Spirit baptism is not a distinct experience subsequent to the new birth.[146] Typically, however, they do not teach that tongues is the initial evidence of the Spirit baptism, or else they offer some exceptions.

At this point, it is important to note that the Oneness pioneers we have cited did not proclaim dogmatically that all who had not experienced Acts 2:38 would go to the lake of fire. Like Parham, Seymour, and Durham, most felt that there still could be a type of salvation outside the New Testament church, similar to that of Old Testament saints, particularly for people who walked in all the "light" they had received. We have already seen examples of this thinking in the quotation from Farrow and in the song "Baptized in the Body" by Haywood.

Thus Ewart could say, "Pastor Durham passed on to glory at a comparatively early age," even though he died without being baptized in Jesus' name. Ewart even called A. G. Garr "a great man of God" while also remarking that he "flatly rejected" the Oneness message.[147]

G. T. Haywood made a distinction between being begotten and being born, similar to one Parham had made earlier. Christians who had faith but who were not born again according to Acts 2:38 could still be considered as "'begotten' by the Word" even though they had not yet been "born of the Spirit." In language reminiscent of the *Apostolic Faith* (Azusa Street), he discussed the question of whether all such people were lost:[148]

> The one question that is so often asked is, "Are all those people who thought they were born of the Spirit, and were not, lost?" No, not by any means. They shall be given eternal life in the resurrection if they walked in all the light that was given them while they lived.

Andrew Urshan likewise made a distinction between

being begotten and born. He described his status at repentance as "a happy, blood-washed, newly conceived child of the King!" He spoke of people being "saved" before they were born again and wrote of some who died in the faith before baptism in Jesus' name. Nevertheless, he taught that baptism in Jesus' name is for the remission of sins. It is necessary to go in the Rapture and escape the Tribulation. He also believed strongly that the baptism of the Holy Spirit is necessary.[149] People who believed in God and lived righteous lives "without ever coming to the light of being born again according to Acts 2:38" will rise in the second resurrection, presumably to live on the new earth.[150]

Conclusions

In chapter 5, we will discuss doctrines of Trinitarian Pentecostals, make comparisons, and draw conclusions about the theology of Pentecostals overall.

5

Trinitarian Pentecostal Organizations

In this chapter we will survey the two remaining branches of the Pentecostal movement—the Second Work Trinitarians and the Finished Work Trinitarians—and draw general conclusions about Pentecostal doctrine. We will briefly identify the major groups, placing the reported worldwide constituency in parentheses after each name.[151]

Second Work Trinitarian Pentecostals

The Second Work Trinitarian Pentecostals teach three distinct crisis experiences associated with God's plan of salvation: (1) conversion (also the time of justification and regeneration), (2) sanctification, and (3) the baptism of the Holy Spirit with the initial sign of speaking in other tongues. This wing of the movement retained the earlier Holiness movement's doctrine of sanctification as a second work of grace.

In recent years, however, the emphasis on sanctification as a second work of grace has diminished significantly. So concluded James Bowers, a Church of God minister in Scottsboro, Alabama, from a study of sermons, articles, textbooks, and other publications:[152]

> Sanctification is conspicuously absent from the preaching and teaching of Church of God pastors. . . . Whatever teaching Church of God members receive on sanctification and holiness is likely to come from some source other than their local church. . . . Sanctification has been largely neglected in denominationally sponsored training opportunity for laity and ministers. . . . Nor did Church of God members receive definitive instruction on sanctification from their prominent authors [in recent years]. With few exceptions, sanctification was left unaddressed or presented in ambiguous language. . . . Many Church of God authors were either non-Wesleyan, ambiguous, or altogether silent where sanctification was concerned.

Most Second Work Trinitarian Pentecostals were part of existing Holiness denominations that joined the Pentecostal movement. (See chapter 2.) The predominantly white groups have grown steadily, although not as fast as the AG and UPCI, the major representatives of the other two wings of Pentecostalism. The major black group has grown rapidly.

The *Church of God in Christ* (COGIC) (6,500,000)

is by far the largest Holiness Pentecostal denomination in the United States. Indeed it is the largest Pentecostal denomination in the country, one of the largest black denominations, and one of the most rapidly growing denominations. In the U.S. it grew from a reported 733 churches and 30,263 adherents in 1926 to 15,300 churches and 5,499,875 adherents in 1991. We should note, however, that church growth researcher C. Peter Wagner and others believe that its currently reported constituency is considerably overstated—it is over 350 per church—and should be reduced by about one-half for comparison with other denominations.[153]

The church officially emphasizes seven major doctrines: the Bible, the trinity, the Rapture, salvation, healing, the baptism of the Holy Ghost, and sanctification. The statement on salvation stresses the importance of repentance, faith, water baptism, and the Holy Ghost: "We believe that the only means of being cleansed from sin is through repentance, faith in the precious Blood of Jesus Christ and being baptized in water. We believe that regeneration by the Holy Ghost is absolutely essential for personal salvation." The church emphasizes sanctification, but its official statement does not clearly define it as a second work: "The doctrine of sanctification or holiness is emphasized, as being essential to the salvation of mankind. . . . We believe in the sanctifying power of the Holy Spirit, by whose indwelling, the Christian is enabled to live a Holy and separated life in this present world."[154]

Originally COGIC "held to strict standards of dress and personal conduct," but after the death of the founder, C. H. Mason, in 1961, there was a "blurring of doctrinal and disciplinary distinctives."[155] Unlike other black denominations, COGIC has been quite willing to have fellowship with the Charismatic movement.

The *Church of God (Cleveland, Tennessee)* (CG) (4,000,000), is the largest predominantly white organization among Second Work Pentecostals. Its foreign missions efforts have benefited greatly from mergers with several large indigenous Pentecostal churches. In the U.S. it grew from 202 churches and 7,784 adherents in 1916 to 6,060 churches and 753,230 adherents in 1996.

The CG has a number of black members. In 1936, 42 of 1081 churches were identified as black. From 1920 to 1966, black and white congregations were segregated in the official structure. Today, however, there are no such barriers, and the Council of Eighteen (international governing body) must always have black membership.

R. G. Spurling, the founder of the Christian Union in 1886 (which became the CG), was opposed to creeds of any kind. By 1910, however, the church found it necessary to publish its basic beliefs. A committee report, which became the official teachings, stated, "The Church of God stands for the whole Bible rightly divided. The New Testament as the only rule for government and discipline." It then listed twenty-five prominent teachings, as follows (excluding Scripture references):[156]

(1) Repentance. (2) Justification. (3) Regeneration. (4) New Birth. (5) Sanctification subsequent to Justification. (6) Holiness. (7) Water Baptism by immersion. (8) Baptism with the Holy Ghost subsequent to cleansing: The enduement of power for service. (9) The speaking in tongues as the evidence of the baptism with the Holy Ghost. (10) The full

restoration of the gifts to the church. (11) Signs following believers. (12) Fruits of the Spirit. (13) Divine healing provided for all in the Atonement. (14) The Lord's supper. (15) Washing the saints' feet. (16) Tithing and giving. (17) Restitution where possible. (18) Premillennial second coming of Jesus: First, to resurrect the dead saints, and to catch away the living saints to meet Him in the air. Second, to reign on the earth a thousand years. (19) Resurrections. (20) Eternal life for the righteous. (21) Eternal punishment of the wicked. No liberation, no annihilation. (22) Total abstinence from all liquor or strong drinks. (23) Against the use of tobacco in any form, opium, morphine, etc. (24) Meats and drinks [citing passages of Scripture granting liberty]. (25) The Sabbath [citing passages of Scripture granting liberty].

In the 1940s a controversy erupted over sanctification as a second work of grace. In response, the church adopted it first official Declaration of Faith, which has remained unchanged. It consists of fourteen points affirming the verbal inspiration of the Bible; the trinity; the deity, humanity, death, burial, resurrection, ascension, and exaltation of Jesus Christ; the sinfulness of humanity and necessity of repentance; justification, regeneration, and new birth by faith in the blood of Jesus; "sanctification subsequent to the new birth, through faith in the blood of Christ; through the Word, and by the Holy Ghost"; holiness as "God's standard of living for His people"; "the baptism of the Holy Ghost subsequent to a clean heart"; speaking in tongues as the initial evidence of the Spirit baptism; water baptism by immersion in the trinitarian formula; divine healing in the Atonement; the Lord's supper and foot washing; the premillennial second coming of Jesus; and the bodily resurrection, with eternal life for the righteous and eternal punishment for the wicked.[157] The statement on sanctification was a compromise that did not clearly define it as a second work of grace but averted a schism.

As noted in chapter 2, when the CG removed A. J. Tomlinson as its leader for life, he broke away and formed a new church in 1923, which he considered the true church. Due to litigation, this church was forced to adopt a distinct legal name. For years it was known as the Tomlinson Church of God, but since 1952 has been called the *Church of God of Prophecy* (CGP) (286,848) in its "secular affairs." In the U.S. it grew from 441 churches and 18,351 adherents in 1936 to 1,961 churches and 72,859 adherents in 1996.

The CGP has a distinctive ecclesiology. It believes that the true church as an organization disappeared in A.D. 325, when the Roman emperor Constantine essentially united church and state. The true church was restored with A. J. Tomlinson in 1903. While members of other churches may be saved, eventually the saved people will recognize that the CGP is the true church.

To commemorate the spot where Tomlinson received his revelation from God to restore the church, the CGP established the Fields of the Wood, a meeting ground named because of a belief that it fulfills Psalm 132:6. The church has erected various religious monuments on the site, which are maintained by the Church of Prophecy Marker Association.

The *International Pentecostal Holiness Church*

(IPHC) (378,538) resulted from a merger of three holiness denominations that embraced the Pentecostal experience: the Fire-Baptized Holiness Church (founded 1895), the Holiness Church of North Carolina (founded 1898), and the Tabernacle Pentecostal Church (founded 1898). The Fire-Baptized Holiness Church taught an especially strict standard of holiness, even prohibiting the eating of pork and the wearing of neckties.

The five "cardinal doctrines" of the church are justification by faith, sanctification as a second work of grace, the baptism of the Holy Spirit with the evidence of speaking in tongues, divine healing in the Atonement, and the imminent, premillennial return of Jesus Christ.[158] In accordance with its Methodist roots, the IPHC allows baptism by sprinkling.

The IPHC revised its statement on sanctification in 1997 to acknowledge the progressive nature of sanctification instead of merely presenting "entire sanctification" at one point in time, yet the statement still confesses sanctification as a "definite, instantaneous work of grace." Its Articles of Faith now explain sanctification as follows:[159]

> Jesus Christ shed His blood for the complete cleansing of the justified believer from all indwelling sin and from its pollution, subsequent to justification. . . .
>
> While sanctification is initiated in regeneration and consummated in glorification, we believe that it includes a definite, instantaneous work of grace achieved by faith subsequent to regeneration.

In the U.S. the IPHC grew from 192 churches and

5,353 adherents in 1916 to 1,653 churches and 157,163 adherents in 1996. In addition to the reported worldwide constituency, it has two large indigenous churches as its affiliates—the Pentecostal Methodist Church of Chile and the Wesleyan Methodist Church of Brazil.

Over the years, the IPHC has moderated its Holiness and Pentecostal distinctives and identified closely with the Evangelical movement. Many members have transferred to non-Pentecostal denominations while not renouncing their Pentecostal identity. The most notable example is Oral Roberts, who became a Methodist minister. In many cases, upward social mobility or a job transfer was the catalyst for the change. As of 1988, researcher David Barrett estimated that there were 150,000 IPHC adherents in the U.S. but another 450,000 former adherents in other denominations.[160]

A small black Holiness organization founded in 1886, the *United Holy Church of America* (50,000), also accepted the Pentecostal experience. It teaches that speaking in tongues is one of the spiritual gifts but not necessarily the initial evidence of the Holy Spirit baptism.

There are a number of smaller groups in this branch of Pentecostalism, mostly offshoots of the groups we have already discussed. Also in this category are the *Apostolic Faith* (Baxter Springs, KS) (4,000), founded by Charles Parham, and the *Apostolic Faith Mission* (Portland, OR) (4,100), founded by Frances Crawford.

Finished Work Trinitarian Pentecostals

The second branch of Pentecostalism accepted William Durham's doctrine that sanctification was not a second work of grace but a process that began at conversion. The Oneness movement arose within this branch, but the groups we will discuss rejected that doctrine and remained trinitarian.

The largest Pentecostal denomination in the world is the *Assemblies of God* (AG) (30,000,000). It was founded in 1914 as the first Finished Work group. (See chapter 3.) The AG did not explicitly exclude those who believed in sanctification as a second work, however.

The Assemblies of God is the first or second largest Protestant church in about thirty countries of the world. Its total constituency includes 16,000,000 in Brazil. The church there is actually an indigenous church founded in 1911 that later affiliated with the AG but retained its own government.

In the U.S. the AG had 118 churches and 6,703 adherents in 1916. For 1996 the AG reported 11,823 churches, 32,314 ministers, 1,573,108 in Sunday morning attendance, 1,407,941 members, and an estimated 2,467,588 constituents ("persons of all ages who identify with an A/G church"). Of the total churches, 14.7 percent identified themselves as Hispanic and 1.4 percent as black. Average annual water baptisms per reporting church were 15.2, and average annual Spirit baptisms were 12.2.[161]

In 1916, in response to the Oneness controversy, the AG adopted a Statement of Fundamental Truths. The preamble explained:[162]

> This Statement of Fundamental Truths is not intended as a creed for the Church, nor as a basis of fellowship among Christians, but only as a basis of unity for the ministry alone. . . . The human phraseology employed

in such statement is not inspired nor contended for, but the truth set forth in such phraseology is held to be essential to a full Gospel ministry. No claim is made that it contains all truth in the Bible, only that it covers our present needs as to these fundamental matters.

The statement consisted of seventeen points, with the following headings:

(1) The Scriptures Inspired. (2) The One True God. (3) Man, His Fall and Redemption. (4) The Salvation of Man. (5) The Promise of the Father. (6) The Full Consummation of the Baptism in the Holy Ghost. (7) Entire Sanctification, the Goal for All Believers. (8) The Church a Living Organism. (9) The Ministry and Evangelism. (10) The Lord's Supper. (11) Baptism in Water. (12) Divine Healing. (13) The Essentials as to the Godhead. (14) The Blessed Hope. (15) The Imminent Coming and Millennial Reign of Jesus. (16) The Lake of Fire. (17) The New Heavens and New Earth.

Section 2 stated that God has "revealed Himself as embodying the principles of relationship and association, i.e., as Father, Son, and Holy Ghost." Section 13, which was about the same length as all the other sections combined, expressly taught the doctrine of the trinity and refuted the doctrine of Oneness. It said that God is "a Trinity" or "one Being of three Persons." The distinction of persons "is an eternal fact, but as to its mode it is inscrutable and incomprehensible, because unexplained.

(That is, it is not explained as to how there can be three persons in the Godhead.)"

This section denounced the Oneness doctrine in strong terms:

> It is a transgression of the Doctrine of Christ to say that Jesus Christ derived the title, Son of God, either from the fact of the incarnation, or because of His relation to the economy of redemption. . . . To deny that the Father is a real and eternal Father, and that the Son is a real and eternal Son, is . . . a denial of the Father and the Son; and a displacement of the truth that Jesus Christ is come in the flesh.

Some of the scriptural references cited as support were I John 2:22-23 and II John 9, which speak about the spirit of antichrist, false prophets, and not having God.

Sections 5 and 6 explained that the baptism in the Holy Ghost is "the normal experience of all in the early Christian Church," and "the full consummation . . . is indicated by the initial sign of speaking in tongues, as the Spirit of God gives utterance." However, "this wonderful experience is distinct from and subsequent to the experience of the new birth."

Section 7 proclaimed the importance of "a life of holiness without which no man shall see the Lord" and "entire sanctification [as] the will of God for all believers." "Entire sanctification" is Wesleyan language; thus, in principle, a believer in the second work could subscribe to the statement.

Section 12 taught that divine healing is in the Atonement. While the document affirmed the Lord's supper and water baptism, there was no mention of foot washing and no mention of a required baptismal formula.

The Statement of Fundamental Truths was revised in 1983. It now consists of sixteen points. Most of the language remains essentially the same as in 1916, with a significant exception: the entire section entitled "The Essentials as to the Godhead" has been deleted. Instead there is a brief statement that Jesus is "the eternal Son of God." Some other significant clarifications are as follows: (1) The current statement eliminates the term "entire sanctification." (2) It further describes speaking in tongues as "the initial physical evidence of the baptism in the Holy Ghost" and "the initial physical sign." (3) It says the Rapture is "the imminent and blessed hope of the church," indicating a pretribulation Rapture.[163]

In position papers adopted in the 1970s through 1990s, the AG defined its position on a number of controversial issues.[164] The papers affirm the inerrancy of Scripture, tongues as the initial evidence of the Holy Ghost and as real languages spoken as the Spirit gives utterance, pastoral authority, ministry in the body, women in ministry, the pre-tribulation Rapture, and divorce and remarriage in the case of marital unfaithfulness only. One paper prohibits the licensing of ministers who have divorced and remarried (regardless of the reason). Other papers refute the doctrines of unconditional eternal security, annihilation or liberation of the wicked in eternity, divine healing as automatic upon faith or as incompatible with medical assistance, and various doctrines that are prominent in the Charismatic movement. (See chapter 10.) Finally, with some position papers the AG opposes abortion, alcoholic beverages, gambling, homosexuality, and transcendental meditation.

Shortly after the Oneness controversy, the AG faced a challenge to the doctrine of tongues as the initial evidence of the Holy Spirit baptism. F. F. Bosworth, one of the original delegates in 1914 and later an executive presbyter, began to teach that tongues was only one of many possible signs of the Spirit baptism. The AG reaffirmed its position that tongues is the only initial sign. Consequently, Bosworth withdrew from the AG in 1918.

He joined the Christian and Missionary Alliance (CMA), which had lost numerous ministers and members to the Pentecostal movement, many of whom entered into the AG. The CMA allowed speaking in tongues and other supernatural gifts but did not promote them. In later years, however, it has distanced itself from Pentecostal manifestations. Bosworth held many healing campaigns and was an important influence on the post–World War II healing revival. He joined William Branham in several of his campaigns.

Over the years, many other influential ministers were part of the AG but left for other organizations or ministries. Examples are Aimee Semple McPherson, Finis Dake (author of *Dake's Annotated Reference Bible*), Kenneth Hagin, A. A. Allen, Jim Bakker, Jimmy Swaggart, and Paul Crouch.

The *International Church of the Foursquare Gospel* (ICFG) (2,500,000) was founded by Aimee Semple McPherson (1890-1944). Born in Ontario, Canada, she married a Pentecostal evangelist named Robert Semple. They were ordained by William Durham in Chicago and worked with him for a time. They went to China as missionaries, but Robert soon contracted malaria and died. Aimee returned to the U.S. in 1910. A year later she married Harold McPherson, but this marriage ended in divorce in 1921.

"Sister," as she became known, joined the Assemblies of God in 1919. She started a church in Los Angeles, known as Angelus Temple, that grew rapidly. When she began erecting a church building, the largest auditorium in America at the time, the AG asked for an assurance that the property would not be placed in her name. She declined to give it, voluntarily left the AG in 1922, and started her own organization in 1923.

She chose the name for her organization from a fourfold emphasis on Jesus as Savior, baptizer in the Holy Spirit, healer, and coming king. This message was similar to the earlier teaching of A. B. Simpson, founder of the CMA, except where he spoke of Jesus as sanctifier she spoke of Him as baptizer with the Holy Ghost.

Aimee McPherson was a flamboyant preacher who used theatrical techniques. For example, she once rode into church on a motorcycle dressed as a policeman and exclaimed, "Stop, you're going to hell!" She became one of the best-known preachers in America, "the first Pentecostal well-known to the public at large."[165] During the Depression, the ICFG provided 1,500,000 people with food, clothing, and other assistance.

McPherson was also quite controversial. In 1926, she suddenly disappeared, apparently drowning while swimming at the beach. A month later she was discovered in Mexico, and she explained that she had been kidnapped. Her detractors alleged an affair with a former employee, but she steadfastly denied it. In 1930 she suffered a nervous breakdown, and in 1931 she married David Hutton. (The marriage ended in divorce.) In 1944 she died of an apparently accidental overdose of a medical prescription.

Aimee McPherson was the "lifetime president" of the ICFG. After she died, her son, Rolf McPherson, served as leader until his retirement.

Today the IFCG has grown beyond its controversial past. It has a large overseas constituency due to mergers with indigenous groups. In the U.S. it grew to 1,742 churches and 227,307 constituents in 1996.

Compared to other Pentecostal organizations, historically the ICFG has had a high percentage of women ministers, has been less concerned with outward holiness, and has been the most receptive to the Charismatic movement. While the church officially proclaims that tongues is the initial evidence of the Holy Spirit, this doctrine is not universally held. One of the best-known ICFG pastors in recent years is Jack Hayford.

The *Pentecostal Church of God* (PCG) (301,786) was founded in 1919 by some trinitarian ministers in the AG who did not want a statement of faith such as the AG adopted in 1916. Its first leader was John C. Sinclair (1863-1936), one of the AG's executive presbyters in 1914. He later withdrew from the PCG, however, and became independent.

In 1933 the PCG adopted a statement of faith similar to that of the AG. Over the years it has been considered more liberal than the AG in matters such as holiness and divorce and remarriage. In the U.S., the PCG has grown from 81 churches and 4,296 constituents in 1936 to 1,224 churches and 119,200 constituents in 1996.

The *Open Bible Standard Churches* (46,000) resulted from a merger of two groups in 1935. The first group withdrew from Florence Crawford's Apostolic Faith Mission in 1919 on the ground that she was too strict in matters of holiness, fellowship, and church government. The second withdrew from the Foursquare Gospel in 1932 after Aimee McPherson's remarriage as a divorcee.

A small group that is quite similar to the AG is the *Christian Church of North America* (13,500), which was originally composed of Italian-Americans. The first congregation was started in 1907 by Luigi Francescon, an immigrant who received the Holy Spirit under William Durham in Chicago, and his friend Pietro Ottolini.

The *Full Gospel Fellowship of Churches and Ministers International* (195,000) is a loosely structured organization that provides credentials for independent ministers and churches. It began in 1962 with the (unrealized) hope of providing leadership to the Charismatic movement. The primary organizers were Gordon Lindsay (1906-73) and W. A. Raiford. Lindsay was a convert of Charles Parham, the manager for William Branham's healing campaigns for a time, the publisher of *Voice of Healing* (later *Christ for the Nations*), and the founder of Christ for the Nations Institute in Dallas.

Over the years, the Trinitarian Pentecostal organizations of the U.S. and Canada maintained some fellowship with one another, forming the Pentecostal Fellowship of North America (PFNA). No black organizations were included, however. In 1994, the "Memphis Miracle," a significant step toward racial reconciliation, took place. Pentecostal leaders meeting in Memphis dissolved the PFNA and formed the Pentecostal/Charismatic Churches of North America, which included black organizations. No Oneness organizations were invited to participate.

Trinitarian Pentecostals around the World

From the Azusa Street Mission in Los Angeles, the Pentecostal movement spread rapidly around the world. The February-March 1907 issue of *The Apostolic Faith*, published by the mission, reported outpourings of the Holy Spirit in London, Stockholm, Oslo, and Calcutta. Later issues gave reports from Africa, Australia, Canada, China, Denmark, Jerusalem, and elsewhere.

The earliest missionaries from Azusa Street were A. G. Garr and his wife, who went to India and Hong Kong. American missionaries in various parts of the world received their Pentecostal experience either by attending Azusa Street or reading the news about it, and the Holy Spirit began to fall in their missions. Notable revivals occurred in India, China, and Japan as a result.

A key figure in the spread of Pentecostalism to Europe was Thomas Ball Barratt (1862-1940) of Norway, a Methodist pastor. While in the United States in 1906, he heard of the Azusa Street revival, corresponded with the mission, and received the Holy Spirit in New York City. He returned to Oslo, where he conducted the first modern Pentecostal meeting in Europe and founded the Filadelfia Church.

Pastors from across Europe came to visit Barratt's services in Oslo and were filled with the Spirit. Notable converts, who in turn established Pentecostal movements in their own countries, were Alexander Boddy, an Anglican pastor in Sunderland, England; Jonathan Paul, a

Holiness leader in Germany; and Lewi Pethrus, a Baptist pastor in Stockholm, Sweden. Pethrus's Filadelfia Church in Stockholm became the largest Pentecostal church in the world.

In Canada, the Pentecostal movement began in Toronto, Ontario, when an independent Holiness evangelist from England, Ellen Hebden, received the Holy Ghost. Soon afterwards, her husband, James, also a preacher, received the Spirit as well. They apparently had no prior contact with Pentecostals. Ellen Hebden testified that she received the Spirit while seeking God in prayer but without any expectation of what would happen. She began speaking in tongues, and then she sang in tongues for three hours. The Hebdens soon learned of the Azusa Street Mission and sent a report that was published in *The Apostolic Faith*. While the influence of the Hebdens was great initially, they did not believe in organization, so other workers ultimately had a greater impact.

After the peak of the Azusa Street revival (1906-09), the center for worldwide revival shifted to William Durham's work in Chicago. A. H. Argue received the Holy Spirit there in 1907 and spread the Pentecostal message in western Canada.

The *Pentecostal Assemblies of Canada* (218,782) was founded in 1919. (See chapter 4.) It briefly affiliated with the Assemblies of God (1920-25) but soon chose to become a separate organization. It suffered major losses in 1947-48 due to the Latter Rain movement, which began in its ranks. (See chapter 9.)

The *Pentecostal Assemblies of Newfoundland* (30,992) developed as a separate organization, for until 1949 Newfoundland was a separate dominion from

Canada in the British Commonwealth. The founder was Alice Belle Garrigus (1858-1949), a Pentecostal evangelist from Boston, Massachusetts, who started a mission in St. John's in 1911 and served as the first leader.

Two Italian immigrants, Luigi Francescon and Giacomo Lombardi, received the Holy Spirit under William Durham. In 1908, Lombardi held the first Pentecostal service in Italy. On periodic trips back to Italy, he and Francescon established a strong Pentecostal following there; today it is by far the largest Protestant grouping in that country. About 200,000 people are in the AG, and 200,000 are with other Pentecostal organizations. Francescon also established large Italian Pentecostal churches in Argentina (1909) and Brazil (1910).

Two Swedish immigrants to America, Daniel Berg (1884-1963) and Gunnar Vingren received the Holy Spirit in South Bend, Indiana, near Chicago. Commissioned as missionaries by William Durham, they went to Brazil and began a national church there in 1911, which they called the *Assemblies of God*. It began before the American organization of that name, as a distinct entity, but it later affiliated with the American AG while remaining independent in government. It is the largest Protestant church in Brazil and the largest AG church in any country. It reports 16,000,000 constituents, but some researchers say 8,000,000 is more accurate.[166]

In Chile, a Methodist missionary named Willis C. Hoover (1856-1936) received the Holy Ghost in 1909 after reading about a Pentecostal revival at a mission in India. He organized the *Pentecostal Methodist Church of Chile* and later the *Evangelical Pentecostal Church of Chile*, the two largest Protestant denominations in the country. Their combined adult membership in 1975 was 350,000.[167] These churches do not teach that speaking in tongues is the sole initial evidence of the baptism of the Holy Spirit.

John G. Lake (1870-1935), a convert from Zion City and a noted healing evangelist, went to South Africa in 1908 and established two large Pentecostal churches there: the *Apostolic Faith Mission* (white) (440,000) and the *Zion Christian Church* (black) (5,250,000). The latter is the country's largest Christian denomination.

Holiness and Christian Living

All Pentecostals have historically had a great concern for holiness of life, both inwardly and outwardly. Steven Land, a theologian in the Church of God, has explained this concept well:[168]

> With regard to salvation and the daily walk of holiness, faith and works, "talk and walk," love and obedience, gospel and law are fused. Love obeys. . . . Faith alone justifies through grace. But the faith which justifies is never alone; it is always, in the Spirit, the faith which works through love. To be in the faith is to be faithful. To be unfaithful is to be an adulterer who has fallen out of love with God.
>
> Pentecostals believe that Christians can and have defected or "backslid.". . . They call upon those crucified with Christ to crucify the "affections and lusts.". . . They do not see this as works-righteousness. . . .
>
> As a result of this emphasis Pentecostals often practiced a very strict discipline which recognized very few indifferent matters. . . . Holiness prohibi-

tions against dancing, attendance at movie theatres (worldly amusement), wearing jewelry (worldly luxury and adornment, or vainglorious displays) and so on became tests of fellowship. . . . When the apocalyptic fervor was high, of course, most people were glad to submit to these lists of rules or holiness practices. However, as the fervor subsided and incomes rose, more became affordable; and, as a result, many third- and fourth-generations believers went to other more lenient churches. For most of the early believers however, these practices . . . were seen as being consistent with a full commitment to the God who was looking for a people who were holy and blameless before him in love. These practices also served to give a social identity and sense of distinction between the church and the world. . . . The plain, simple life of sacrifice, consecration and witness was consistent with the vision of the kingdom that must shine brightly from within to a watching world.

The fruit of the Spirit and the gifts of the Spirit were fused as were the salvation experiences of regeneration, sanctification and Spirit baptism. . . . The fullness of salvation [was] regeneration, sanctification, and Spirit baptism. . . .

To be of the world was to be motivated by the lust of the eye, lust of the flesh and pride of life. Worldliness and godliness were mutually exclusive. To become a Christian is to receive the Spirit of God and to reject the spirit of the world. Men and women were called upon to come out of the world, to be delivered from all binding vices, to leave worldly luxuries, intoxicating beverages, harmful habits (such as smoking) and to cease frequenting worldly amusements where there were lewd displays contrary to the Spirit of holiness. . . .

Their differences in conversation, dress, worship, witness, and so on were . . . important to their sense of identity and belonging. Their intense sense of the otherness of God and his coming kingdom seemed to drive them to find ways in which to bear witness to that in their daily life. . . .

Dramatic conversions and deliverances were the rule. It was eventful because of the sharp distinction and the costs that had to be counted. But if there were tears and travail as one was born into the new "world" on the way to consummation, there was also great joy. . . . Witnessing drew the line between the church and the world and invited the world to cross the line.

In his early Pentecostal ministry, Charles Parham purposed to live by faith, not to incur debts, not to solicit money, to share all things with coworkers and people in need, and to love those who opposed him. He taught the paying of tithes. He opposed worldly practices such as theater attendance, dancing, and warfare.[169] He did not specifically discuss matters of adornment and dress in his writings, however. Apparently he was not opposed to the wearing of some jewelry,[170] although pictures of his early followers reveal a conservative, modest appearance.

Holiness was an important theme at Azusa Street. Seymour was moderate on specific issues, not wanting to divert the preaching of the gospel into excessive emphasis on rules. *The Apostolic Faith*, however, did report about converts who gave up their jewelry, and it warned against various worldly amusements such as gambling, playing cards, and going to horse races. (See chapter 1.)

Florence Crawford, a leader at Azusa Street and later founder of her own organization, took a strict stand on a number of matters:[171]

> Ministers could neither solicit funds nor receive regular offerings. An offering box near the church entrance sufficed. Her members not only relinquished dancing, card playing, theater attendance, smoking, and drinking, they also distanced themselves from those who practiced such activities. Proscribing all makeup and short hair for women, Crawford enjoined modest apparel and insisted that slacks, shorts, and short sleeves were inappropriate for women.

The Second Work Trinitarians historically took a strict stand on holiness of conduct and dress. In recent years, most of them have moderated or abandoned these positions, although a minority of members still adhere to them.

As an example, the Church of God formerly opposed all jewelry. In the 1950s a controversy arose over wedding bands, and the church decided to allow them. There was a steady relaxing of the "practical commitments," until in 1988 the church officially eliminated its rules against going to movies, wearing makeup, wearing jewelry, and women cutting their hair.[172]

The Church of God of Prophecy maintained a more conservative position on these issues than its parent body. In the 1950s it took a stand against members owning televisions. In its "Advice to Members" (1968), it specifically prohibited shorts in public, rings, lipstick, going to movies, and public swimming. Women did not cut their hair or wear pants. No one was accepted for membership if he or she wore any jewelry, including a wedding band.[173]

The Finished Work Trinitarians were not as strict as the Second Work Trinitarians, but even so the Assemblies of God was quite conservative on matters of lifestyle, dress, and amusements in comparison to the rest of society. Over the years, it has abandoned most of its outward expressions of holiness, however, as AG historian Edith Blumhofer has explained:[174]

> In 1914, Pentecostals generally agreed with other fundamentalist evangelicals about what separation meant: modesty in dress and appearance, as well as abstinence from alcohol, smoking, gambling, dancing, theater attendance, and other such amusements. . . .
>
> While some matters were left to individual conscience, there was a general agreement about acceptable and unacceptable behavior.
>
> As time passed, however, and cultural standards changed, a new generation in the Assemblies of God questioned what they saw as "legalism" in the older generation. Although a range of "acceptable" behavior (depending to some degree on geographical location) still exists, Assemblies of God people are less outwardly conspicuous in society than they once were.

Carl O'Guin, an AG minister in 1915, said the ministers preached for people to dress modestly, but the people "wanted to do it anyway; it was their frame of mind." Women wore long dresses and long sleeves and did not wear makeup or jewelry. No woman would wear pants or cut her hair. Preachers were "death" on the theater. The AG was not as strict as some groups, for it allowed engagement and wedding bands.[175]

Pictures on display in the historical center at AG headquarters show that the gradual abandonment of holiness standards of outward appearance (hair, ornaments, makeup, dress) took place in the 1950s and especially the 1960s. During this time, many ministers tried to stem the tide. For example, *Call to Holiness*, a tabloid published in Lorain, Ohio, by AG members contained articles against television, movies, tobacco, alcohol, makeup, and excessive jewelry (such as beads, bracelets, and earrings). In 1961 it reprinted an article from the *Pentecostal Evangel* (the official AG organ)—"There Is Beauty in Holiness" by Carl Brumback—that taught inward and outward holiness and opposed makeup and jewelry.

In 1963, Ralph Riggs, general superintendent from 1953 to 1959, wrote *A Call to Holiness*, a tract that was also printed as an article in *Call to Holiness*. In it he urged Christians not to attend movies, use tobacco or alcohol, wear makeup, or dress immodestly. He also spoke of a "twilight zone of public ball games, newsreels in a downtown theater, and public roller-skating rinks where a person mixes with a crowd of sinners" and recommended abstaining from such activities also.

In 1961 the Rocky Mountain District of the AG amended its bylaws to read, "We unitedly declare ourselves against all forms of worldliness, such as wearing of slacks and shorts, lipstick, paint, earrings, and excessive jewelry. We further declare ourselves against mixed bathing, use of tobacco and alcoholic beverages." In 1963, the Ohio District reaffirmed, with only one dissenting vote, its standard of holiness as stated in its constitution and bylaws: "We oppose all appearance of evil . . . such as immodesty in dress, bobbing or undue dressing of the hair; . . . attendance at picture shows, dances, roller rinks, places where mixed bathing is permitted, use of tobacco, and the use of cosmetics which change the natural appearance." Also in 1963, the Southern Missouri District (home of Springfield, the headquarters) added a statement against makeup in its list of qualifications for church membership: "Applicant must disapprove of, and refrain from participation in worldly amusements, theaters, movies, cards, dancing and use of make-up, etc."[176]

Oneness Pentecostals have remained the most conservative on issues of practical holiness, although there is some variation in beliefs and in the local implementation of standards. In its Articles of Faith, the UPCI opposes "theaters [movies], dances, mixed bathing or swimming, women cutting their hair, make-up, any apparel that immodestly exposes the body, all worldly sports and amusements, and unwholesome radio programs and music" and ownership of television. A position paper on holiness further explains the meaning of modest apparel: people are not to wear ornamental jewelry or clothing associated with the opposite sex. Other position papers take a stand against abortion, gambling, homosexuality, transcendental meditation, and ungodly, worldly use of computers, the Internet, video equipment, and other technology.[177]

Most of the other major Oneness groups have had similar teachings. For instance, in 1963 the PAW opposed "all unnecessary jewelry, such as rings (not including wedding rings), bracelets, earrings, stick-pins, and flashy breast pins . . . showy colors in dress, attractive hosiery, short dresses, low necks, short sleeves (that is, above the elbow), and bright ties."[178] In recent years, however, there has been greater variation among many of these groups. The PAW, for example, has many members who wear jewelry and makeup and many others who do not. To some extent, this trend has extended to doctrine, with a few PAW ministers espousing unconditional eternal security and even elements of trinitarianism.

Many early Pentecostals, especially those who came from the Holiness movement, opposed all remarriage after divorce. The wife of J. H. King, IPHC leader from 1900 to 1946, left him shortly after their marriage in 1890. Because of his conviction against divorce and remarriage, he remained celibate until she died, remarrying only in 1920. While the AG allows divorce and remarriage in the case of marital unfaithfulness, it will not license anyone who has divorced and remarried and has a previous companion still living. The UPCI allows remarriage for the "innocent party" and will grant ministerial license in such a case, although it recommends that ministers do not remarry after divorce.

Most of the early Pentecostals were pacifists. For example, the AG, PAW, and UPCI adopted official statements supporting the government but opposing the taking of human life in warfare.[179] The AG eventually abandoned this position, however. The UPCI retains this view in its Articles of Faith but treats the matter as a "conscientious scruple," and today many ministers and members are not pacifists.

All major Pentecostal groups teach that tithes and offerings are God's plan for the church.

Summary of Pentecostal Beliefs

In summary, all three branches of classical Pentecostalism affirm most of the basic doctrines of conservative Protestantism, including the existence of one true God; the creation of the universe by God; the inspiration and authority of Scripture; the existence of angels, the devil, and demons; the fall and sinfulness of humanity; the Incarnation; the Atonement; salvation by grace through faith in Jesus Christ; water baptism; the Lord's Supper; the New Testament church as the people of God; the priesthood of believers; the rapture of the church; the second coming of Jesus Christ to earth; the Millennium; the last judgment; eternal punishment for the unrighteous; and eternal life for the righteous.

We have already discussed the most significant differences among Pentecostals, namely, on sanctification, water baptism, the Godhead, and the experience of the new birth.

The unique doctrine that Pentecostals hold in common is *the baptism of the Holy Spirit* with the initial sign of speaking in tongues (speaking miraculously in languages unknown to the speaker, as the Spirit gives utterance). They also teach that miracles and gifts of the Spirit, including healing for the body, are for the church today.

From the beginning, one of the major tenets of Pentecostals has been the *soon return of Jesus Christ to earth.* In accordance with Joel 2 and Acts 2, they associate the great outpouring of the Holy Spirit with the latter days. They teach that the Lord has restored apostolic doctrine, experience, and power in order to produce a worldwide revival that will prepare people for His coming. Pentecostals affirm that the Second Coming is drawing near and that it will occur before the Millennium. Most expect the Rapture to take place before the Tribulation, but some believe it will occur during or at the end of the Tribulation.

If we must single out the most distinctive tenets of Pentecostalism as a whole, historically it would be these two: the baptism of the Holy Spirit with tongues and the soon coming of the Lord Jesus Christ. While other conservative Christians have proclaimed the second point as well, for Pentecostals it is so intertwined with the first as to be an essential part of their identity.

All three branches of Pentecostals affirm that *divine healing* is part of the Atonement. In other words, Christ's redeeming work has made physical healing available to the church. As a result, some early Pentecostals shunned all medical care, but the general practice has been to trust God for healing while also recognizing that God can use doctors and medicine.

A few people taught that if a person had enough faith he would always receive healing. Some even taught that by faith it was possible to have perfect health and never die. This doctrine tended to be self-defeating, as all proponents eventually died. In general, Pentecostals stress the importance of believing God for healing, but they do not say that healing is automatic or that if someone does not receive healing then he does not have faith. They acknowledge that God is sovereign and that they will not receive some benefits of the Atonement until the resurrection.

A few Pentecostals interpreted Mark 16:17-18 to mean that Christians should deliberately handle snakes as a test of faith, and a few even extended the test to the drinking of poison. The latter was rare because it was usually fatal. For a time, A. J. Tomlinson and the early Church of God were the main proponents of snake handling. Today, the practice exists primarily among a few independent churches in Appalachia. To most Pentecostals, the passage in Mark simply speaks of divine protection and deliverance in times of unsolicited danger or satanic attack.

Pentecostals celebrate *the Lord's Supper*, typically once or a few times a year. They teach it to be symbolic, but they expect the Lord to meet with them in a special way. As they partake, they exercise faith for the forgiveness of sins, healing, and deliverance. In practice, then, their view of communion approximates Calvin's teaching of the spiritual presence of Christ in the sacrament.

The Second Work Trinitarians and the Oneness believers traditionally have conducted *foot washing* in conjunction with the Lord's Supper at least once a year. Most of the Finished Work Trinitarians, notably the Assemblies of God, do not follow this practice, however.

Demonstrative, spontaneous worship has always characterized Pentecostals. Important elements of public worship are preaching, singing, testifying, and praying. Evangelistic services typically end with an altar call, extended prayer by the congregation, and laying on of hands. Common expressions of worship include exuberant singing, vocal expressions of praise, praying aloud, raising of hands, clapping of hands, dancing ("shouting"), shaking, crying, and speaking in tongues. Sometimes there is leaping, running, falling ("being slain in the Spirit" by the power of God), "holy laughter," and singing in tongues. Early Pentecostals found this type of worship in the Scriptures, and to a great extent they inherited it from English and American revivalism and African-American churches.

Almost all Pentecostals accept *the ministry of women*. In most cases, however, women do not fill positions of top leadership. The COGIC and the CG do not allow women to be ordained or to become pastors, but the AG and UPCI allow both. Compared to the early days, there are fewer women pastors, as significantly more men entered the movement and as many women now exercise their ministry in conjunction with their husbands.[180]

Pentecostals are diverse in *church government*. The Second Work groups generally have an episcopal form like their Methodist forebears, and so do most black and Hispanic groups. The other major groups, notably the AG and UPCI, are mostly congregational with some presbyterian elements. The local church controls its own affairs, with strong pastoral leadership; a district organization handles the licensing and discipline of ministers; and the general organization supervises and promotes world missions efforts.

A few small groups are neither Oneness nor trinitarian but espouse a two-person view in which the Son is subordinate to the Father. Sometimes called "duality," it is essentially a form of *Arianism*.[181] The three major branches of Pentecostalism strongly reject this view, however.

In characterizing the Pentecostal movement as a whole from a historical perspective, Steven Land has concluded, "The streams of Pietism, Puritanism, Wesleyanism, African-American Christianity and nineteenth-century Holiness-Revivalism form a confluence which has today become a sea of Pentecostal believers. . . . Perhaps the two most important spiritualities which formed the originators of Pentecostalism [were] Wesleyan and African-American."[182]

Significant Changes

In recent decades, the Pentecostal movement has undergone significant changes away from its roots, particularly among the Second Work Trinitarians and Finished Work Trinitarians. The most important change concerns the baptism of the Holy Spirit.

First, the initial evidence doctrine is increasingly under attack. Some indigenous churches in Europe and Latin America have departed from this teaching, and the Charismatic movement does not generally adhere to it. (See chapter 10.) Even in the classical Pentecostal denominations that affirm this doctrine, many theologians and ministers now question or deny it.

In a related development, the number of members who receive the Holy Spirit with the sign of tongues has steadily declined. Overall, it is estimated that only 35 percent of the members of classical Pentecostal denominations have received this experience,[183] and in the Charismatic movement the percentage is far less. In the Assemblies of God, the number is estimated at 30 percent (by some scholars) to 50 percent (by denominational officials). The AG has established a commission to investigate this problem and propose remedies.

As we have noted, there has also been a significant departure from practical expressions of holiness in lifestyle, dress, and amusements. Many countercultural beliefs and practices, such as pacifism and foot washing, have been abandoned by some groups and are gradually declining in groups that still affirm them. Worship is generally more subdued and sedate than in times past.

Why are these changes occurring? We can identify at least three major factors.

First, there is *the generational effect*.[184] In any revival movement, the first generation experiences a dramatic encounter with God that results in radical changes of belief and lifestyle. This generation has a high commitment to the distinctive tenets of the group, because they discovered these truths for themselves, defended them in the face of great opposition and at great cost, and experienced first-hand the spiritual benefits of their newfound commitments.

Typically, most of the second generation adheres to the same tenets because they were molded by the dedication, spirituality, sacrifice, and sincerity of the first generation. They observed or at least heard direct testimonies of the transformation of their elders, and they observed first-hand the spiritual blessings that resulted. In many cases, however, they are not as effective in transmitting the core values to the next generation.

Consequently, the third generation often inherits a tradition without the full inward experience that molded the tradition. They neither observe nor experience the transition from the old life to the new. Living realities of the first generation become monuments in the second generation and relics in the third. Godly disciplines become legalisms and then archaic practices. Of course, this trend can be countered by personal revival and renewal and by a continual influx of converts who embrace the original spiritual realities.

The second influence that has prompted changes in the Pentecostal movement is *upward social mobility* with a corresponding increase in the *desire for social acceptance.* Like most revival movements and like Christianity in the beginning, Pentecostalism appealed first and foremost to the common people, especially to the socially disadvantaged, the dispossessed, and the oppressed.[185] Such people had the least to lose and the most to gain by taking the step of faith.

As Pentecostals experienced the blessings of God upon their lives, however, they began to move upward in society and had the means to enjoy greater participation in society. As their churches grew, they drew the attention of the establishment and were able to influence the establishment to some extent. At this point, they acquired a greater stake in society and thus a greater concern for how society viewed them. As part of the price of participating in and influencing the larger religious and secular communities, however, they encountered greater pressure to conform to the expectations of those communities.

In connection with this process, the Trinitarian Pentecostals particularly sought *to identify with conservative Protestantism—Fundamentalism and later Evangelicalism—*and this association in turn became a third catalyst for change. When the Assemblies of God rejected the Oneness movement in 1916, they chose ecclesiastical tradition over apostolic precedent. In essence, they drew back from the full application of the restorationist idea that had produced Pentecostalism in the first place. Had all Pentecostals devoted several years to Bible study, discussion, and prayer over the matter, perhaps the outcome would have been significantly different, but in 1916 the die was cast that would mold future generations.

Trinitarian Pentecostals thus consciously sought to identify more with Fundamentalists who did not receive the Spirit—and indeed who denounced the move of the Spirit—than fellow Pentecostals with whom they had been closely associated. In fact, early leaders such as AG editor Stanley Frodsham spoke of themselves as Pentecostal Fundamentalists—Fundamentalists whose only important difference from the others was that they spoke in tongues.[186] J. R. Flower—AG orchestrator of the anti-Oneness wing and a key denominational leader from the beginning in 1914 until his retirement in 1959—said, "We are fundamentalists, but we are more than that." When the AG was invited to help form the National Association of Evangelicals in 1943, he led the AG in doing so, noting that some Pentecostals kept their "fingers crossed" lest they lose this "good fortune."[187] From the 1940s onward, the influence of Evangelicals became stronger. As we shall see in chapters 9 and 10, the Latter Rain movement in the 1950s and the Charismatic movement in the 1960s and beyond also had a significant impact in diluting Pentecostal uniqueness.

As a result, Trinitarian Pentecostals gradually adopted many Evangelical positions and methodologies. For example, one of the arguments that arose against certain holiness practices was that other Christians—including prominent ministers to whom the Pentecostals looked for instruction and leadership—did not see the need for them. When the Pentecostal Fellowship of North America was formed in 1947, it simply adopted the statement of faith of the National Association of Evangelicals and added a Pentecostal paragraph.[188]

In recent years, both Pentecostal and non-Pentecostal scholars have urged Pentecostals to resist the "evangeli-calization" of their movement and instead draw inspiration and guidance from their own unique identity, experience, and theology. In arguing for a "distinctive Pentecostal self-understanding" in theology and spirituality, Steven Land has asserted, "Pentecostalism cannot and should not be simply identified with a rationalist or scholastic type of evangelicalism. Further, it cannot, without funda-mental alteration and accommodation, be assimilated into any and every Christian denomination without eventually bringing fundamental changes."[189]

The Oneness movement has not been immune to the motivators for change that we have discussed, although its theological isolation has served to minimize the third factor. Consequently, Oneness Pentecostals have preserved more of the doctrinal approach, experience, worship, and lifestyle of the early Pentecostals than Trinitarian Pentecostals have.

First of all, regarding doctrine, it is true that the Oneness views of the Godhead and the new birth were a development in the second decade of the Pentecostal movement. They were a logical progression of the earliest Pentecostal thought, however, and in many cases the prac-tical emphasis and effect have been remarkably similar.

For example, Trinitarian Pentecostals today assume that their doctrine of salvation is the same as that of the early Pentecostals, but in practice many of them empha-size a Baptist-style sinner's prayer more than the baptism of the Holy Ghost. While Parham, Seymour, and Durham spoke of a person as being justified before receiving the

Holy Ghost, they stressed the necessity of receiving the Holy Ghost. Early Trinitarian Pentecostals typically said that believers were born again before receiving the Holy Spirit but needed to receive the Spirit in order to have full salvation, to enter the New Testament church, and to go in the Rapture. Early Oneness Pentecostals typically said that believers needed to receive the Holy Spirit to be born again, to enter the New Testament church, and to go in the Rapture, but those who did not could still receive a degree of salvation (such as life on the new earth) if they walked in all the light they knew. While the doctrines were different, the effect upon preaching, witnessing, and praying was much the same, and both stand in contrast to the Trinitarian Pentecostal approach today.

In particular, it is the norm for Oneness Pentecostals to receive the Holy Spirit with tongues, and it is generally a requirement for church membership. By one estimate, 90 percent of people ages ten or over who regularly attend a United Pentecostal Church have spoken in tongues.[190] Thus, a UPCI church of 100 adult members has about the same number of Spirit-filled people as an AG church of 300 adult members. In the U.S., the reported AG constituency is at least 300 percent more than that of the UPCI, but the number of active Spirit-filled believers is probably only about 55 percent greater.[191]

It seems clear that doctrinal emphasis is an important factor in the disparity. The UPCI places a much greater emphasis on the baptism of the Holy Spirit. It is a focal point of every evangelistic service, and it is taught as an integral part of salvation and God's plan for all believers. In the Apostolic Church of the Faith in Christ Jesus, a Oneness church in Mexico that has a greater diversity of views on the essentiality of the Holy Spirit, only 72 percent of members have spoken in tongues—still higher than trinitarian churches but very low for a Oneness group. In the Pentecostal Methodist Church of Chile, a trinitarian group that does not teach tongues as the sole initial evidence, only 50 percent of the *ministers* have spoken in tongues.[192]

On secondary doctrinal issues, Trinitarian Pentecostal denominations have gradually solidified their position in a way that corresponds to Fundamentalism, while Oneness Pentecostals allow greater diversity, as was characteristic of early Pentecostals. For example, the AG officially teaches the pretribulation Rapture, while the UPCI has no official position. The AG officially opposes the doctrine of annihilation, while the UPCI has generally treated it as a part of eschatology and therefore open to different interpretations. In the 1980s, however, the UPCI passed a rule against licensing new ministers who teach the doctrine, while still allowing ministers to hold the view.

Longtime participants in Trinitarian Pentecostalism have told UPCI audiences and ministers that UPCI camp meetings and conferences are quite similar to early Pentecostal services in the fervency of worship, racial integration of audiences, and physical demonstrations.[193] Some of them state that they no longer experience the intensity of the move of the Spirit in their groups that they did in early times.[194] Some of them even urge Oneness Pentecostals to maintain their original zeal, consecration, worship, and emphasis on the Holy Ghost, and not follow the example of groups such as the AG and CG, who have in many ways become more

Evangelical than Pentecostal.[195] Oneness Pentecostals who visit Trinitarian Pentecostal churches often remark that the prayer, worship, and move of the Spirit there is less fervent, demonstrative, and intense than what they typically experience in their own churches.

In sum, Second Work Trinitarian Pentecostals and Finished Work Trinitarian Pentecostals adhere to the basic doctrines of early Pentecostalism, but their teaching, preaching, worship, and lifestyle have gradually become less distinctive, less zealous, more Evangelical, and more middle-class American. Oneness Pentecostals retain much of the earlier characteristics of the Pentecostal movement as a whole, but their distinguishing doctrines have caused them to remain relatively isolated from other Pentecostals and Evangelicals to this day.

6

Liberalism and Neo-Orthodoxy

In chapters 1-5 we have traced the most significant development within Christianity in the twentieth century, as measured both by theological innovation (or restoration) and by numerical growth. In the early part of the century, however, the Pentecostals were a very small segment of Protestantism that had sprouted from Holiness groups that in turn had separated from Methodism. In this chapter and the next, we will look at the developments within mainline Protestantism. Due to space limitations, we can only present a brief overview of various theologies and cite some representative examples.

The most important development within mainline Protestantism was Liberalism, also known as Modernism, and the reactions to it. Liberalism was a continuation of a trend that began in earlier centuries and became quite strong in the nineteenth century, but to a great extent it captured the mainline Protestant denominations in the twentieth century.

In essence, Liberalism questioned the truthfulness of the Bible and undermined its authority. The eighteenth and nineteenth centuries had seen the emergence of a post-Christian mindset as the Western world emphasized scientific methods, rationalism, and experiential knowledge. (See volume 2, chapter 12.) Many theologians and philosophers began to apply these methods to traditional religion, eliminating the supernatural elements and retaining what they deemed to be rational and humanly comprehensible.

In a way, we can regard both Liberalism and Holiness-Pentecostalism as reactions to formal Protestant orthodoxy, albeit at opposite ends of the spectrum. By the seventeenth century, Protestantism had settled into rival theological camps, each with its own well-defined confession of faith and each of whom labeled the others as heretics. They seemed to focus on doctrinal identity more than on personal faith and spiritual experience. By the eighteenth century, the Pietists in continental Europe and the Methodists in England were seeking to refocus attention on a personal relationship with God and a lifestyle of holiness. The Holiness movement of the nineteenth century (which arose from Methodism) and the Pentecostal movement of the twentieth century (which arose from the Holiness movement) perpetuated that emphasis.

Liberalism

Whereas the Pietists, Methodists, Holiness movement, and Pentecostals all sought a more fervent personal relationship with God on the basis of scriptural teachings, Liberalism sought a more personal theology by questioning scriptural teachings. Liberal theologians in the nineteenth century began to view the Bible as a human book that contained divine principles. To them, it was inspired much like other great writings of philosophy, poetry, and literature. In other words, the human element predominated in the writing of Scripture.

Instead of seeing Scripture as infallible, they saw it as full of errors. Instead of being the direct revelation of God to humanity, it was a reflection of human thinking about God. It was not the authoritative Word of God; it simply described human efforts to understand ultimate reality.

Liberal theologians began to deny, one by one, the supernatural elements of Scripture, including the miracles, the deity of Jesus, the virgin birth (conception) of Jesus, the atoning work of Jesus, the resurrection of Jesus, and the second coming of Jesus. They regarded these beliefs as mythical or prescientific elaborations that arose from the superstitious nature of the people who wrote the Bible. Now that the human race had developed a rational understanding of the universe, miracles were no longer an acceptable explanation of reality.

These theologians thus sought to remove the miraculous from Christianity and yet perpetuate what they considered to be its spiritual, moral essence. As volume 2 has discussed, theologians who attempted this task in the nineteenth century included Friedrich Schleiermacher, a Reformed pastor in Germany and the starting point for Liberalism; Søren Kierkegaard, a Danish existential philosopher (existentialism relates to individual existence and discovery of truth); and Albrecht Ritschl, a German professor and son of a Lutheran bishop. By the early twentieth century, Liberalism was in the process of taking over seminaries, universities, and mainline denominations.

In general, Liberalism denied that humans have a sinful nature, instead holding that they are basically good. Therefore, it denied the need for salvation in the traditional Christian sense of atonement, redemption, justification, and regeneration. Instead of proclaiming personal deliverance from the penalty of sin, it reinterpreted salvation in terms of improving individuals and bettering society. Heaven and hell became states of being or states of mind rather than literal places.

To understand Liberalism, let us briefly examine three prominent theologians at the beginning of the twentieth century. *Adolf von Harnack* (1851-1930) of Germany was the foremost church historian in his day and a theological professor in Berlin. In 1901 he published an influential book, *What Is Christianity?* He proposed that one could express the essence of Christianity by three essential points: the fatherhood of God, the brotherhood of man, and the infinite value of the human soul. He discarded the other elements, particularly the miraculous. In effect, he reduced Christianity to a philosophical religion, something that could appeal to everyone and not be offensive to anyone.

In the U.S., *Walter Rauschenbusch* (1861-1918), a German Baptist pastor, was the most prominent proponent of the *social gospel*, which stressed the importance of social action. Of course, conservative Christian groups, including the Methodists and Holiness people, had long engaged in practical works such as establishing orphanages, feeding the poor, rehabilitating alcoholics, and so on. The primary motivation for the antislavery and temperance movements of the nineteenth century was religious conviction.

The social gospel went beyond these kinds of actions, however, and offered a redefinition of Christianity. It said that the goal of Christianity is not the spiritual salvation of individual souls from sin and hell, but the transformation of society on earth. Christians are not to look for the physical return of Christ to earth, the literal reign of Christ for a thousand years, or eternal life in a place called heaven. Rather, the gospel calls them to establish the kingdom of God in this world—the kingdom of justice—through social and political means. The church's priority should be to work for justice, freedom, and a better society.

Albert Schweitzer (1875-1965), a German theologian and philosopher, became famous as a missionary doctor in Africa. He published *The Quest of the Historical Jesus* (1906). In it, he tried to strip away the myths about Jesus and discover who He really was as a man. He concluded that Jesus mistakenly believed the end of the world was near in His day, and thus He proclaimed that the kingdom of God was at hand. In order to fulfill His predictions, Jesus unsuccessfully tried to provoke the end of the world. He believed He would precipitate the end of all things, and His death would be the climactic moment. In Schweitzer's view, Jesus miscalculated and was killed too soon to implement His plans. In essence, He failed in His mission. Early Christianity was thus an attempt to reinterpret the failure of Jesus and turn it into a spiritual success.

Associated with Liberalism was *higher criticism* of the Bible, in which scholars studied the Bible as they did uninspired literature.[196] They analyzed the total historical situation of the biblical books, including dating, verification and writing of history (historical criticism). They also studied the structure and style of the books (literary criticism) and the literary sources and composition of the books (source criticism). Some of them investigated the presumed process by which oral tradition moved from stage to stage, became modified, and was finally incorporated in Scripture (tradition criticism).

While some study of this sort is necessary for a full understanding of the biblical text, and while these methods did yield some positive, productive results, many scholars employed them in a way that undermined the Bible's message. They typically denied the miracles of the Bible, questioned the accuracy of biblical accounts, and disagreed with what the Bible said about itself. This type of destructive criticism of Scripture developed in the nineteenth century in Germany with F. C. Baur, David Strauss, Julius Wellhausen, and the Tübingen school, but it came to full fruition in the twentieth century.

In the view of conservative Christians then and now, Liberalism actually cut the heart out of Christianity. It undermined or destroyed essential biblical doctrines such as the deity of Jesus Christ, the Atonement, justification by faith in Jesus Christ, and the new birth. Nevertheless, to a greater or lesser extent, its ideas became predominant in mainstream European and American Protestantism.

Liberalism provoked a sharp counterattack from people who accepted the Bible as the infallible, inerrant Word of God, including its miracles. This response became known as Fundamentalism, which we will discuss in chapter 7. There was also a more moderate reaction in the scholarly world, called Neo-Orthodoxy, which we discuss next.

Karl Barth and Neo-Orthodoxy

Neo-Orthodoxy developed in the 1920s through 1940s as a response to Liberalism. It defended historic Christian doctrines against Liberalism, yet it did not return completely to earlier beliefs such as the infallibility of Scripture in all things. Thus, it adopted an intermediate stance between Liberalism and traditional Protestant orthodoxy, with various theologians being closer to one side or the other. In the eyes of more conservative Christians, this movement did not completely return to the "orthodox" Protestant theology of the sixteenth-century Reformers, yet they welcomed its critique of Liberal theology and its defense of many biblical concepts.

Neo-Orthodox theologians realized that the Liberal agenda was bankrupt, yet they still tried to take into account the rationalism of modern society. They sought to blend biblical supernaturalism and modern rationalism so as to affirm the essential doctrines of Scripture in a modern context. Ancient doctrines were rephrased and reinterpreted.

We can mark the beginning of the Neo-Orthodox movement with the publication of Karl Barth's *Commentary on Romans* in 1919. Barth (1886-1968) was a Reformed pastor in Switzerland and the foremost theologian in the first half of the twentieth century. His major publication was *Church Dogmatics* (1932-64). It was the most comprehensive theological work of the century, with twenty-one volumes in English.

Barth emphasized the "otherness" of God and the "strange new world" of the Bible. In other words, God is so different from us that we could never learn about Him simply by human reason. Rationalism is insufficient to establish religion. Rather, we must learn about God by revelation, and God's Word is His revelation to us. Thus, the basis of Christianity is revelation, not reason.

Clearly, Barth rejected the central tenet of Liberalism— the idea that we can approach God and construct religion through rationalism. He fell short of going back completely to earlier Protestant orthodoxy, however, because he did not fully uphold the infallibility of the Bible and he employed the methods of higher criticism, with its denial of the Bible's literal accuracy.

He avoided the apparent conflict between his emphasis on biblical revelation and his failure to uphold biblical infallibility by stressing that God uses the Bible to speak to us individually when we encounter Him personally. Instead of viewing the Bible as the absolute Word of God, he said it "becomes" the Word of God when humans encounter God. The objective statements of Scripture, then, are not as important as what the Bible means to us subjectively. Here he built upon the existential philosophy of Kierkegaard even while rejecting Liberalism itself.

Barth proclaimed the sovereignty of God. God is in control of the world. We cannot remake God in our image, for God is who He is.

In contrast to Liberalism, Barth emphasized the sinfulness of humanity. Because of their sinfulness, humans must have God's illumination to understand truth, and they must have the grace of God at work in their lives.

Barth drew considerably from Luther and Calvin, especially the latter. He stated many of the same doctrines as earlier Protestants but not with the same commitment to the inspiration and infallibility of the Bible that they had presupposed. He presented his teachings in a fresh, original way, and he was willing to challenge traditional formulations. Yet, in the final analysis, he did not wish to breach ecumenical tradition.

On the doctrine of God, Barth did not like the traditional terminology of "three persons," because it made too great of a distinction in the Godhead. He was willing to speak of three eternal "modes of being," "the triune God," and "the Trinity," however. His doctrine of God bears similarities to Oneness thought—so much so that some critics have called him a modalist.[197] "For Barth there is only one revelation of God—in Jesus Christ."[198] Jesus Christ is the unique revelation of God Himself in flesh, and His atoning sacrifice is the work of God Himself:[199]

God is the One whose name and cause are borne by Jesus Christ. . . .

Who and what is the God who is to be known at the point upon which Holy Scripture concentrates our attention and thoughts? . . . From first to last the Bible directs us to the name of Jesus Christ. . . . Under this name God Himself became man. . . . There is no greater depth in God's being and work than that revealed in these happenings and under this name. For in these happenings and under this name He has revealed Himself. . . . When the bearer of this name becomes the object of our attention and thoughts, when they are directed to Jesus Christ, then we see God, and our thoughts are fixed on Him. . . .

God has not withheld Himself from men as true being, but . . . He has given no less than Himself to men as the overcoming of their need, and light in their darkness—Himself as the Father in His own Son by the Holy Spirit. . . .

God Himself, in His deep mercy and its great power, has taken it upon Himself to exist also in human being and essence in His Son. . . . We have to do with God Himself as we have to do with this man. . . . God Himself has assumed and made His own our human nature and kind in His Son, just because God Himself came into this world in His Son. . . .

The Holy Spirit is the coming of the man Jesus, who is the Son of God, to other men who are not this but with whom He still associates. . . .

It is the eternal God Himself who has given Himself in His Son to be man, and as man to take upon Himself this human passion. . . . He gives Himself to be the humanly acting and suffering person in this occurrence [on the cross]. He Himself is the Subject who in His own freedom becomes in this event the object acting or acted upon in it.

If we truly know God, said Barth, then we will obey God. "Knowledge of God is obedience to God. . . . Knowledge of God as knowledge of faith is in itself and of essential necessity obedience. . . . This is obedience, the obedience of faith."[200]

Barth attributed great significance to water baptism. He said that it relates us to "the one divine act of salvation and revelation." Believers are baptized into the following expectations: [201]

(1) The coming to pass of the kingdom and rule of God in their lives, (2) their baptism and endowment with the Holy Spirit, (3) the execution of God's judgment on them too, (4) the receiving of remission of sins, (5) their membership of the new people of God of the last time, and (6) their existence in the unity of Jews and Gentiles in common judgment and blessing.

Despite his Reformed heritage, Barth opposed the baptism of infants since they could not have the personal encounter with God that baptism represents.

He identified the inward work of salvation as the baptism of the Holy Spirit. It is related to, but distinct from, water baptism.

Based on passages in Acts and the Epistles, Barth taught that baptism is an identification with the saving work of Jesus. He was not willing to say that any specific baptismal formula was uniform in the early church. He acknowledged that, theologically, a simple baptismal formula that invoked the name of Jesus would be the most appropriate, but since the trinitarian formula is used everywhere we should not abandon it, even though we cannot otherwise justify its necessity:[202]

The name "Jesus" as the basis and goal of the apostolic message and apostolic baptism shows that the divine act had taken place and the Mightier [than

John] had come. . . . Proclamation of the name of Jesus in which all salvation is enclosed, and baptism in His name, are thus the distinguishing mark of the apostolic preaching and baptism which began on the Day of Pentecost. . . .

What may not be presupposed, however, is that from the very first a specific formula was used . . . and even less still that it was always and everywhere the same. If a formula of this kind was required, it is hard to see why the simple "into Jesus Christ" of Gal. 3:27 and Rom. 6:3 did not contain all that was needed, or why it would not have been enough to include the term *onoma* [name] as in most of the relevant verses, e.g., "into the name of Jesus Christ" or "of the Lord Jesus Christ." In the most solemn passage of all, however, though with no change of meaning, this short statement took the familiar Trinitarian form (Mt. 28:19) and this form . . . established itself in all parts of Christendom as the ecclesiastically normal and obligatory formula . . . It may be noted that what we have here is a custom that should be observed for the sake of ecumenical peace even though its exegetical, dogmatic and theological necessity cannot be demonstrated. . . . The only thing which is unconditionally necessary from a theological standpoint is that baptism should be a washing with water . . . and that whatever is said . . . should characterise it unequivocally as a movement into Jesus Christ, into the washing of man accomplished in Him. . . .

The name of Jesus Christ, the place of salvation and the origin of all the related action, is here the object and goal of Christian action, which is referred and orientated to the name of Jesus Christ as this goal. In faith, love and baptism the Christian moves towards the name of Jesus Christ, towards Jesus Christ Himself. . . .

When the community baptises, and when its candidates are baptised, they are on the way into that strong tower [Proverbs 18:10], on the way to the One who enters Jerusalem, the Lord, their Creator, Reconciler and Redeemer. One might also think here of the virgins who go to meet the Bridegroom with their lamps. . . . Baptism is a going forth to Jesus Christ.

Barth explained that the wording of Matthew 28:19 actually points to Jesus Christ and His saving work. For him, the three titles do not refer to three names but to the one name of God. They signify God's redemptive work in Jesus Christ in light of the past (salvation history, the plan of God through the ages), the present (Christ's act of atonement as applied to the believer), and the future (the ongoing work of God in the individual and in the world):[203]

Mt. 28:19 . . . is an extension of the christological formulae of Acts and Paul. . . .

The apostles are to baptise them, not into three names, but into one name expounded in three different ways. . . .

If the mention of Father, Son and Holy Ghost is to be regarded as an enumeration, it is the enumeration of the dimensions of the one name of God, i.e., of His one work and word, of His one act of salvation and revelation, with a view to which, if there is to be faith, love, obedience and service, so the nations are to be made disciples, summoned to conversion, and led to enter and pursue the way of Jesus Christ. The words Father, Son and Holy Ghost, in their inseparability and distinction, together indicate the expansion of the one name, work and word of God. . . .

The Father is the basis of the history of Jesus Christ, of the history of Israel and of all world history. . . . [Jesus] is invested with the glory of His name, work and word, with His *exousia* [authority] in heaven and on earth. . . .

"And of the Son": . . . The one work and word of God which forms the goal of baptism is decisively the work and word of this Servant of God, of Jesus Christ. . . .

"And of the Holy Ghost"—this is, from the centre, the forward extension: God's one act of salvation and revelation in the dimension which points to future time. . . . The name, work and word of the Holy Spirit is again the one name, work and word—now in its future and eschatological aspect—which is the goal of baptism.

Rudolf Bultmann and Form Criticism

Toward midcentury, the influence of Barth was eclipsed by Rudolph Bultmann (1884-1976), a German, who perhaps had the greatest impact on theology of anyone in the twentieth century. He stood in the Neo-Orthodox tradition, but he pushed it toward Liberalism. He criticized Liberalism, yet his theological system is clearly unacceptable to conservatives.

An important critical tool that Bultmann employed and

popularized is *form criticism*. This approach assumes that much of the biblical material was originally in various oral forms, and it seeks to understand the text by investigating these forms. Bultmann particularly applied this method to the Gospels. The idea is that Matthew, Mark, Luke, and John did not simply sit down and write their Gospels, but they collected various bits and pieces of information, stories, parables, sayings, teachings, sermons, and legends that were preserved orally. While some of the material originally came from the life of Jesus Himself, many of the words and deeds that the Gospels attribute to Jesus actually came from other sources and are not historically accurate.

To understand Christianity, then, we cannot simply read the Gospels at face value, but we must ascertain where the various pieces of the story came from and then evaluate their relative significance and their purpose. Some passages, for example, are Jewish fables or legends that perhaps predated Christ, but the Gospel writer appropriated them for his purpose of glorifying Christ. We should not regard them as history, but they provide insight as to what the early church believed.

Bultmann concluded that the Gospels are not very reliable historically and that we can know almost nothing about the historical Jesus. In essence, the Gospels reflect early theology, not actual history. They reveal what the early Christians taught about Christ, not what really happened in Christ's life. Thus, it is not necessary for us to believe in the miracle accounts; we can simply extract the truth they teach. We should focus on the Christ of faith.

For Bultmann, then, what is important is what the

Bible means for our present experience with God. In Bible days, people believed in angels, demons, and miracles, so of course they wrote in those terms. But today, we realize that these things are fanciful, so we need to translate the stories into modern terms. We need to strip away the mythological elements and focus on the true message of Christianity. Bultmann called this process "demythologizing" the Bible.

This method creates a huge problem, however: where does one stop demythologizing? Who is to say what is true and what is false, what is historical and what is not, what is the true message and what is just the disposable wrapping that surrounds the message? Who decides what is the essential core? The bottom line is that no objective determination is possible. The reader is the one who decides subjectively.

At this point, it appears that we are almost back to old-time Liberalism and its fallacies. If the Bible is God's revelation to humans, how can humans sit in judgment on it? Once again, it appears that in trying to accommodate to twentieth-century rationalism, theologians fatally compromised the Word of God. Indeed, Bultmann discarded the historical reality of the Incarnation, substitutionary Atonement, Resurrection, and Second Coming. In essence, he retained only "justification by (personal existential) faith alone and not by history (the saving events recorded in the Gospels)."[204]

We cannot simply dismiss Bultmann as a Liberal, however, because he did emphasize personal faith in Jesus Christ. He taught the importance of a definite, personal experience with God. He did not completely eliminate the Cross or the uniqueness of Christ, but he presented what he considered to be the challenge and offense of the Cross to sinful humans. Clearly, however, he erred in deleting the miraculous from the Bible, discarding essential doctrines, and emphasizing experience and ethics over doctrine.

Bultmann stands between Liberalism and Evangelicalism. Many conservative theologians employ some of his methods while rejecting his extreme conclusions. People from both sides of the spectrum thus draw from his work, perpetuating his influence.

Other Neo-Orthodox Theologians

Closely associated with Karl Barth was *Emil Brunner* (1889-1965), also from Switzerland. Like Bultmann, he represented the more liberal side of Neo-Orthodoxy. For example, he taught universalism, the doctrine that everyone will be saved in the end. He also criticized the doctrine of the virgin birth of Jesus.

In the United States, a prominent Neo-Orthodox theologian was *Reinhold Niebuhr* (1893-1971). Like Barth, he reacted against Liberalism, but he considered that Barth had gone too far the other way in that he failed to deal adequately with ethics. While Niebuhr did not accept the social gospel, he sought to work out a proper Christian ethical system. For example, he taught that Christians must actively oppose the exploitation of minority groups and that Christians have a duty to take part in politics. He adapted positive elements in the teaching of Liberal theologians and sought to implement them in a more conservative theological system.

Reinhold's brother, *H. Richard Niebuhr* (1894-1962), was also a significant figure. His description of Liberalism has become a classic critique: "A God without wrath brought men without sin into a kingdom without judgment through the ministration of a Christ without a cross."[205] By this statement he highlighted that Liberalism does not believe in eternal punishment, the last judgment, the sinfulness of humanity, or the atoning sacrifice of Jesus Christ, and thus robs Christianity of its most meaningful and distinctive tenets.

Dietrich Bonhoeffer (1906-45), a German pastor and theologian, wrote *The Cost of Discipleship* (1937), in which he proclaimed the importance of acting upon our faith and living a committed life. While salvation is free, he said, discipleship will cost us everything. He deplored what he called "cheap grace"—the false notion that people can receive God's grace and then continue in a disobedient, self-willed, sinful lifestyle:[206]

> Cheap grace . . . amounts to the justification of sin without the justification of the repentant sinner who departs from sin and from whom sin departs. . . . Cheap grace is the grace we bestow on ourselves.
>
> Cheap grace is the preaching of forgiveness without requiring repentance. . . . Cheap grace is grace without discipleship, grace without the cross, grace without Jesus Christ.

In what serves as a critique of both Liberalism and much of Evangelicalism, Bonhoeffer explained that obedience is essential:[207]

> The response of the disciples is an act of obedience, not a confession of faith. . . .

> *Only he who believes is obedient, and only he who is obedient believes. . . .*
>
> It is faith which justifies, and not the act of obedience. . . . From the point of view of justification it is necessary thus to separate them, but we must never lose sight of their essential unity. For faith is only real when there is obedience, never without it, and faith only becomes faith in the act of obedience.
>
> We should completely misunderstand the nature of grace if we were to suppose that there was no need to take the first step, because faith was already there. Against that we must boldly assert that the step of obedience must be taken before faith can be possible. Unless he obeys, a man cannot believe.

Bonhoeffer practiced what he preached. During the Nazi regime in Germany, most Christians, including pastors and theologians, supported Adolf Hitler out of national pride and fear of the consequences of opposing him. Bonhoeffer felt that he needed to oppose Hitler by whatever means he could. Thus, he joined a conspiracy to assassinate Hitler, but the plot was discovered and he was arrested. He was executed by the special order of Himmler just a few days before his concentration camp was liberated by the Allies.

Bonhoeffer taught that we must learn to live for others, not just for ourselves. We must learn to live without constantly relying on God for comfort and help, instead taking responsibility for our own lives. Rather than merely focusing on a personal experience with God and having a self-contained religion, we must develop our character, our personality, and our relationships with others. He described this concept as "religionless Christianity."

Paul Tillich (1886-1965), a German Lutheran immigrant to America, tried to provide theological answers to secular questions. The basis of his theology was what he called "the ultimate"—the ultimate reality, the ultimate truth. He said it is located in God, who is the "ground of being" and can only be encountered by experience. Humans reject God only because they have never really encountered Him; if they ever encountered God, then they would respond accordingly.

Tillich's theology was existential, that is, focusing on personal experience and subjective beliefs. His approach undermined the authority of Scripture, and it even called into question the personality of God by its focus on the search for "the ultimate."

Neo-Orthodox theologians began to make use of another tool of higher criticism called *redaction criticism* ("redaction" means "editing"), an outgrowth of form criticism. Under this view, each biblical writer had his own reasons for writing and selected and shaped his material accordingly. The Gospel writers, for instance, did not simply record history but selected material in accordance with their own theology or agenda. Redaction criticism tries to investigate the mind of the writer to determine why he included certain elements and omitted others.

It is true that the Gospel writers emphasized certain important themes, but conservative theologians say that God inspired them to do so. Redaction criticism, however, underscores the human element in the process. The result is that it typically finds different—even competing and conflicting—theologies in the New Testament itself.

Evaluation of Neo-Orthodoxy

In summary, Neo-Orthodoxy was not an organized movement but a grouping of theologies that reacted against Liberalism yet used many of the critical tools of Liberalism. The key beliefs were the sovereignty of God, the grace of God, the sinfulness of humanity, the necessity of divine revelation for people to know God, the revelation of God in Christ, the Scriptures as containing (but not being identical to) the Word of God, and the need for a personal encounter with God.

The Neo-Orthodox theologians clearly identified the errors of Liberalism. In this they were aided by the First and Second World Wars, which for many people shattered the humanistic notions that people are basically good, can perfect themselves, and can establish the kingdom of God on earth.

On the other hand, the Neo-Orthodox theologians were willing to question traditional beliefs and terminology. They were more interested in basing their views on Scripture rather than historic creeds. The doctrine of the trinity is a case in point. Some were critical of traditional trinitarian terms. Others continued to use them but reinterpreted them. They were often more frank and insightful than Evangelicals in acknowledging the historical development of the doctrine of the trinity, because they did not feel bound to defend every traditional formulation.[208]

In the final analysis, however, the Neo-Orthodox theologians did not return completely to biblical truth, because they did not fully accept the authority of the Bible as the Word of God. While they refuted the central tenets of Liberalism and discarded some aspects of non-biblical tradition, they failed to acknowledge in full the supernatural message of the Bible. They emphasized a personal encounter with God, but they failed to discover the biblical experience of the baptism of the Holy Spirit.

Other Philosophical and Theological Developments

A man who had a tremendous impact upon twentieth-century religious views was *Sigmund Freud* (1856-1939), an Austrian Jew. He founded the modern study of *psychology* and the practice of psychotherapy. Many of Freud's ideas are quite controversial even today, notably his tracing of most psychological problems to childhood experiences and his attribution of almost every motivation to sexuality (often unconscious or repressed). Freud was an atheist, and he labeled religion as a neurosis. In his view, only an unhealthy mind would believe in God or depend upon religion for assistance.

Christian thought was a significant force in the *Civil Rights movement* in the United States in the 1960s, which secured political and social rights for blacks. The moral leader of this movement was Martin Luther King, Jr. (1929-68), a Baptist minister who was committed to nonviolent protest in order to achieve equality and integration. He worked through the Southern Christian Leadership Conference to achieve his goals. King organized the massive March on Washington in 1963 and was assassinated in 1968.

A philosophical development that affected modern theology is *positivism*. This philosophy stresses the analysis of language, and it tries to determine which logical propositions have factual meaning. It says that all valid knowledge comes through the scientific method. Since metaphysical language cannot be verified by the scientific method, it is meaningless.

In the 1960s, some theologians drew from the ideas of positivism and the implications of Bultmann, Tillich, and others to formulate *secular theology*. They sought to apply theology to the secular world and to answer the questions of secular philosophy. Carried to its extreme, this movement said that language about God is meaningless. It is impossible to talk intelligently about God, and it is even impossible to think of God as a personal being. This movement became characterized by the phrase "God is dead." What was left was to apply theology to society—a reduction of theology to philosophy.

In this line of thought, Joseph Fletcher became the foremost exponent of *situation ethics*. Under this view, there are no moral absolutes. What is true and right depends upon the situation. What is moral in one situation may not be moral in another. Fletcher went so far as to say that, in certain cases, such things as prostitution or fornication may not be wrong. To make a moral decision on these matters, we have to look at the background of people, the influences on them, their motivation, their purpose, and the alternatives available to them.

Liberation theology arose in Latin America among Roman Catholics who were influenced by Marxism. It looks at salvation largely in terms of political and economic liberation, sounding much like the social gospel in a revolutionary setting. According to liberation theologians, the church's goal should be to create a just society, and therefore it should be active in promoting political, economic, and social changes. They typically define social justice to include the redistribution of wealth and means of production, and some of them, like the communists, attack the notion of private property. Pope John Paul II has spoken against liberation theology, but it is quite influential in both Catholic and Protestant circles.

Another recent development is *process theology*. Drawing from modern scientific theory, it says that all reality, including God, is in a state of flux, a state of becoming, or a state of evolution. Even God is changing, progressing, and "becoming" something that He is not. He does not know the future because it does not yet exist and has not yet been determined.

Wolfhart Pannenberg (born 1928) of Germany is characterized by a *theology of history*. He reacted against Barth and Bultmann in stating that God's revelation comes within human history rather than outside it. It is necessary to study Jesus historically instead of simply accepting the Christ of faith. In particular, we should acknowledge the resurrection of Jesus as a historical event.

Jürgen Moltmann (born 1926) of Germany is characterized by a *theology of hope*. In contrast to Neo-Orthodoxy and secular theology, Moltmann embraced eschatology (the doctrine of the last things) and anticipated that the future will bring theological answers. He emphasized that faith must be socially relevant, applying faith to the problems of modern society. He also taught a social doctrine of the trinity, stressing the supposed threeness of God and making this concept the foundation of human relationships.

In Africa, some have formulated a distinctively *African theology*, blending elements of traditional African religion with Christianity. There are many indigenous Christian or quasi-Christian organizations. They run the gamut in religious beliefs from conservative Christian to almost totally African. Some of these groups are Pentecostal in character, encouraging moves of the Spirit, spiritual gifts, and demonstrative worship. At the same time, many include practices and concepts from tribal religions, such as ancestor worship, animism, sacrifices, and polygamy.

Feminist theology has developed as a means of proclaiming the equality of men and women. In its mildest form, it seeks to make the language of worship inclusive rather than masculine. Many feminist theologians seek to eliminate all references to God as masculine, or at least balance them with references to God as feminine. For example, prayers may be addressed to "our heavenly Parent" or "our heavenly Father and Mother." Jesus may be called "the Child of God." Some seek to make these changes in the Bible and in official liturgy. For instance, in 1999 the Methodists in England included the first prayer to "God the Mother" in their new worship book.[209] Radical feminists worship the "Goddess" or "Sophia" (Greek for "wisdom"). They draw inspiration from the pagan worship of female deities. They celebrate female sexuality and endorse lesbianism.

As an example, a feminist church in San Francisco called Weave of Faith, "a Christian feminist worshipping community," described its worship as follows:[210]

> While our rituals may borrow from women's spirituality and non-christian religions, the divinity which we worship is grounded in the judeo-christian tradition, more often than not with feminine names and

attributes which are biblically based. Our liturgies try to provide a model for using inclusive language. Also, we are committed to providing a safe environment for theological exploration and open spiritual experience: there are no "heresies" in our worshipping community. We are all exploring greater understanding of the divine and our relationship to the world, each other, ourselves, and that which is greater than ourselves (who can be called She, He, It or Them): whatever provides a meaningful connection.

The twentieth century also saw the rise of the *ecumenical movement*, the attempt to unite various branches of Christendom in fellowship and ultimately in organization. The worldwide movement began with the World Missionary Conference in Edinburgh in 1910. The foremost example of ecumenism today is the World Council of Churches (1948), which we discuss in the next section. The sister organization in the United States is the National Council of the Churches of Christ in the U.S.A. (NCCC). The NCCC is the successor to the Federal Council of Churches of Christ, founded in 1908.

In addition, there are other significant examples of ecumenism that we will discuss in subsequent chapters, including the National Association of Evangelicals, Catholic-Protestant dialogue, the Pentecostal/Charismatic Churches of North America, and the Charismatic movement itself.

The World Council of Churches

The World Council of Churches (WCC) is a "fellowship of churches which confess the Lord Jesus Christ as

God and Saviour according to the Scriptures and therefore seek to fulfil together their common calling to the glory of the one God, Father, Son and Holy Spirit."[211] Most Protestant and Orthodox churches have joined it, but the Roman Catholic Church, most Evangelical churches, and most Pentecostal churches have not. From the beginning, the leadership and the agenda have been dominated by liberal theology of one sort or another. It was too liberal for Karl Barth, who addressed the opening conference and sharply criticized it for departing from essentials of the Christian faith.

Christianity Today, the leading Evangelical Christian magazine, offered the following critique of the WCC in 1984:[212]

The gospel soon became lost in all sorts of political and social causes with which the World Council identified. . . . From 1960 through 1980, this seemed to be the permanent direction of the council.

Most troubling to biblically oriented evangelicals were the following: (1) The deity of Christ was left undefined, though the council's constitution gave it lip service. Vastly differing views on the person and work of Christ flourished equally within the leadership of the council. (2) The New Testament gospel became lost—the gospel that Jesus Christ, the divine Savior and Lord, became incarnate, died on the cross and rose again bodily from the dead to redeem mankind from sin through personal faith in himself. (3) The Bible was an honored book from which proof texts were selected when they supported views considered relevant on other grounds, but no attempt was made to deal seriously with scriptural teaching. (4) Universalism—the view that all will be saved regardless of faith, religion, or moral condition, became standard doctrine. (5) World history was interpreted in Marxist terms, superficially glossed with traditional Christian vocabulary. (6) Left-wing offenses against human rights and human freedom were seldom noted, and rarely rebuked. By contrast, right-wing oppression was made a *cause célèbre*; and the council actively opposed efforts to further human rights and political democracy in the Marxist countries.

In 1984, at its sixth assembly at Vancouver, the WCC attempted to woo Evangelicals. *Christianity Today* reassessed the council at that time and concluded that its theology still fell far short of biblical truth in five major areas:[213]

1. *Its equivocal stand on the deity of Christ.* . . .

2. *Its failure to diagnose the predicament of mankind* [human sinfulness]. . . .

3. *Its wrong diagnosis surely leads to a wrong remedy.* . . . In the WCC study volume prepared for the Vancouver assembly, John Paulton lists as one *unlikely* option, that "only those calling upon Jesus as their personal savior, can be saved.". . .

4. *Its almost exclusive concern for the horizontal dimension of salvation* . . . communal salvation, one that leads to a new humanity and a restoration of society rather than to personal faith in Jesus Christ, a right relationship to God, and the new birth. . . .

5. *Its religious pluralism.* . . . Its official pre-assembly study guide [said], "In the end the great communities of faith will not have disappeared. None will have 'won' over the other. Jews will still be Jews; Muslims still Muslims; and those of the great Eastern faiths, still Buddhists or Hindus or Taoists. Africa will still witness to its traditional life view; China to its inheritance. People will still come from the east and the west, the north and the south, and sit down in the Kingdom of God without having first become 'Christians' like us.". . . [A] stern warning [was] presented by World Council official D. C. Mulder *against* evangelizing because it imposed an obstacle to dialogue with other religions.

Moreover, the World Council study guide on the Bible stated:[214]

There are diverse literary traditions in the biblical writings. . . . Some of these traditions may be contradictory. The church is in dialogue with Scripture, but has been fed from many sources, in the light of which, biblical statements may have to be declared inadequate, or erroneous. . . . We are not to regard the Bible primarily as a standard to which we must conform in all the questions arising in our life.

In 1998, the WCC held its eighth assembly in Harare, Zimbabwe. It faced considerable dissent from Orthodox bodies, which make up about 30 percent of the membership and are concerned about the increasingly liberal drift of the organization. *Christianity Today* reported, "Both

Orthodox and mainline evangelicals generally are unhappy with the liberal Protestant ethos they say dominates WCC debate on issues such as feminism, inclusive language in Bible translation, same-sex unions, ordination of homosexuals, abortion, environmentalism, and population control."[215]

Interestingly, the WCC has discussed water baptism in the name of Jesus Christ. Its study of water baptism advocated the traditional trinitarian formula. In response, two member organizations—both in areas where the United Pentecostal Church International has large national churches—asked that the WCC recognize the validity of the Jesus Name formula. The Church of North India stated:[216]

> In view of the fact that there is strong biblical evidence for baptism performed/received in the name of Jesus/Jesus Christ as well as the fact that certain Christian denominations still baptize in the name of Jesus (which is more *personal* and evocative of discipleship than the metaphysical Trinitarian formula) the churches should be urged to recognize as valid baptisms in the name of Jesus.

The National Council of Churches in the Philippines made a similar proposal:[217]

> There are churches which are using the Trinitarian formula as found in Matthew 28:19. . . . Most of the member churches of NCCP are using this formula. There are those who use 'in the name of Jesus' only. Both practices have scriptural support. Among the NCCP member churches the issue of baptismal

validity is not very intense at this very point. Other sectarian groups would consider this point very vital to the question of baptism's validity.

As of 1999, the WCC consisted of 339 Protestant and Orthodox organizations, with a total constituency of about 500 million, or 25 percent of the almost 2 billion professing Christians worldwide. The remainder are mostly Roman Catholics and Pentecostals.[218] The NCCC had 35 denominations with 52 million constituents.[219]

Liberal Trends

By century's end, liberal ideas about the infallibility of the Bible and other essential doctrines dominated most mainline Protestant denominations, including the Presbyterians and Reformed, Lutherans, Methodists, United Church of Christ, Episcopalians, Anglicans, United Church of Canada, and some Baptists. In the United States, the two major exceptions are the Southern Baptist Convention and the Lutheran Church–Missouri Synod. There are some conservative organizations in the denominational groupings we have mentioned, and even in the liberal organizations there are significant conservative minorities.

A survey of 10,000 Protestant ministers by sociologist Jeffrey Hadden indicated the extent of liberal thinking among mainline Protestant clergy in 1982. He obtained the following results from 7,441 who responded:[220]

Jesus born of a virgin?
60% of Methodists said no
49% of Presbyterians said no

44% of Episcopalians said no
19% of American Lutherans said no

Bible—inspired Word of God? [infallibility of Scripture]
82% of Methodists said no
81% of Presbyterians said no
89% of Episcopalians said no
57% of American Lutherans said no

Existence of Satan [as a personal being]?
62% of Methodists said no
47% of Presbyterians said no
37% of Episcopalians said no
33% of Baptists said no
14% of American Lutherans said no

Physical resurrection of Jesus?
51% of Methodists said no
35% of Presbyterians said no
30% of Episcopalians said no
33% of Baptists said no
13% of American Lutherans said no

A notable example of liberal thinking in the mainline denominations is the increasing acceptance of extramarital sex and homosexual activity as compatible with Christianity, even though the Bible clearly teaches otherwise. (See Leviticus 18:22; Romans 1:26-27; I Corinthians 6:9-11.)

In 1988, the Newark (New Jersey) Episcopal Diocese voted to receive a fifteen-page report entitled "Changing

Patterns of Sexuality in Family Life." The report stated: "It is our conclusion that by suppressing our sexuality and by condemning all sex which occurs outside of traditional marriage, the church has thereby obstructed a vitally important means for persons to know and celebrate their relatedness to God." The presiding bishop of the Episcopal Church, Edmund Lee Browning, praised the Newark Diocese for being "at the cutting edge" of church issues, although he did not officially endorse the report.[221]

In 1989, John Spong, bishop of the Newark Episcopal Diocese, ordained J. Robert Williams, a confessed practicing homosexual, as a priest. At the time, Williams had lived with a male companion for four years. Spong said, "We need to be honest. We have gay priests in every diocese."[222] Six weeks after his ordination, Williams stated publicly, "Monogamy is as unnatural as celibacy. It is crazy to hold up this ideal." He also advised the famous Roman Catholic nun Mother Teresa to get a lover and thereby improve herself.[223]

In 1988, the United Church of Canada, that country's largest Protestant denomination, agreed to allow the ordination of practicing homosexuals. It affirmed the right of church membership "regardless of sexual orientation" and the right of all church members to "be considered eligible" for ordination.[224]

In 1989, in a poll of the Presbyterian Church in the U.S.A., 50 percent of the pastors and 56 percent of the specialized clergy said the Bible teaches that it is possible to be a Christian and engage in homosexual activities.[225]

In 1998 and 1999, controversy erupted in the United Methodist Church, as some ministers performed "marriage" and "blessing" ceremonies for homosexuals. On

January 16, 1999, 95 United Methodists "blessed" a lesbian couple before 1,500 people in Sacramento, California. The two lesbians were lay leaders who had lived together for fifteen years.[226]

Summary

Two significant trends characterized mainline Protestantism in the twentieth century. First, it became predominantly and increasingly liberal in theology and ethics. That is, the majority of denominational leaders, clergy, and laity no longer accepted some of the fundamental doctrines of Christianity, such as the infallibility of the Bible, the miracles of the Bible, the virgin birth of Jesus, the true deity of Jesus, the substitutionary atoning work of Jesus for our salvation, the physical resurrection of Jesus, and the second coming of Jesus to earth.

Second, church membership in these denominations declined significantly over the century. For instance, from 1965 to 1989, the United Church of Christ decreased by 20 percent, the Presbyterian Church by 25 percent, the Episcopal Church by 28 percent, the United Methodist Church by 18 percent, and the Christian Church (Disciples of Christ) by 43 percent.[227] Increasing numbers of people with Protestant backgrounds no longer attended church or identified with Christianity but became secularists. In addition, the loss in the mainline denominations translated into moderate gains for Evangelical churches and significant gains for new religious movements (such as Mormons and Jehovah's Witnesses), the Pentecostal movement, and the Charismatic movement.

7

Fundamentalism and Evangelicalism

In the early twentieth century, conservative Protestants began to rally against Liberalism (Modernism) and its higher criticism of the Bible. They defended a traditional understanding of the Bible and affirmed fundamental doctrines that Christians of all branches had held over the centuries. They also stood against Darwinian evolution and Marxist socialism.

The Fundamentalists

From 1910 to 1915 prominent conservative Protestant scholars wrote a series of twelve pamphlets called *The Fundamentals*, which defended key doctrines that were under attack. The result was a new movement called Fundamentalism. Of course, the basic doctrines were not new, but the movement itself was.

The editors of *The Fundamentals* were A. C. Dixon and R. A. Torrey. The authors included Benjamin B. Warfield, H. G. Moule, James Orr, Charles Erdman, and others. They came from the United States and the United Kingdom and from many denominations.

For a number of years, the Fundamentalists and the Modernists struggled for control of the major Protestant denominations and seminaries. Eventually Liberal and Neo-Orthodox views won the day. As a result, many Fundamentalists left their denominations and institutions and formed their own. For example, John Gresham Machen, a Presbyterian professor, left Princeton Theological Seminary and founded Westminster Theological Seminary in Philadelphia. He was also instrumental in founding what became known as the Orthodox Presbyterian Church (1936). Other Fundamentalist organizations that came into existence were the Independent Fundamental Churches of America (1930), the General Association of Regular Baptist Churches (1932), the Bible Presbyterian Church (1938), and the Conservative Baptist Association of America (1947).

These denominations have remained small. In addition to them, there are many independent Fundamentalist churches, including the independent Bible churches and Baptist churches. The largest defender of Fundamentalist doctrine became the Southern Baptist Convention, one of the few major groups to maintain its conservative theological identity.

The first attempt at forming an association of Fundamentalists was the World's Christian Fundamentals Association (1919). In 1941, Carl McIntire, a fiery radio preacher, organized the American Council of Christian Churches (ACCC). In 1948, the International Council of Christian Churches (ICCC) came into being as a counterweight to the World Council of Churches. Today, the ACCC supports another international organization instead of the ICCC—the World Council of Biblical Churches.

The ACCC is the largest association of historic Fundamentalism today, but it is relatively small. In 1987, its member organizations claimed a total constituency of only 1.5 million, compared to 40 million for the National Council of the Churches of Christ and 5 million for the National Association of Evangelicals.[228]

In 1925, the Fundamentalists received national notoriety as a result of the so-called Scopes Monkey Trial. Tennessee had recently passed a law forbidding the teaching of evolution in the public schools. John Scopes, a high school biology teacher in Dayton, was put on trial for violating this law. Scopes was convicted by a jury, but the real significance of the trial was in the debate between two of the most prominent lawyers in America and the resulting press coverage.

William Jennings Bryan, a three-time Democratic presidential candidate, aided the prosecution and upheld the biblical account of creation. Clarence Darrow, a famous criminal defense attorney, represented Scopes. In an unusual maneuver, Darrow was allowed to call Bryan as a witness for the defense and subjected him to harsh attacks and ridicule. By asking questions on science and biblical interpretation that required expert knowledge, he was able to make Bryan look somewhat foolish, and he called the proponents of creationism "bigots and ignoramuses." The national press painted a distorted picture of Bryan and his allies as fools, calling them "peasants, yokels, morons, hillbillies." Of course, Darrow and his allies were depicted as educated and enlightened.[229]

The Scopes Trial gave Fundamentalists an undeserved national reputation for being ignorant, anti-intellectual, anti-science, and anti-education. This negative impression exists to this day, and the media still show heavy bias in this regard.

Unfortunately, too many Fundamentalists reacted to this type of ridicule by becoming defensive and antagonistic. As a result, they helped perpetuate the stereotype.

In addition to the organizations we have mentioned, prominent institutions that used the Fundamentalist label over the years include Bob Jones University, Moody Bible Institute, and Dallas Theological Seminary. A popular Fundamentalist evangelist was Billy Sunday (1863-1935), a former professional baseball player and a Presbyterian minister. Leading Fundamentalist writers and media personalities today include Jerry Falwell, Tim La Haye, and Hal Lindsey.

Key Doctrines of Fundamentalism

In opposition to Liberalism, Fundamentalism emphasized five major doctrines:

1. *The verbal inspiration and inerrancy of Scripture.* As we have seen, Liberalism was really an attack on the authority of Scripture. In response, the Fundamentalists affirmed the divine inspiration and infallibility of the Bible. This doctrine became the basis for all the others, for they are derived from a straightforward interpretation of Scripture.

"Verbal" means pertaining to words. By "verbal inspiration," the Fundamentalists did not mean that Scripture was verbally dictated, but that every word of the Bible was inspired of God and therefore true. Not only are the thoughts and themes of Scripture inspired, but so is the choice of words.

Verbal inspiration means that the Bible is infallible (incapable of error or mistake) and inerrant (without error). Every word is true. While a scribe, translator, or printer could make an error in transmitting a particular text, the original writings were given by inspiration of God and thus were completely true. Consequently, the Fundamentalists rejected any higher criticism that would attribute errors to the original text of Scripture.[230] (A few Fundamentalists, such as James Orr, were willing to concede that there could be factual errors on matters such as geography, but no theological errors.)

Perhaps the strongest, clearest exponent of the verbal inspiration of Scripture at this time was Benjamin Warfield (1851-1921). He was a professor at Princeton Theological Seminary, which in the nineteenth century and early twentieth was a bastion of conservative Reformed theology. The Princeton theologians of that era, including Charles Hodge, A. A. Hodge, Warfield, and Machen, were noted for their exposition and defense of the inerrancy of the Bible.

2. *The deity and virgin birth of Jesus*. Jesus is not merely a man, but He is truly God manifested in the flesh. Moreover, as a human He was conceived in the womb of the virgin Mary by a miracle of God's Spirit. (Some Fundamentalists listed the deity of Christ as the essential element, some listed the virgin birth, and some listed both. All affirmed both teachings.)

3. *The substitutionary atonement.* Jesus Christ died for the sins of the human race, paying the penalty for our sins so that we might be saved through Him. Thus the only means of salvation is by grace through faith based on the atoning sacrifice of Jesus.

4. *The physical resurrection of Jesus.* Jesus arose from the grave with a glorified human body, and He lives forever.

5. *The bodily return of Jesus to earth.* Jesus is physically coming back to earth again in fulfillment of biblical prophecy. (Some Fundamentalists identified the fifth essential as the historicity of biblical miracles, which all Fundamentalists agreed upon as a consequence of the inerrancy of Scripture.)

Of course, these five doctrines were not the only ones that the Fundamentalists espoused, nor were they the only doctrines addressed in *The Fundamentals.* These five, however, were the essential doctrines that characterized the movement as a whole. These were the major points of controversy with Liberalism, which denied each of them.

Most Fundamentalists also espoused *premillennialism,* meaning the Second Coming will take place before the Millennium. Christ will return to earth and then establish a kingdom on earth for a thousand years, after which will come the last judgment. (See Revelation 20.) The alternative proposed by more liberal-minded theologians was either postmillennialism or amillennialism. Postmillennialism says the church will establish the Millennium first, and after a thousand years of peace Christ will return. Amillennialism says there will be no literal kingdom for a thousand years; the prophecy of Revelation 20 simply refers to the rule of God in our hearts.

As time went on, most Fundamentalists also accepted the doctrine of *dispensationalism*. This system of interpreting the Bible makes a strong distinction between Israel and the church. Consequently, the nation of Israel will yet receive the fulfillment of promises that God made to them in the Old Testament which have not yet been fulfilled; the promises are not simply fulfilled in the church. Dispensationalists identify different ages, called dispensations, in which God worked with people in distinct ways. Most dispensational schemes identify seven such ages. An important part of dispensationalism is the doctrine of the secret, pretribulation Rapture.

John Nelson Darby (1800-1882), leader of the Plymouth Brethren (a Separatist group in England), systematized dispensationalism and became its most prominent advocate. He was the first to teach clearly that Christ's second coming will occur in two phases: (1) Before the Tribulation, He will come in the air to catch away the saints. (2) After the Tribulation, He will come to the earth with His saints to rescue Israel at the close of the Battle of Armageddon and to establish His millennial kingdom.

Dispensationalism was made popular among Fundamentalists in America by Cyrus I. Scofield (1843-1921). He taught the doctrine in the notes to the *Scofield Reference Bible*, which he published in 1909.

On matters of *lifestyle*, the early Fundamentalists were quite conservative. They advocated strict morality, modesty of dress, and abstention from smoking, drinking, dancing, gambling, attending movies, and worldly amusements. Unlike the Holiness movement, however, most of them did not take an absolute stand against the wearing of jewelry or (when it became popular) makeup.

205

When it became common in society for women to cut their hair and wear pants, many Fundamentalist were initially opposed to these practices, but most eventually accepted them. Some of them, notably independent Baptists, maintained their opposition, however. Prominent examples were independent Baptists John R. Rice and Jack Hyles.

We clearly see Fundamentalism's major doctrinal themes and separatist stance in the ACCC's official characterization of itself:[231]

> Among the fundamental doctrines of the Faith are: the inspiration and inerrancy of Scripture; the deity of Jesus Christ, His virgin birth, substitutionary blood atonement, His literal bodily resurrection and His Second Coming "in power and great glory." We as Fundamentalists also affirm that the Bible teaches separation from unbelievers and erring brethren. . . .
>
> We need to stand together to expose Liberalism, New Evangelicalism, the Charismatic movement, and compromise in all areas of life and ministry. . . .
>
> No church or individual can be a part of the ACCC and at the same time be connected in any way with the National Council of Churches (NCC) with its liberal theology, ecumenical apostasy, and leftist sociopolitical agenda. Neither can one be a part of the ACCC and be associated with the National Association of Evangelicals (NAE), which is noted for its compromise, confusion and inclusion of Charismatics.

The ACCC has adopted the following doctrinal statement:[232]

Among other equally biblical truths, we believe and maintain the following:

a. The plenary [full] divine inspiration of the Scriptures in the original languages, their consequent inerrancy and infallibility, and, as the Word of God, the supreme and final authority in faith and life;

b. The Triune God: Father, Son and Holy Spirit;

c. The essential, absolute, eternal deity, and the real and proper, but sinless, humanity of our Lord Jesus Christ;

d. His birth of the Virgin Mary;

e. His substitutionary, expiatory death, in that He gave His life "a ransom for many";

f. His resurrection from among the dead in the same body in which He was crucified, and the second coming of this same Jesus in power and great glory;

g. The total depravity of man through the fall;

h. Salvation the effect of regeneration by the Spirit and the Word not by works but by grace through faith;

i. The everlasting bliss of the saved, and the everlasting suffering of the lost;

j. The real spiritual unity in Christ of all redeemed by His precious blood;

k. The necessity of maintaining, according to the Word of God, the purity of the Church in doctrine and life.

Fundamentalists and Pentecostals

As we saw in chapter 5, early leaders in the Assemblies of God described themselves as Fundamentalists who spoke in tongues. Actually, however, the Pentecostal movement and the Fundamentalist movement are quite distinct. Historically, the former began in 1901, while the latter began in 1910, among two entirely different groups of people. The Pentecostals arose primarily from the edges of the Holiness movement, and they developed their own organizations in the first two decades of the century. The Fundamentalists arose primarily among Presbyterians, Baptists, and other large Protestant bodies. They fought for control of their denominations for years and did not form their own organizations until the 1930s.

More importantly, as a matter of theology, the early Fundamentalists flatly rejected the Pentecostal movement. They typically said that speaking in tongues is of the devil, or at best a psychologically induced phenomenon.

The reaction of the two editors of *The Fundamentals* is a good example. A. C. Dixon discussed the baptism of the Holy Ghost with William Durham but rejected the doctrine as an indictment against Christianity. He said the Pentecostal movement was "wicked and adulterous."[233]

In his 1895 book *The Baptism with the Holy Ghost*, R. A. Torrey had promoted the Keswick concept of the baptism of the Holy Ghost as an endowment of power. He had even speculated that tongues could be the initial sign but ultimately rejected this idea:[234]

> In my early study of the Baptism with the Holy Spirit, I noticed that in many instances those who were so baptized "spoke with tongues," and the question came often into my mind: if one is baptized with the Holy Spirit will he not speak with tongues? But

I saw no one so speaking, and I often wondered, is there anyone today who actually is baptized with the Holy Spirit. This 12th chapter of 1st Corinthians cleared me up on that, especially when I found Paul asking of those who had been baptized with the Holy Spirit: "Do all speak with tongues?"

When the Pentecostal movement came, Torrey rejected it out of hand. He asserted, "God withdrew the gift of tongues from the church back in the beginning of the Church Age, and there is no good reason to say that He ever restored it." He also said that the Pentecostal movement "was emphatically not of God and founded by a sodomite."[235]

Fundamentalists typically held that miracles ceased with the completion of the New Testament. Warfield argued against tongues on that basis. They also used dispensationalism to maintain that God no longer deals with His people through visible miracles, signs, and wonders.

In 1928, the World's Christian Fundamentalist Association officially rejected speaking in tongues and miraculous healing ministries. When it was formed in 1941, the American Council of Christian Churches specifically excluded Pentecostals and those who had fellowship with Pentecostals. In the 1980s, Jerry Falwell suggested that speaking in tongues results from eating too much pizza the night before and getting indigestion.

Thus it is a misnomer to speak of Pentecostals as Fundamentalists. Of course, Pentecostals have historically affirmed the five essential points of Fundamentalism that we have presented—the verbal inspiration and inerrancy of Scripture, the deity and virgin birth of Jesus, the substitutionary atonement, the physical resurrection of Jesus, and the bodily return of Jesus to earth. The overall approach to theology and spiritual experience is considerably different, however, as the Fundamentalists have been quick to point out.

Clearly, then, Pentecostals should not uncritically adopt the Fundamentalist approach to theology, although they have sometimes done so. For example, the second generation of Pentecostal teachers often embraced dispensationalism uncritically. But while this system does offer helpful insights, it has to be modified significantly to be compatible with Pentecostal belief and practice.[236] Even professed Pentecostal dispensationalists have often contradicted the theological system—for instance, speaking of the church as "spiritual Israel"—or otherwise modified it.[237]

Pentecostals are not simply Fundamentalists who speak in tongues. Their respect for the inspiration, infallibility, and authority of the Bible is just as great, and so is their commitment to the fundamental doctrines relating to the identity and work of Jesus Christ in human history. They are quite different, however, in their personal experience with God, understanding of the work of the Holy Spirit, concept of holiness, and interpretation of the New Testament.

While Fundamentalists affirm miracles in the Bible, they reject miracles today. They deny that the church in the Book of Acts is the role model for us to follow. They say that instructions in the Epistles relative to divine healing, spiritual gifts, and spiritual ministry are no longer applicable. Morever, dispensationalists minimize the ethical teachings of the Sermon on the Mount, considering them to be legalistic instructions for the Jews in preparation for their earthly kingdom. Although Fundamentalism's reason for existence is to champion the inspiration and authority of the Bible, in effect it renders large portions of the Bible irrelevant to the church today.

Historically, the Fundamentalists were quite conservative politically, while many early Pentecostals warned both of the dangers of socialism and unbridled capitalism. Fundamentalists typically supported military action by the government, while most early Pentecostals were pacifists. The Fundamentalist movement mainly attracted whites, while the Pentecostals were racially diverse. Of course, both groups have always been conservative morally.

The difference between Fundamentalists and Oneness Pentecostals is particularly great. Fundamentalists reject any modification of the doctrine of the trinity or any idea that the experience of salvation could involve more than a verbal confession of faith. Most of them also advocate unconditional eternal security.

The Evangelicals

By the 1940s some conservatives were dissatisfied with the label "Fundamentalist" because of the negative connotations in society and the adversarial position of many Fundamentalists toward other churches. They wanted to affirm the basic doctrines of Fundamentalism and historic Protestantism, but they wanted a more positive identity, a less strident tone, a more conciliatory approach toward others, and a greater appreciation for culture, education, scholarship, and science. That desire led to the Evangelical movement. In essence, the

Evangelicals are the moderate heirs of the Fundamentalists.

The word *evangelical* comes from the Greek word for "gospel," and historically it has been synonymous with Protestantism. Even today, in continental Europe and in Latin America the term generally refers to all Protestants. In the twentieth century it came to be associated with a definite, identifiable conversion experience—accepting Jesus as one's personal Savior or making a decision for Christ—coupled with efforts to spread the gospel to others. In our context, it denotes "the movement in modern Christianity, transcending denominational and confessional boundaries, that emphasizes conformity to the basic tenets of the faith and a missionary outreach of compassion and urgency."[238]

The modern Evangelical movement became a recognizable force in 1942 in the U.S. with the formation of the National Association of Evangelicals (NAE). The three major leaders who spearheaded the development of the NAE were J. Elwin Wright, Harold Ockenga, and Carl F. H. Henry. A subsidiary, the National Religious Broadcasters (NRB), was formed in 1944.

The NAE was an alternative to the ACCC that was less sectarian and more inclusive. Notably, the ACCC excluded all Pentecostals, while Trinitarian Pentecostals participated in the formation of the NAE.

In 1987, the NAE had a membership in its constituent churches of 5 million, 60 percent of whom were Pentecostals. In 1999, the NAE consisted of 49 denominations, individual congregations from 27 other denominations, several hundred independent churches, and 250 parachurch ministries and educational institutions. These groups ministered "directly or indirectly" to 27 million people.[239] Actual constituency of NAE denominations was about 6 million. The total number of churches was about 43,000.[240]

The ten largest denominations in the NAE are, in order, the Assemblies of God, the Church of God (Cleveland, Tennessee), the Church of the Nazarene, the Christian and Missionary Alliance, the Presbyterian Church in America, the International Church of the Foursquare Gospel, the Baptist General Conference, the International Pentecostal Holiness Church, the Wesleyan Church, and the Conservative Congregational Christian Churches. Four of these groups are Pentecostal (AG, CG, ICFG, IPHC), three are Holiness churches (Nazarenes, CMA, Wesleyans), and three emerged from the Fundamentalist-Modernist controversy in mainline Protestantism (Presbyterians, Baptists, and Congregationalists).

The Southern Baptist Convention is not a member of the NAE, although it is the largest Evangelical denomination. (Indeed, it is larger than all NAE denominations combined.) There are also no black or Hispanic groups in the NAE. Oneness Pentecostals are excluded by the NAE's doctrinal statement, although a Oneness organization—the Bible Way Church—was able to join the NRB.

The Evangelical movement began to grow rapidly after World War II, first in America and then in other parts of the world. The person who did more than any other in this regard, and who is most associated with the term "Evangelical," was Billy Graham (born 1918), a Southern Baptist evangelist. Graham's ministry drew national attention beginning with a crusade in Los

Angeles in 1949. Since then, he has conducted numerous evangelistic crusades around the world, and they have resulted in more than two million decisions for Christ. In the early 1970s, one million people attended a Sunday crusade service in Seoul, Korea. Graham has been a friend of a number of U.S. presidents.

In 1956, Graham founded *Christianity Today* magazine. Now independent of him, it has become the leading Evangelical periodical. Graham was also instrumental in calling the World Congress on Evangelism (Berlin, 1966), the International Congress on World Evangelization (Lausanne, 1974), and two International Conferences of Itinerant Evangelists (1983 and 1986).

Graham epitomized the new Evangelicalism in contrast to the old Fundamentalism. He was one of the first speakers to insist on racial integration of his crusades. Moreover, in planning a crusade in a city, he enlisted help from people of all denominations in the area, including Roman Catholics. As a result, he came under fire from Fundamentalists for compromise.

Well-known Evangelical educational institutions include Wheaton College, Fuller Theological Seminary, and Gordon-Conwell Theological Seminary. Evangelical institutions in the Pentecostal/Charismatic tradition are Evangel University (Assemblies of God), Lee University (Church of God), Regent University, and Oral Roberts University.

There are many other Evangelical institutions and parachurch organizations. One of those at the cutting edge of evangelizing unreached peoples is Wycliffe Bible Translators (1934).

Well-known scholars and authors of the Evangelical

movement include F. F. Bruce, Carl F. H. Henry, George Eldon Ladd, Harold Lindsell, James I. Packer, Bernard Ramm, and John R. W. Stott.

In a class by himself is C. S. Lewis (1898-1963). Although he was not strictly an Evangelical—he did not uphold the infallibility of Scripture, for example—he is one of the most widely read and beloved authors among Evangelicals. A classics scholar and Christian apologist, Lewis was born in Northern Ireland. He converted to Christianity in 1931 while a professor at Oxford, and he later taught at Cambridge. Lewis wrote lucid, logical defenses of classic Christian positions for a lay audience. His seven-volume *Chronicles of Narnia* is an outstanding work of children's literature that incorporates important theological concepts.

In the latter part of the twentieth century, some Evangelical churches grew rapidly by structuring their services in a contemporary, nontraditional format specifically for the unchurched. This "seeker sensitive" approach was pioneered by Pastor Bill Hybels and Willow Creek Community Church in suburban Chicago, where the weekly attendance grew to 14,000.

Exemplifying the growth of Evangelicalism, in 1970 the Southern Baptist Convention surpassed the United Methodist Church to become the largest Protestant denomination in the United States. It now reports over 40,000 churches in the U.S. with a constituency of 15 million. In 1976, a Southern Baptist was elected as president—Jimmy Carter—and he popularized the term "born again." In 1992 and 1996 Southern Baptists were elected as president and vice president—Bill Clinton and Al Gore—although their political, social, and moral views were more liberal than those of most Southern Baptists.

There are also many Evangelicals within the mainline denominations, especially in the southern U.S. Moreover, in Third World countries, Protestants tend to be more conservative than in the West.

Key Doctrines of Evangelicalism

Evangelicals affirm the basic theology of historic Protestantism. In opposition to Liberalism, they affirm the same doctrines as the Fundamentalists, although they usually express them more moderately. As an example, Fundamentalists officially state that the Bible is "inerrant," while Evangelicals typically state that it is "infallible." The dictionary meaning of both words is essentially the same, and most Evangelicals would also affirm that the Bible is "inerrant." The term "infallible" is a little less absolute, however. It allows for the view of some Evangelicals that the Bible could have minor errors of history and geography while still being absolutely trustworthy and authoritative in matters of doctrine and Christian living.

Evangelicals are also much more open to the miraculous work of the Holy Spirit, whereas the Fundamentalists are not. Among Evangelicals who are not part of the Pentecostal/Charismatic movement, there is often an acknowledgment that miracles, including speaking in tongues and divine healing, can still take place today, even if they are not regarded as the norm or the paradigm.

The Southern Baptists and the Holiness groups (such as Nazarenes and Wesleyans) are still overwhelmingly opposed to speaking in tongues. Consequently, the Charismatic movement among them is still small in comparison to that in mainline denominations. Ironically, then, Trinitarian Pentecostals are closely aligned with some groups that discourage speaking in tongues but in theological opposition to other groups that are open to speaking in tongues.

The NAE Statement of Faith is as follows:[241]

1. We believe the Bible to be the inspired, the only infallible, authoritative Word of God.
2. We believe that there is one God, eternally existent in three persons: Father, Son and Holy Spirit.
3. We believe in the deity of our Lord Jesus Christ, in His virgin birth, in His sinless life, in His miracles, in His vicarious and atoning death through His shed blood, in His bodily resurrection, in His ascension to the right hand of the Father, and in His personal return in power and glory.
4. We believe that for the salvation of lost and sinful people, regeneration by the Holy Spirit is absolutely essential.
5. We believe in the present ministry of the Holy Spirit by whose indwelling the Christian is enabled to live a godly life.
6. We believe in the resurrection of both the saved and the lost; they that are saved unto the resurrection of life and they that are lost unto the resurrection of damnation.
7. We believe in the spiritual unity of believers in our Lord Jesus Christ.

Interestingly, the statement does not explicitly affirm salvation by grace through faith. Nor does it issue an explicit call to evangelism. Apparently, the framers were still primarily concerned to establish conservative doctrine against Liberalism.

While Evangelicals are confessional trinitarians, a number of scholars who are considered authorities by the Evangelical world have offered interpretations of the trinity that are remarkably similar to the Oneness view. Frank Stagg, a prominent Southern Baptist seminary professor, essentially embraced the same view of the Godhead as Oneness Pentecostals.[242] Renowned Christological scholars Oscar Cullmann and James D. G. Dunn have described the Incarnation in the same way that Oneness theologians do when distinguishing their belief from traditional trinitarianism.[243] Often, there seems to be little difference from the Oneness view when Baptist ministers preach, teach, pray, lead in worship, and explain the doctrine of God in practical terms, as when former Southern Baptist president W. A. Criswell stated that the only God we will see in heaven is Jesus.[244]

Lordship Salvation

There is a dispute within Evangelicalism over the meaning of faith and repentance. One side says that genuine conversion includes more that a verbal confession of faith; it also involves confession of sin, godly sorrow for sin, and a decision to forsake sin. One must accept Christ both as Savior and Lord in order to be truly converted. This position gives full weight to the biblical definition of repentance. Exponents of this view are A. W. Tozer, John Stott, and John MacArthur. *Christianity*

Today described MacArthur's views as follows:[245]

> MacArthur argued that most contemporary evan-
> gelical teaching on salvation is rife with "easy-
> believism," which he says, is a doctrine that gives bare
> intellectual assent to the redemptive work of Christ
> while failing to call Christians to true repentance and
> a life of obedience and goods works. . . . MacArthur
> holds that the only correct biblical model of the sal-
> vation experience is a doctrine known traditionally
> as "lordship salvation." In essence, it holds that to be
> saved a person "must trust Jesus Christ as Lord of his
> life, submitting to His sovereign authority."
>
> "Easy-believism" [has resulted in] a community of
> professing believers populated by people who have
> bought into a system that encourages shallow and
> ineffectual faith. . . . [Many] sincerely believe they are
> saved but are utterly barren of any verifying fruit in
> their lives . . . [and in the judgment may be] stunned
> to learn that they are not included in the kingdom.

In opposition to this view, many Evangelicals argue
that the only requirement for salvation is a simple decision to accept Christ as Savior, even without any intention
of serving Him. One should also accept Him as Lord and
obey His Word, but this attitude is not a necessary part
of saving faith. Either repentance is synonymous with a
profession of faith, or else it is not required. Defenders of
this view include Charles Ryrie and Zane Hodges.

This view is influenced by a dispensationalist view
of repentance. Some argue that under the law (including
the ministry of John the Baptist), repentance did require

a decision to forsake sin, but under grace, repentance is stripped of this "works" requirement.

Charles Ryrie, a former professor at Dallas Theological Seminary, explained:[246]

> Is repentance a condition for receiving eternal life? Yes, if it is . . . changing one's mind about Jesus Christ. No, if it means to be sorry for sin or even to resolve to turn from sin, for these things *will not save*. . . . Repentance may prepare the way for faith, but it is faith that saves, not repentance (unless repentance is understood as a synonym for faith or changing one's mind about Christ). . . . [A person is saved if he accepts Jesus as Savior] in spite of [an] area of initial unwillingness when he came to Christ and continued disobedience while he lived the Christian life.

Similarly, Zane Hodges, a professor at Dallas Theological Seminary, wrote:[247]

> Faith alone (not repentance and faith) is the sole condition for justification and eternal life. . . . It is an extremely serious matter when the biblical distinction between faith and repentance is collapsed and when repentance is thus made a condition for eternal life. For under this perception of things the New Testament doctrine of faith is radically rewritten and held hostage to the demand for repentance. . . . Though genuine repentance may precede salvation . . . it need not do so. . . . There is no such thing as believing the saving message without possessing eternal life at the same time.

This doctrine flies in the face of Jesus, who said in Luke 13:3, "Except ye repent, ye shall all likewise perish." (See also Acts 2:38; 3:17; 11:18; 17:30; 26:20.) Again, we see the contrast between the heirs of Fundamentalism and the Pentecostals, particularly the Oneness Pentecostals. Many of the former have reduced the concept of saving faith to intellectual acceptance, excluding an active appropriation of or obedience to the gospel. They discount the necessity of genuine repentance, of water baptism for the remission of sins, and of an actual experience of being baptized (immersed) with the Holy Spirit. Oneness Pentecostals, of course, emphasize all three as part of saving faith and full salvation.

Evangelicals Today

By 1920, it appeared that Liberalism was victorious within Protestantism, and the Fundamentalists were fighting to stay alive. In the latter half of the twentieth century, however, the Evangelicals—the moderate heirs of the Fundamentalists—made a remarkable comeback. They grew significantly while the mainline Protestant denominations declined. They established their own colleges, universities, seminaries, publishing houses, magazines, social agencies, evangelistic associations, and other parachurch organizations. They produced biblical scholars and theologians who published first-rate works in defense of the faith. In short, the Evangelical movement has revitalized conservative Protestantism, has grown significantly, and now possesses everything it needs to perpetuate itself.

Liberal trends are developing within Evangelicalism, however. For example, some Evangelicals teach that ultimately God will save everyone, or at least that He will save many people who never confess Christ but have sincere faith according to their traditional religion. Some Evangelical scholars have questioned the infallibility of Scripture and are using the tools of higher criticism in a way that is incompatible with a high view of inspiration. Some advocate the acceptance of homosexual behavior. These trends also affect Pentecostal scholars and institutions that identify with Evangelicalism.

A number of Evangelical leaders are concerned about a disturbing trend of accommodation to secular social mores. For example, in 1988, the Josh McDowell Ministry commissioned the Barna Research Group to survey sexual activity among youth who attend church regularly. The survey covered 1,500 young people aged twelve to eighteen in eight Evangelical denominations, including one Trinitarian Pentecostal denomination. Here are some of the findings:[248]

- 65% of churched youth have had some type of sexual contact by age 18.
- 43% have had sexual intercourse by age 18.
- 20% have participated in some sexual experimentation by age 13.
- 57% said they received at least some of their information about sex from the movies.

These figures are about 10 to 15 percentage points behind the results from secular youth surveys. Nevertheless, they are still disturbingly high. The influence of the movies is noteworthy since Evangelicals formerly opposed movie attendance.

In 1989, the Christian Broadcasting Network commissioned the Gallup organization to survey college students. The survey included students from 100 U.S. colleges, and almost 99 percent of them were unmarried. Here are the results (in *Christianity Today*, 14 July 1989):

Percent . . .	All	Evangelicals
• who believe premarital sex is wrong	24%	52%
• who have sex regularly or occasionally	50%	28%
• who have had more than one sex partner	50%	30%
• who believe abortion is wrong	37%	71%
• of women who have had abortions	9%	4%
• of men with partners who have had abortions	15%	6%

Again the negative results for Evangelicals are significantly lower than for the general population, but in absolute terms they are still quite high. Clearly, the secular society is having a significant impact upon Evangelical youth.

In 1990, the Barna Research Group conducted a survey of the general U.S. population to see how many people considered themselves to be "born again" (a simple indication of Evangelicalism) and how many had an Evangelical view of salvation. Here are the results:[249]

- 34% of American adults considered themselves born again.
- 62% of the respondents said they had made a personal commitment to Jesus Christ, but about half

this number said they would reach heaven because of their good works or because everyone goes to heaven.

- 48% of church attendees considered themselves born again.
- 58% of those holding church leadership positions considered themselves born again.
- 15% of those holding church leadership positions said they had never made a personal commitment to Christ.

Evangelicals and Oneness Pentecostals

Trinitarian Pentecostals consider themselves to be Evangelicals even though the Pentecostals arose primarily from the Holiness movement while the Evangelical movement was a development from Fundamentalism, which rejected the Pentecostal movement. As we discussed in chapter 5, this self-identification has been a significant influence in changing Pentecostals. For better or worse, it appears that the "evangelicalization" of Trinitarian Pentecostals will continue.

What about Oneness Pentecostals? Are they Evangelicals? If we examine the distinctive doctrines that Evangelicals proclaim in contrast to Roman Catholicism and Protestant Liberalism, then Oneness Pentecostals would indeed appear to be Evangelicals. Some Evangelical cult-hunting organizations have argued that they are not, however, because of their distinctive doctrines of the Godhead and salvation, and therefore label them as a cult. Ironically, in making this claim, the cult hunters appeal to "historic orthodoxy" and the creeds, sounding more like Catholics than Protestants. J. L. Hall, editor in chief of the UPCI, has examined their criteria in light of Scripture and has shown that on this basis the Oneness Pentecostals are more truly Evangelical than the mainstream Evangelicals.[250]

Oneness Pentecostals should resist the efforts of those who label them a cult. (See appendixes C and D.) First, it is a prejudicial label designed to thwart a sincere examination of Scripture. Second, as the *Evangelical Dictionary of Theology* notes, it plays into the hands of secularists who would curtail religious freedom for everyone.[251]

At the same time, Oneness Pentecostals should be cognizant of their unique theological identity. They should resist "evangelicalization" but should affirm that in the light of Scripture they are indeed the most evangelical believers in the truest sense of the word. As the motto of the UPCI proclaims, they believe in proclaiming "the whole gospel to the whole world."

Roman Catholicism and Eastern Orthodoxy

The Roman Catholic Church entered the twentieth century with the basic views proclaimed by the Council of Trent (1545-63). It had faced liberal ideas in the nineteenth century and resisted them firmly. In 1864 Pope Pius IX had issued the *Syllabus of Errors*. In it he defended tradition; rejected "modern liberalism" (rationalism and historical criticism of the Bible); and denounced the separation of church and state, freedom for other religions, and public school education.

The nineteenth century also saw the official promulgation of two important doctrines: the immaculate conception of Mary, proclaimed by Pope Pius IX in 1854, and the infallibility of the pope, proclaimed by the First Vatican Council in 1870.

Despite the consolidation of papal power and the papal rejection of liberal theology, rationalism and liberalism began to affect the Roman Catholic Church. As with Protestantism in the early twentieth century, it became common for Catholic scholars to use modern critical methods of studying the Bible. Their reinterpretations of the Bible were not as devastating as those of the Protestants, however, because as Catholics they affirmed the authority of church tradition and the continuing work of the Holy Spirit to lead the church into new doctrinal understandings. Thus, even if they concluded that the Bible did not support a certain doctrine, they could uphold it on the basis of postbiblical tradition and progressive revelation.

For example, many Catholic theologians have acknowledged that the Scriptures do not explicitly teach the doctrine of the trinity. Nevertheless, they maintain that the Holy Spirit progressively revealed it over the centuries through church fathers, councils, and creeds. Some have urged Protestants to accept other doctrines that have developed over the centuries, such as the veneration of Mary, on the same basis that they accept the trinity.

The Doctrine of Mary

The latest development of official Roman Catholic doctrine came in 1950, when Pope Pius XII proclaimed the bodily assumption of Mary. He taught that at the end of her life Mary was taken up into heaven, body and soul. While many Catholics had long believed this doctrine, it did not become official church teaching until 1950. To date, this pronouncement is the only time that a pope has officially invoked the doctrine of papal infallibility since it was defined in 1870.

The pope did not specify whether Mary actually died before she was taken up into heaven, but most Catholic theologians believe that she did. There is a Roman Catholic church in Jerusalem that commemorates the place where she was supposedly laid to rest.

Pius XII's official pronouncement, *Munifidentissimus Deus*, states:[252]

> The majestic mother of God . . . finally achieved, as the supreme crown of her privileges, that she should be preserved immune from the corruption of the tomb and, like her Son before her, having conquered death should be carried up, in body and soul, to the celestial glory of heaven, there to reign as Queen at the right hand of her Son, the immortal king of the ages.

This doctrine is the latest in a series of steps that have elevated Mary almost to the status of a goddess. From the Middles Ages onward, Catholics have often called her Queen of Heaven and Mediatrix. In 1891, Pope Leo XIII stated that "nothing is bestowed on us except through Mary, as God himself wills. Therefore as no one can draw near to the supreme Father except through the Son, so also one can scarcely draw near to the Son except through his mother."[253]

The Second Vatican Council (1962-65) resisted efforts to further define and exalt Mary's position, but as the end of the century drew near, a movement arose to take yet another step in glorifying Mary. By 1997 the pope received petitions from 157 nations on every inhabited continent with over four million signatures asking him to exercise papal infallibility to declare a new official doctrine, namely that Mary is "Co-Redemptrix, Mediatrix of All Graces and Advocate for the People of God." Supporters were Mother Teresa of Calcutta (an Albanian nun known internationally for her humanitarian work in India), 500 bishops, and 42 cardinals. Among the cardinals were John O'Connor of New York, Joseph Glemp of Poland, and six at the Vatican itself. This doctrine would mean "that Mary participates in the redemption achieved by her son, that all graces that flow from the suffering and death of Jesus Christ are granted only through Mary's intercession with her son, and that all prayers and petitions from the faithful on earth must likewise flow through Mary, who then brings them to the attention of Jesus."[254]

Supporters hoped that Pope John Paul II would be sympathetic, for he adopted the papal motto of "Totus tuus" ("All yours"), referring to Mary. Many Catholic theologians, however, opposed the proposed doctrine, and Protestants were highly critical. Nevertheless, this discussion reveals the level of devotion that many Catholics have for Mary.

Many of them claim to have seen apparitions of her, and the sites of these alleged visits have become shrines where pilgrims congregate. The most famous occurrences were in Lourdes, France (1858); Fatima, Portugal (1917); and Medjugorje, Bosnia and Herzegovina (1981 to present). Ten to twenty million pilgrims have visited Medjugorje.

Vatican II

The most important development in Roman Catholicism in the twentieth century was the Second Vatican

Council, which met from 1962 to 1965. Convened by Pope John XXIII and concluded by Pope Paul VI, this council made the most significant changes since the Council of Trent. It set a new tone for the church.

We can identify five major characteristics of the council's work:

1. *Pastoral, rather than dogmatic, discussion.* The council affirmed traditional Catholic theology. Unlike the Council of Trent's dogmatic presentation, however, it offered a more nuanced approach, with the goal of relating to modern needs and concerns.

2. *Conciliatory, rather than confrontational, approach.* Whereas Trent pronounced anathemas on key Protestant positions, Vatican II adopted a conciliatory tone toward Eastern Orthodox and Protestants, speaking of them as "separated brethren." It acknowledged the work of God in their midst and offered the hope of peaceful reunion:[255]

> The Church recognizes that in many ways she is linked with those who, being baptized, are honored with the name of Christian, though they do not profess the faith in its entirety or do not preserve unity of communion with the successor of Peter. . . . They are consecrated by baptism, in which they are united with Christ. . . . Likewise we can say that in some real way they are joined with us in the Holy Spirit, for to them too He gives His gifts and graces whereby He is operative among them with His sanctifying power. . . . In all of Christ's disciples the Spirit arouses the desire to be peacefully united, in the manner determined by Christ, as one flock under one shepherd, and He

prompts them to pursue this end. Mother Church never ceases to pray, hope and work that this may come about.

Before this time, it was considered a sin for Catholics to visit a Protestant church, but now the church offered dialogue and even fellowship. Moreover, it said that people of other religions could also be saved, specifically mentioning Jews, Muslims, and others:[256]

> Whosoever, . . . knowing that the Catholic Church was made necessary by Christ, would refuse to enter or to remain in it, could not be saved.
>
> Those also can attain to salvation who through no fault of their own do not know the Gospel of Christ or His Church, yet sincerely seek God and moved by grace strive by their deeds to do His will as it is known to them through the dictates of conscience. Nor does Divine Providence deny the helps necessary for salvation to those who, without blame on their part, have not yet arrived at an explicit knowledge of God and with His grace strive to live a good life.

3. *Enhancement of the bishops' role.* Ever since Vatican I proclaimed papal infallibility in 1870, the pope was practically the only source of doctrinal teaching, but to a limited extent Vatican II revived the influence of the bishops. The pope remained the undisputed ruler, but with the pope's consent, the council made important decisions for the future of the church.

4. *New emphasis on the Bible.* Vatican II continued to maintain that Scripture and church tradition are equal

in authority and that the church hierarchy is the only correct interpreter of Scripture. Thus it proclaimed:[257]

It is clear, therefore, that sacred tradition, Sacred Scripture and the teaching authority of the Church, in accord with God's most wise design, are so linked and joined together that one cannot stand without the others, and that all together and each in its own way under the action of the one Holy Spirit contribute effectively to the salvation of souls.

Nevertheless, the council decided to incorporate more Scripture readings and quotations in the liturgy, placing them in the language of the people. It also encouraged laymen to read and study the Bible.

This attitude contrasted sharply with the traditional Roman Catholic position. Under the old view, laymen were not capable of understanding the Bible properly; it could be confusing and even dangerous for them. Thus they were to leave the study of Scripture to the priests and theologians. The church would interpret the Bible authoritatively for them and tell them what they needed to know. Indeed, in 1229 the laity were forbidden to read the Bible.

5. *Modernization and reform of liturgy and canon law*. Vatican II changed many practices that had been standard for four hundred years. The primary purpose was pastoral, that is, to become more relevant to modern people and to meet their needs more effectively. For instance, the council decided that priests should recite the mass in the vernacular—the common language of the people—instead of Latin. Now the people could understand what was being

said when they went to church, and they could benefit from the Scripture readings in the liturgy.

Another change was the eating of meat on Fridays. By longstanding tradition, Catholics had abstained from eating meat on Fridays in commemoration of the day of Christ's crucifixion. They were allowed to eat fish, since most of the apostles were fishermen. Even the public schools in America typically served fish on Fridays to accommodate their Catholic students.

The list of saints and the church calendar were revised to reduce the number of saints that were venerated. Those who appeared to be mythical—evidence for their historical existence was lacking—were removed from the list. For example, St. Christopher, the patron saint of travel, was deleted.

In summary, Vatican II did not make major doctrinal changes, but it did change many traditions, and it opened the door for further debate. People began to think about the potential for additional changes. If the church could suddenly modify or overturn traditions that were hundreds of years old, then more changes were also possible. For example, the celibacy of the priesthood had become an official rule in the early Middle Ages. In principle, it could be overturned. Before Vatican II, such a change was unthinkable, but after Vatican II many people began to think it was possible.

Vatican II shook the faith of some traditionalists. Many devout people had difficulty adjusting to the changes. People who had abstained from eating meat on Fridays now learned that it was no longer a sin. People who had prayed for years to St. Christopher, who were named after him (traditionally a Catholic's first or middle name was that of a saint), and who had medals or statues of him for their protection, now learned that he was not a saint after all. Some people became disillusioned and cynical.

Some Catholics insisted on celebrating the old Latin mass of the Council of Trent, called the Tridentine mass. A few bishops even broke away from the church in order to perpetuate more conservative views and practices.

Catholic Theologians

Probably the most influential Catholic theologian of the century was *Karl Rahner* (born 1904), a Jesuit and a German. He defended orthodox Catholic dogma, such as the trinity and papal infallibility, but he did so in the spirit of Vatican II. Indeed, he was one of the leading thinkers behind that council.

One of Rahner's best-known concepts was that of the "anonymous Christian"—a person who can be saved even without an explicit religious commitment. Rahner taught that God's grace can bring salvation through non-Christian religions, and a person can be saved if he allows this grace to work in him even though he does not understand what it is. Rahner went so far as to say, "Even an atheist . . . is not excluded from attaining salvation, provided that he has not acted against his moral conscience."[258]

Pierre Teilhard de Chardin (1881-1955), another Jesuit, was a paleontologist from France. He developed a mystical theology whereby he sought to integrate Christian thought with evolution. He described creation as the process of evolution and sin as the imperfections that arise within evolution. He emphasized faith in the "cosmic Christ," describing the mystical body of Christ as evolving in the context of human evolution and identifying this process as the true meaning of redemption. He believed that humanity is evolving toward the "omega point" of perfection, of unification under the commitment of love, and he identified this destiny as Jesus Christ.

Hans Küng (born 1928) of Switzerland became a professor at Tübingen. In his doctoral thesis, he analyzed Karl Barth's doctrine of justification by faith and concluded that it was compatible with the teaching of the Council of Trent. He further stated, "Today there is a fundamental agreement between Catholic and Protestant theology, precisely in the theology of justification—the point at which Reformation theology took its departure."[259] Most Catholic theologians accepted his conclusion and no longer see the Protestant doctrine of justification by faith alone as a heresy.

In 1970, Küng attacked the doctrine of papal infallibility. Instead, he proposed a doctrine of the "indefectibility" of the church. That is, God keeps the church in the truth, preserving the gospel, despite errors in the church. Similarly, he argued that the Bible is not infallible but indefectible. Küng acknowledged the pope as the leader of the church, but as the chief servant rather than the sovereign.

As a result of these ideas, under the direction of Pope John Paul II, the church stated that Küng was no longer a Catholic theologian. He was not excommunicated or removed from the priesthood, but he was banned from holding a post as professor of Catholic theology. Despite this restriction, he continued to teach at Tübingen and to exert enormous influence.

Current Issues in Catholicism

Today there is probably as much *theological diversity* within the Roman Catholic Church as there is within mainstream Protestantism. There are liberal Catholic theologians who question the basic doctrines of Scripture and Catholic tradition and who question historic moral and social stands. There are also conservatives who uphold the inerrancy or at least the infallibility of Scripture and who advocate strict morality. Just as in Protestantism, there are many proponents of modern approaches such as historical criticism, situation ethics, liberation theology, and feminist theology.

Under the leadership of Pope John Paul II, the Roman Catholic Church has remained officially conservative on *moral issues*, standing firm against artificial birth control, abortion, divorce, extramarital sex, and homosexuality. It opposes women in the priesthood, and it insists on celibacy of the priesthood. Catholic laity, however, have abandoned many of these moral stands, particularly in the West. For example, almost all Catholics in the West practice some form of birth control, and the rates of divorce, premarital sex, and abortion are about the same for Catholics as for the general population. Moreover, many bishops in Europe and the U.S. are working toward changes in some of these areas, although they remain in submission to the pope.

In particular, there is pressure to rethink the *rules regarding the priesthood*, due to a severe shortage of priests in the U.S. and Europe. In some cases, parishes have been consolidated, and in others, lay persons have had to take over many functions that were traditionally reserved for the priests. Many observers believe that a major reason for the shortage is the requirement of celibacy.

In addition, there is quite a bit of evidence that the celibacy rule is not effective but is a factor in the high incidence of moral failure in the priesthood. Of course, this problem goes back to the early Middle Ages.

A. W. Richard Sipe, a former Benedictine monk who became a psychotherapist, studied the problem of sexual misconduct in the priesthood and published his findings in *A Secret World: Sexuality and the Search for Celibacy.* He conducted a study for twenty-five years (1960 to 1985) with over one thousand priests and with five hundred other men and women, many of whom had been involved as sexual partners of priests. He estimated "that half the 53,000 Roman Catholic priests in the U.S. are breaking their vow of celibacy." According to him, about twenty-eight percent of all priests are engaged in relationships with women, many of them long-term; an additional ten to thirteen percent have relationships with men; and about six percent pursue adolescents or children, usually boys.[260]

The Roman Catholic Church says that these figures are far too high. For one thing, half the priests that Sipe interviewed were already in therapy, so presumably they had problems and were not representative of all priests. Even if we reduce Sipe's numbers by one-half, however, there is still a significant problem. In recent years, the church has been sued many times and has paid many millions of dollars in claims to victims of sexual misconduct and child molestation by its clergy.[261]

In *Latin America*, the Roman Catholic Church faces both conservative and liberal challenges. On the left are the liberation theologians, who redefine the gospel in terms of social justice and revolutionary action. Pope John Paul II denounced these views, but they are still quite influential.

On the right are the Evangelicals, of whom eighty percent or more are Pentecostals. The Evangelicals are growing rapidly in Latin America at the expense of the Catholics. Even though the Catholic Church has become quite ecumenical, in Latin America it has taken a strong stand against non-Catholic denominations, calling them cults or sects. At times there has been strong persecution, even resulting in violence and murder. In the 1950s, the United Pentecostal Church suffered severe persecution of this nature in Colombia. In recent years, Evangelicals in remote areas of Mexico have also endured such persecution. Of course, the Catholic Church does not officially endorse violence, but bishops and priests in various locations have incited followers to harass, hinder, or expel non-Catholics.

A dramatic development in the Roman Catholic Church is the *Charismatic movement*, which entered the church in 1967. (See chapter 10.) Officially, the Catholic Church has been open to this movement. The prevailing philosophy is that as long as the Charismatics stay within the Catholic Church, continuing to acknowledge its authority and doctrines, then they can conduct and attend private Charismatic prayer meetings. In this way, the church has been able to retain most of these people.

Conflict occurred, however, when Archbishop Emmanuel Milingo of Lusaka, Zambia, embraced the Charismatic movement. He "experienced a trancelike vision after meeting Italian priests in the Catholic charismatic movement" in Rome. "Back in Africa, Milingo began praying for cures of ailing supplicants, and soon hundreds were reporting miracles."[262] Critics accused him of promoting tribal magic instead of modern medicine, and the Vatican ordered him to Rome for a year of rest and psychiatric evaluation. Milingo denied that he used charms, spells, or witch doctor's techniques or that he opposed modern medicine. Instead, he said that the healings took place by the power of God. Nevertheless, in 1983 he resigned his position.[263]

Despite the dramatic changes that the twentieth century brought to Roman Catholicism, Pope John Paul II sought to maintain a conservative stance on its distinctive doctrines. For example, in a 1984 document entitled *Reconciliation and Penance*, he attacked the idea that Catholics can receive forgiveness "directly from God" without going through the church. He emphasized the importance of the sacrament of penance, which he said Jesus instituted, and the importance of confession to a priest in order to obtain forgiveness.[264] In 1985, the Vatican announced that Catholics can receive a plenary indulgence by hearing their bishop's Christmas or Easter blessing on radio or television if they are unable to hear it in person.[265] According to Catholic theology, a plenary indulgence remits the temporal penalty for all confessed sin and is paid for by the "treasury of merits" built up by Christ, Mary, and saints.

Ecumenical Dialogue

The twentieth century saw a considerable convergence of thinking and practice among mainline Protestants and mainline Catholics. Key doctrinal differences that had long separated these two movements in the past grew relatively unimportant.

Vatican II's characterization of Protestants as "separated brethren" opened the door for ecumenical dialogue with various denominations. As we have seen, Catholic theologians now generally agree that the doctrine of justification by faith, which caused the Protestant Reformation in the 1500s, is no longer a problem.

The Roman Catholic Church and the Church of England have made much progress in ecumenical dialogue. The Church of England has always been diverse theologically, with a strong Anglo-Catholic element. The biggest issue separating the two churches is papal supremacy. (King Henry VIII broke away from Rome and formed the Church of England in 1534 for this very reason.) In 1982, however, the Anglicans made a major concession, agreeing that the pope should be the supreme bishop in any future united church. "Both sides agree that there is no doctrinal barrier to reunification, and that even the most difficult problem—the office of the Pope—need not stand in the way." One of the Anglican negotiators, Cambridge professor Henry Chadwick, stated, "We have agreed that the papacy should be the focus of Eucharistic communion of all the churches."[266]

In 1987 the Second Anglican–Roman Catholic International Commission said it had reached agreement "on the essential aspects of the doctrine of salvation and on the church's role within it." According to Kortright Davis, a member of the Anglican delegation, the agreement makes clear that "salvation is from beginning to end God's activity. . . . The notion of [human] merit has been transformed so that it is no longer merit that is at issue, but the response of faith." The goal of the dialogue is eventually to bring both churches to fully accept each other's sacraments and ministries.[267]

A significant new problem, however, is that in recent years the Anglicans have begun to ordain women to the priesthood, which Rome refuses to do. Papal infallibility and the doctrine of Mary also remain obstacles.

The Catholics have also conducted a significant dialogue with Lutherans. Some theologians on both sides have signed a statement saying that the central issue of justification by faith, which caused the Lutherans to leave the Catholic Church in the 1500s, is no longer an issue—that both Lutherans and Catholics believe justification is by faith and is shown by works. In 1983, the Lutheran–Roman Catholic Dialogue Group in the United States announced that it had reached a "fundamental consensus" on the doctrine of justification by faith. It stated, "Our entire hope of justification and salvation rests on Christ Jesus and on the gospel whereby the good news of God's merciful action in Christ is made known." While differences remain, some of the Catholic scholars stated that Luther was essentially right and that Vatican II essentially vindicated him.[268]

In the 1990s, Roman Catholics and Evangelicals conducted a similar dialogue. Some prominent theologians and leaders on both sides have signed a joint statement of agreement in key doctrinal areas, including justification. There is considerable debate within the Evangelical community, however, as to whether the dialogue and the joint statement are appropriate.

Interestingly, the Roman Catholics started dialogue with Pentecostals beginning in 1972. Pentecostal participants included leading scholars and ministers of the Assemblies of God, the Church of God (Cleveland, Tennessee), the Church of God of Prophecy, the Church of God in Christ, the International Church of the Foursquare Gospel, the International Pentecostal Holiness Church, and the Pentecostal Assemblies of Canada. One Oneness Pentecostal church was represented: the Apostolic Church of the Faith in Christ Jesus (Mexico). Also participating were Charismatics from the American Baptist, Anglican, Catholic, Episcopal, Lutheran, Orthodox, and Presbyterian churches.

In the final report of the dialogue that took place from 1985 to 1989, the participants explained the basis of their desire for unity:[269]

> For the Roman Catholic Church, the basis of ecumenical dialogue with Pentecostals, properly speaking, is found in the Catholic recognition of the baptism performed by Pentecostals in the name of the Father, Son, and Holy Spirit. This implies a common faith in the Lord Jesus Christ. This recognition by Roman Catholics of Pentecostal baptism means, in consequence, that Roman Catholics believe that they share with Pentecostals a certain, though imperfect *koinonia* [fellowship, communion]. . . . The unity of baptism constitutes and requires the unity of the baptized. . . . Our agreement on the trinitarian basis of baptism draws and impels us to unity.
>
> Pentecostals do not see the unity between Christians as being based in a common water baptism. . . . Instead, the foundation of unity is a common faith and experience of Jesus Christ as Lord and Savior through the Holy Spirit. This implies that to

the extent that Pentecostals recognize that Roman Catholics have this common faith in and experience of Jesus as Lord, they share a real though imperfect *koinonia* with them.

In this statement and in the Vatican II documents, we find that Roman Catholics seek institutional unity based on a common trinitarian faith and baptism. At this point it is not clear how far Pentecostals and other Protestants will be willing to go to fulfill this vision of unity. That Pentecostals have participated in sustained ecumenical dialogue is itself quite significant, since early Pentecostals of all kinds generally viewed the Roman Catholic Church as an apostate church or at least a church of false doctrine whose members needed to be saved.

Eastern Orthodoxy

The Eastern Orthodox Church officially broke from the Roman Catholic Church in 1054. While it has a similar theology of the sacraments, it does not recognize the sovereignty of the pope, and it considers itself to be the original, pure church. Culturally, theologically, and liturgically, it has a Greek, rather than Latin, heritage. A contemporary Greek Orthodox writer has explained the differences as follows:[270]

Some of the major differences between the Orthodox and the Roman include the following: The primacy and the infallibility of the Roman Pope; the *filioque* clause [procession of Holy Spirit from both Father and Son instead of the Father only]; the teachings on purgatory; the immaculate conception and the bodily ascension of the *Theotokos* ["mother of God"]; all these are rejected by the Orthodox. In addition there are other doctrinal, ecclesiastical, and administrative differences. The Greek Church recognizes only a primacy of honor to the Bishop of Rome, to the Bishop of Constantinople and then to other church leaders for historical reasons. . . . In the matter of the ecumenical dialogue the Orthodox Church would have no hesitation to accept the bishop of Rome as the *primus inter pares*, the first among equals. But she would yield no other ground on this important subject.

Eastern Orthodoxy is not monolithic but consists of autocephalous (self-governing) national churches that have mutual fellowship under the patriarch of Constantinople. It is the dominant religion of Greece, Romania, Georgia, Russia, Bulgaria, and Yugoslavia (Serbia and Montenegro). It is strong in other Slavic countries, and it has ancient churches in the Middle East. In the West, its adherents are primarily people whose ethnic origins are in the Middle East and Eastern Europe.

In addition, several ancient churches are generally classified with Eastern Orthodoxy even though they operate independently. On one side are the Monophysites, notably the Coptic Church in Egypt, the Ethiopian Orthodox Church (also called Coptic), and the Armenian Apostolic Church. They reject the Council of Chaldecon (451), believing that Christ has only one nature (primarily divine) instead of two complete natures (human and divine) in one person. On the other side are the Nestorians, notably the Assyrian Church in the Middle

East. The Council of Chalcedon denounced Nestorianism for emphasizing too greatly the distinction between the divine and human in Christ and for refusing to call Mary the mother of God.

Apart from these deviations, the theology and liturgy of these churches are similar to the other Eastern churches. The Egyptian Copts and the Assyrian Church are minority faiths, since their lands are dominated by Muslims.

Overall, Eastern Orthodoxy is traditional, conservative, and hierarchical. Where it is the majority faith, it closely aligns itself with the state and the culture. In these countries, the church benefits from special legal status and promotion, and for people to deny the faith is to deny their culture.

Under communism, the Russian Orthodox Church and the Orthodox churches in other communist countries cooperated closely with the state. Their leaders were appointed with the approval of the Communist Party. Orthodoxy lost much credibility in these countries because of its accommodation and collaboration. Since the fall of communism, Orthodoxy has sought to reestablish political power and exclude or limit other religious faiths and denominations, especially Evangelicals and Pentecostals.

The Greek Orthodox Church takes a similar position. In Greece, it is against the law to proselyte (seek to convert) someone from Greek Orthodoxy. Occasionally Evangelical ministers and members are persecuted and charged with illegal activity because of their evangelistic efforts.

Theologically, Eastern Orthodoxy has remained relatively static, in part because the Muslims conquered its ancient strongholds in the Middle East. When the Byzantine Empire fell in 1453, the Turks took control of Constantinople (now Istanbul), the imperial capital and the traditional seat of Orthodoxy.

The Orthodox churches are members of the World Council of Churches, and they exert a conservative influence on both doctrine and social ethics. In many ways, their stance is similar to that of the Roman Catholic Church. Moreover, there were Orthodox observers at Vatican II, and in recent years Catholic and Orthodox leaders have engaged in dialogue as "separated brethren."

In the 1980s and 1990s, a number of Evangelicals converted to Eastern Orthodoxy. Notable examples are Franky Schaeffer, son of a well-known Evangelical author and teacher, Francis Schaeffer; and Michael Harper, Anglican Charismatic pioneer. Converts explained that they were attracted by several features: (1) ancient heritage and tradition, (2) liturgical worship, (3) conservative morality, and (4) authoritative voice yet without the difficult Roman Catholic position of papal supremacy and infallibility. It appears that these Evangelicals were looking for a more meaningful, mystical, awe-inspiring worship experience in contrast to simple, unemotional, rational Evangelical forms, and a more certain doctrinal sound in the face of Evangelical fragmentation and liberal trends.

Conclusions

Roman Catholicism, with almost 1.1 billion adherents, and Eastern Orthodoxy, with about 200 million adherents, are major forces in world Christendom, encompassing over twenty percent of the world's population. Although separated by the papacy, to a great extent they are theological and ideological twins. While both advocate traditional doctrines and moral positions, most of their members have adopted the values and lifestyle of modern, secular society.

The Catholics and the Orthodox are in ecumenical dialogue with each other, with the Protestants, and even with non-Christian religions. It is possible that in the future Roman Catholicism could be the basis of a worldwide communion of Christians of many denominations, and ultimately it could become the foundation for one worldwide church.

9

The Healing Revival and the Latter Rain Movement

After World War II, events in the classical Pentecostal movement resulted in two related developments: the Latter Rain movement and the Charismatic movement. Setting the stage for these movements was a post-war healing revival, the peak of which occurred from about 1946 to 1958.

Background of the Healing Revival

Throughout the history of Christianity, there have been various revivals of divine healing. The New Testament clearly teaches that healing is one of the spiritual gifts that God has given to the church (I Corinthians 12:8-10).[271] It instructs the church to pray for the healing of those who are sick (James 5:14-16). The

Gospels contain many accounts of people who were healed in the earthly ministry of Jesus, and the Book of Acts contains many account of people who were healed through the prayers of the apostles and the early church. In history, whenever people have proclaimed and believed the healing message of the Scriptures, God has performed miracles of healing.

Even before the great outpouring of the Holy Spirit in the twentieth century, there were significant healing revivals in the nineteenth century, both in Europe and in America. In the late 1800s, many preachers and teachers in the Holiness movement proclaimed the message of divine healing. They taught that Christians could receive healing by praying to the Lord in faith.

Most of these leaders also began to teach that healing is part of the Atonement. That is, just as Christ purchased our justification and sanctification by His death, burial, and resurrection, so He purchased our healing. He came to reverse all the consequences of our sins, including sickness and disease. They appealed to the scriptural statement that "with his stripes we are healed" (Isaiah 53:5). (See also I Peter 2:24.) They noted that Matthew 8:16-17 clearly applies the Atonement passage in Isaiah 53 to physical healing.

A number of Holiness evangelists, both men and women, became noted for their message of healing. While most taught a balanced view of healing that respected the sovereignty of God and acknowledged that healing did not always come instantly or as people desire, a few went to extremes in their teaching. Some insisted that healing would always come instantaneously if a person had sufficient faith, just as they believed sanctification to be an instantaneous experience. Others held that if someone had enough faith to be saved then he had enough faith to be healed. The corollary was that if a person did not receive healing then his salvation was also questionable. Some rejected all use of medicine and doctors, saying it was contrary to faith.

One of the most famous healing preachers was John Alexander Dowie, whose ministry reached its apex from 1894 to 1905. From Australia, he immigrated to the United States and attracted a national following. As we noted in chapter 1, he founded his own denomination (the Christian Catholic Church) and his own town (Zion, Illinois).

Many early Pentecostal leaders received inspiration from Dowie. Before the Pentecostal movement began in 1901, Charles Parham visited Dowie's operation and learned from his methods. In 1906, Parham brought the Pentecostal message to Zion and converted many of Dowie's followers to the new movement. A number of them became Pentecostal leaders, including L. C. Hall, D. C. O. Opperman, John Lake, and F. F. Bosworth. Lake and Bosworth were noted for their healing ministry as Pentecostals. The parents of Gordon Lindsay, who was to figure prominently in the post-war healing revival, were also followers of Dowie.

Parham preached healing before the outpouring of the Holy Ghost came. Afterwards, he continued to emphasize healing, and some of his early breakthroughs came as a result of dramatic healings. Some well-known Holiness healing preachers entered the Pentecostal movement, including Carrie Judd Montgomery and Maria Woodworth-Etter. Other well-known healing campaigners in the early Pentecostal movement were Smith Wigglesworth (England), Aimee Semple McPherson, and Charles Price, who received the Holy Spirit under McPherson.

In short, healing was a prominent theme among the later Holiness preachers and among the early Pentecostals. Moreover, the decade immediately after World War II saw the emergence of several nationally prominent ministries that focused on divine healing.

William Branham

The father and pacesetter of the post-war healing revival was William Marrion Branham (1909-1965). As a young person, Branham received a personal healing and became an independent Baptist preacher. Later he received the Holy Spirit and became a Pentecostal. He also accepted water baptism in the name of Jesus Christ and adopted a nontrinitarian, Oneness view of the Godhead.[272] He preached for both trinitarian and Oneness churches, but he remained independent.

Branham stated that he had received visitations from God at ages three and seven. Then, in 1946, he testified that an angel visited him and announced that God would give him a gift of divine healing. He said this angel guided him from that time forward. As evidence, Branham's followers displayed a 1950 photograph of Branham preaching in Houston. Above his head is something that appears to be a halo or flash of light.

Branham began his healing campaigns in 1946, and the results were amazing. In his heyday, he filled the world's largest auditoriums and stadiums. Perhaps the most outstanding and widely attested miracle occurred in 1951. William Upshaw, a U.S. congressman from

California who had been crippled for many years, was healed in one of Branham's campaigns. This notable event catapulted Branham to international fame.

Branham had an unusual ability to discern people's illnesses. He would call them out of the audience, reveal details about them, inspire their faith, and pray for their healing. Many people were healed. Walter Hollenweger, who later became the secretary of evangelism for the World Council of Churches, gave the following description and analysis:[273]

> The angel gave him signs to help him in his task. The most important was Branham's ability to name with astonishing accuracy the sickness, and often also the hidden sins, of people whom he had never seen. The author, who knew Branham personally and interpreted for him in Zurich, is not aware of any case in which he was mistaken in the often detailed statements he made. It was characteristic of Branham's kind-heartedness that he gave certain personal revelations to those who were seeking healing in a whisper, so that they were not picked up by the microphone and revealed to the spectators. . . .
>
> Much that was written about him in Pentecostal journals seems to be exaggerated, but there are a number of well-attested cases of miraculous healings. . . .
>
> However generously he is judged, it must be admitted that his sermons were not merely simple, but often naïve as well, and that by contrast to what he claimed, only a small percentage of those who sought healing were in fact healed. The Pentecostal pastor

Leonhard Steiner had a poor opinion of Branham's campaign in Zurich. He wrote that the call to make a decision for Christ was "disturbingly vague. No real call to repentance could be distinguished."

Branham assembled a management team of three men: Jack Moore, Gordon Lindsay, and W. J. E. "Ern" Baxter. Moore was a United Pentecostal pastor in Shreveport, Louisiana, who was so impressed with Branham that he devoted himself to managing Branham's campaigns.

Moore contacted his friend Gordon Lindsay, who was a minister of the Assemblies of God and a convert of Charles Parham. Lindsay resigned his position to become Branham's full-time manager. He wrote a book about him entitled *A Man Sent from God*, and he started a magazine called *Voice of Healing* to promote Branham's ministry. Lindsay soon expanded coverage to other healing ministries that were quickly springing up, however, which caused Branham to part company with him. Ultimately Lindsay adopted the name of Christ for the Nations for his ministry, his magazine, and the Bible institute he founded in Dallas, Texas.

Ern Baxter was an independent Pentecostal who traveled with Branham for a time. He was greatly influenced by the Latter Rain movement a few years later, although he eventually became concerned about errors in it. He ultimately joined the Charismatic movement and became one of the foremost leaders of the Shepherding movement. (See chapter 10.)

F. F. Bosworth, who had left the Assemblies of God because he rejected the initial evidence doctrine, joined

Branham's campaigns in 1948-50.

The Full Gospel Businessmen's Fellowship International, founded in 1951, became a major promoter of William Branham in the 1950s and early 1960s. Branham was a personal friend of the founder, Demos Shakarian, an Armenian Pentecostal and lay church leader in California.

Branham's central message was healing and prosperity. During the time of his greatest popularity he did not place great emphasis on doctrine. For instance, he believed that everyone needed to be baptized in the name of Jesus Christ, including those already baptized with the trinitarian formula, but he did not stress this belief to his mass audiences. Instead, during this time he conducted most of his ministry among trinitarians.

For Branham's first three meetings, Nathaniel Urshan, a UPCI evangelist and later general superintendent, preached the opening message, after which Branham conducted his healing ministry. When Urshan proclaimed baptism in the name of Jesus Christ, Branham asked him not to do so, and Urshan ended his association with the campaign.[274]

Branham's ministry began to decline in the mid 1950s. He encountered severe financial difficulties, and when the Charismatic movement began, he had difficulty adapting to it. He was from a rural background with a limited education, while most Charismatics were urban middle-class people from mainline denominations, and Branham was not very successful in attracting them.

In his later ministry, he began to emphasize doctrine, including several unusual, aberrational beliefs. His following narrowed to those who embraced these views. In particular, he taught what is known as the *serpent seed doctrine*. This doctrine asserts that the original sin of the human race was sexual. In the Garden of Eden, Eve committed sin and became spiritually polluted by having a sexual relationship with the devil. By having sexual relations with her after this time, Adam likewise became polluted. In this way, the whole human race came under sin and perpetuates sin to future generations.

Branham further maintained that Eve conceived a child by the devil, namely Cain. Cain and his descendants were therefore predestined to damnation. This satanic bloodline survived the Flood because one of Noah's daughters-in-law was supposedly a descendant of Cain. Thus even today some people are literally children of the devil and cannot be saved. They will be annihilated in the end of time.

Of course, nothing in Scripture teaches or implies anything like the serpent seed doctrine. However, Sun Myung Moon and the Unification Church ("the Moonies") promote essentially the same view today.

Branham understood the seven churches of Asia Minor in Revelation 2-3 to be representative of ages in church history. He interpreted each church's "angel" (which literally means "messenger" in Greek) to be God's special prophet to the respective age. For example, he identified Martin Luther as the messenger or prophet for the age of the Reformation. He concluded that his day was the last church age, the age of Laodicea, and he was the prophet for that age. Indeed, on his grave is a pyramid that lists the seven ages and seven prophets, and it identifies Branham as the end-time prophet.

Those who accepted Branham's message would constitute the bride of Christ in the end time and would go up in the Rapture. Organized religion was a mark of the beast. Although people in various denominations could be saved, they would suffer through the Tribulation. Branham predicted that the Millennium would begin by 1977.

Branham identified himself as the coming of Elijah before the great and dreadful day of the Lord. (See Malachi 4:5.) He also understood himself to be the angel of Revelation 10 and one of the two witnesses in Revelation 11.

Branham maintained that the zodiac and the pyramids contained hidden messages of prophetic significance. He referred to the Western zodiac, apparently not knowing about the completely different Eastern zodiac system. He believed that the dimensions of the pyramids were significant because God had inspired their building.

Based on his prophetic role, Branham advocated what he called the *spoken word ministry*. According to this view, when he preached under the anointing of God, God actually inspired him to speak authoritative words. Thus, even today, his followers study his books and tapes, believing that they are the special message of God for this age. One of their major methods of evangelism is to distribute his messages in transcribed and taped form.

Branham died on December 24, 1965, as a result of injuries sustained in an automobile accident some days earlier. His followers expected that he would soon rise from the dead, like the two witnesses in Revelation 11, so they embalmed and refrigerated his body and delayed his funeral for one month. Some even believed him to be born of a virgin or to be God incarnate. Even after the memorial service on January 26, 1966, Branham's followers delayed his burial until after Easter in hopes that he would rise on that day like Jesus. Finally, their hopes dashed, they buried him on April 11, 1966.

At the memorial service on January 26 in Phoenix, Arizona, the main speaker was T. L. Osborne, a prominent evangelist in his own right. Some of his remarks demonstrate the unusually high regard that Branham's followers had for him:[275]

God . . . clothed Himself in flesh, came, and showed us the new creation—how it would be when everything was taken care of. The price was paid. All claims were satisfied. He walked here in a human body, a Godman—Whom we call Jesus. . . .

The man we know as William Branham was sent to demonstrate God AGAIN in the flesh.

Some are going to think I am sacreligious or off doctrinally (and it doesn't really matter), but God came again in human flesh and said, "Apparently I must show them again. I must remind them again. They must see one more time. Once again they must know what God is like. And He stepped down and sent a little man, a prophet, but more than a prophet this time, a Jesus-man this time!

Here comes Brother Branham along in the twentieth century and does exactly the same way. GOD IN THE FLESH, again crossing our paths; and many did not know. THEY WOULD NOT HAVE KNOWN HIM IF THEY WOULD HAVE BEEN HERE-: WHEN GOD CROSSED THEIR PATH IN THE BODY THEY CALLED JESUS CHRIST! . . .

This is a matter to give glory to our God, Who has come in the flesh again in our generation. He has come in the flesh in all of us, but in a particular way in this man who was His prophet for this generation.

Although Branham's end-time prophecies were not fulfilled and although he did not rise from the dead, his teachings are still influential to this day. His followers, generally called Branhamites, teach repentance, baptism in Jesus' name, the baptism of the Holy Spirit, and holiness of life. In a few locations they are the largest group that advocates Jesus Name baptism. Unfortunately, they also zealously promote the serpent seed doctrine, the spoken word doctrine, and the necessity of accepting William Branham as the prophet of the end time.

The Branhamites exist in thirteen loosely organized fellowships and in many independent churches. In the U.S. there are about 300 churches with 86,000 constituents and another 400 house churches with 10,000 constituents. Worldwide, there are an estimated 1,150 churches with 191,000 constituents, and 1,380 house churches with 109,000 constituents.[276]

Many Pentecostal observers have concluded that Branham was a man whom God used greatly to inspire faith in people to receive divine miracles, particularly in the early half of his ministry. He was not pretentious, he lived simply, and he exhibited a real concern for people and their needs. Unfortunately, over time he developed an exaggerated opinion of his role. This exalted view of self, theological naiveté, and an independent spirit led him into false and destructive doctrines that seriously damaged his effectiveness and legacy. Even so, his emphasis on healing and prosperity, his methods of operation, and his emphasis on the prophetic spoken word greatly influenced later healing evangelists, the Latter Rain movement, and the Charismatic movement.

Oral Roberts

The second major figure in the post–World War II healing revival was Granville Oral Roberts (born 1918). Roberts was originally a member of the Pentecostal Holiness Church. At age seventeen he was healed of tuberculosis and stuttering. In 1947, one year after Branham, he began a healing ministry. Roberts met Branham on a number of occasions, ministered with him, and was influenced by him to some degree. Oral Roberts soon became the foremost healing evangelist in America.

The main emphasis of Roberts's ministry has been health, prosperity, and hope. In 1955, when television was first becoming widespread in America, he began a national weekly television program; thus he was one of the earliest religious figures to use television.

In 1968, Roberts joined the United Methodist Church. By this time, he had a great following outside the confines of traditional Pentecostalism, and the Charismatic movement was growing rapidly within Protestantism. It seemed to his advantage to identify himself with mainline Protestantism and thus maximize his appeal to the broadest spectrum of Christianity. Since the Methodists were theologically diverse, he could take this step without abandoning his Pentecostal beliefs. Since the Pentecostal Holiness Church had its roots in Methodism, there were many similarities of overall philosophy and structure. Nevertheless, many classical Pentecostals at the time saw this as a compromising, backward step, for the United Methodists did not teach the baptism of the Holy Spirit and were dominated by Liberalism.

Oral Roberts was one of the catalysts of the Charismatic movement, for he attracted many people from mainline churches and introduced them to Pentecostal concepts. He was a key influence in the formation of the Full Gospel Businessmen's Fellowship in 1951. At century's end, he was still one of the leading figures in the Charismatic movement.

Between 1947 and 1968, Roberts conducted over 300 crusades and personally prayed for millions of people. In the 1950s, his radio program was on more than 500 stations, his Sunday morning television program was the number-one syndicated religious program in America for three years, his monthly magazine reached a circulation of one million, and 674 newspapers carried his monthly column. In the 1970s, his prime-time television show reached an estimated 64 million viewers. A survey in 1980 concluded that he was the best-known Pentecostal in the world. An amazing 84 percent of Americans who were surveyed recognized his name. By the 1980s, he had written 83 books, with over fifteen million copies printed, and his mail averaged about five million letters per year.[277]

In 1965, Roberts founded Oral Roberts University in Tulsa, Oklahoma. By 1988, it was worth 250 million dollars and had an enrollment of 4,600 students.

In 1981, Roberts opened another 250-million-dollar project in Tulsa, called the City of Faith Medical and Research Center. It was a hospital, medical center, and research facility, in which he planned to combine medical expertise with healing ministry. The medical community in the city opposed the project, saying there were already excess hospital beds there, but Roberts persevered. His ministry suffered financially because of the stupendous investment, and he had to make dramatic appeals for money to keep the project afloat. On one occasion, he announced that he had seen a 900-foot vision of Jesus telling him to complete the work. He even stated that God would "take him home" if he did not raise the remaining eight million dollars that he needed.[278] Critics responded that this claim in effect made God a hostage taker. At the last moment, the owner of a race track in Florida gave Roberts a sizable donation from gambling income that enabled him to meet his goal.

Ultimately, however, Roberts had to close the City of Faith because it could not sustain itself financially. Tulsa did not need another hospital after all, and there were not sufficient patients coming from around the country as Roberts had expected. Roberts leased the facilities to tenants and concluded that God intended all along for this to take place as a means of supporting Roberts's ministry financially.

Other Healing Evangelists

A number of other healing evangelists also established significant ministries after World War II. *Kathryn Kuhlman* (1907-76) became the world's most widely known female evangelist. She never openly identified with the Pentecostal movement, and she did not allow public speaking in tongues in her services. In this regard, no one knows exactly where she stood in her theology or experience.

Early on, she established a large church in Denver,

but she had to leave it when she married a man who divorced his wife for her. They evangelized together, but after about six years she left him and launched out on her own again.

Kuhlman's healing ministry began in 1946. She focused primarily on people from mainline churches. Pentecostals were somewhat reluctant to follow her because they did not know where she stood doctrinally. In the 1960s, she became popular among Charismatics, and she attracted many mainline Protestants into the Charismatic movement.

In her services, Kuhlman would often announce that a certain type of illness or condition would be healed in a certain part of the auditorium. Someone with the relevant problem would soon identify himself. In addition to healings, her services were noted for people being "slain in the Spirit."

Kuhlman was dramatic in ministry and flamboyant in lifestyle. Her biographer and personal friend Jamie Buckingham noted, "She loved her expensive clothes, precious jewels, luxury hotels, and first class travel."[279]

Another well-known healing evangelist was *Jack Coe* (1918-56). He got his start in the Assemblies of God (AG). He became successful about 1950, but the AG expelled him in that year because of questionable methods and teachings. He died suddenly of polio at age thirty-eight.

A. A. Allen was another healing revivalist who started with the AG. He also began achieving success about 1950, although he too found himself at odds with the AG over questionable and exaggerated claims. He left the AG in 1955 after he was arrested for drunken driving.

Allen was one of the first evangelists to emphasize financial blessings for those who donated money to his ministry. He was also one of the first to introduce gospel rock music into his services. In addition to healing, he also specialized in casting out demons.

He divorced his wife in 1967, which caused him to lose much credibility. He died of sclerosis of the liver in 1970.

Tommy Lee Osborne (born 1923) was inspired by William Branham to begin a healing ministry. He also focused on evangelism and missions, conducting mass evangelism crusades overseas and raising funds to support indigenous churches around the world. He taught the concept of "seed faith" in giving—God would grant a financial harvest to those who planted a "seed" by contributing to his ministry.

In the 1960s, T. L. Osborne sought to appeal to youth by growing a beard and wearing youth-oriented clothing. He began stressing that his wife, Daisy, was an equal partner in pulpit ministry and organizational leadership. She became known as Daisy Washburn-Osborne and became president of the Osborne Foundation.

The Latter Rain Movement

Almost simultaneously with the surge of healing campaigns arose another movement from within Pentecostalism, called the New Order of the Latter Rain. Its peak was from 1948 to 1956.

The Latter Rain movement began among classical Pentecostals who desired revival and a greater exercise of spiritual gifts. There was a perception among Pentecostals in some areas that in the 1930s and 1940s their movement had lost momentum, had gotten somewhat dry, and perhaps even had stagnated. Many people longed for a fresh move of the Spirit. William Branham tapped into this desire with his healing ministry in 1946, sparking renewed faith and spiritual hunger among many people.

Another man who inspired great expectations was Franklin Hall, a teacher who particularly emphasized fasting and healing. He went to extremes in both areas, proclaiming, in essence, that a person could receive whatever he wanted from God if he would invest enough time in fasting. Moreover, a truly spiritual person could be delivered from the potential for sickness, tiredness, and even body odor.

In this atmosphere of desire for a new move of God, some people appealed to the prophecy of Joel 2:23, which speaks of the former rain and the latter rain. Most early Pentecostals had interpreted the former rain to be the first-century outpouring of the Holy Spirit (as Peter indicated in Acts 2:16) and the latter rain to be the end-time outpouring from 1901 onward. Now, some people considered that the latter rain was yet to come. They also appealed to Isaiah 43:19, where God promised to do a new thing, and applied these words to their day.

Another biblical source for the new movement was the Old Testament typology of the three major feasts—Passover, Pentecost (Weeks), and Tabernacles. Some said that Passover was fulfilled by the Atonement, and Pentecost by the outpouring of the Spirit, but the Feast of Tabernacles had not yet been fulfilled. There would soon come a new work of God in addition to the Pentecostal revival that would fulfill the Feast of Tabernacles.

As a distinct movement, the New Order of the Latter

Rain began in February 1948 at Sharon Orphanage and Schools in North Battleford, Saskatchewan, Canada. Three men were key figures in this initial stage: George Hawton, P. G. Hunt, and Herrick Holt. Hawton and Hunt had recently been involved in a dispute with the Pentecostal Assemblies of Canada and had resigned from that organization. They began working in North Battleford with Holt, an independent minister who had been associated with the International Church of the Foursquare Gospel.

During this time, these men and their students began seeking God for a fresh outpouring of the Holy Spirit. They began intense fasting and prayer, and soon they reported a great anointing of the Spirit, many healings, and many personal prophecies—something that would become a characteristic of the Latter Rain movement. People began to lay hands on one another and give detailed prophecies and instructions concerning each other's lives.

The Latter Rain movement swept through classical Pentecostalism, drawing people out of their existing churches. It drew both trinitarians and Oneness believers, but its impact was much greater among the former. It was especially strong in Canada and in the northwestern United States. The Pentecostal Assemblies of Canada suffered a split.

Some prominent Trinitarian Pentecostals who became associated with or endorsed the Latter Rain movement were as follows:

Myrtle Beall (1896-1979), an AG pastor who founded Bethesda Missionary Temple in Detroit. The church became a headquarters for Latter Rain teaching. Her son, James E. Beall (born 1925), later became pastor. He wrote *Rise to Newness of Life*, a book that teaches the necessity of water baptism and advocates baptism in Jesus' name while retaining a trinitarian view of God.

Ivan Q. Spencer (1888-1970), founder of Elim Bible Institute (1924) in upstate New York and Elim Fellowship (1933), an alliance of people who were trained at the institute. Before 1924, Spencer had been a member of the AG. He was introduced to the Latter Rain by Myrtle Beall, and Elim Fellowship became one of the foremost propagators of the movement.

Stanley Frodsham (1882-1969), an AG pioneer and editor of AG publications, who identified with the Latter Rain movement for a while. He considered it to be a renewal of the early Pentecostal movement. In 1949 he resigned as the AG editor and an AG minister in order to participate in the Latter Rain. He taught at Elim Bible Institute for a time, but ultimately he became disenchanted with the excesses of the movement and disassociated himself.

Lewi Pethrus (1884-1974), founder of Filadelfia Church in Stockholm, Sweden, and a leading European Pentecostal pioneer. His church was the largest Pentecostal church in the world until about 1975, and his organization was the largest free (nonestablished) church in Sweden.

Some Oneness Pentecostals who joined the Latter Rain movement were as follows:

David ("Little David") Walker (born 1934), a child evangelist who began preaching at age nine and held great evangelistic, healing campaigns. Eventually, however, he joined the AG.

Raymond Hoekstra, well-known United Pentecostal (UPCI) pastor at Calvary Tabernacle in Indianapolis, Indiana. He resigned his church to be the manager for Little David. Subsequently, he established a successful radio and prison ministry under the name of Chaplain Ray.

W. E. Kidson, a UPCI pastor in Houston and long-time general secretary of the Pentecostal Church, Incorporated (PCI). Accused of financial misdealing, he began to work with William Branham and to have fellowship with the Latter Rain people.[280] He left the UPCI to found the International Ministerial Association.

Leonard W. Coote, missionary to Japan and founder of International Bible College in San Antonio, Texas, a UPCI institution for a short time.

Harry F. B. Morse, a Oneness Pentecostal pioneer, the founder of an influential missionary training institute in Oakland, California, a foreign missions director for the PCI, and a UPCI minister. He believed in keeping Saturday as the Sabbath. Many influential pastors and missionaries, such as David Gray and Ellis Scism, were trained under him.

A. O. Moore, a UPCI minister who had been foreign missions director for the PCI at the time of the merger.

Ted Fitch, an independent minister and author of a book that spoke of the man Christ as preexisting in angelic form.

The main organizational representatives of the Latter Rain movement today are Elim Fellowship (90 churches), the International Ministerial Association (a Oneness group with 635 churches worldwide), and the Independent Assemblies of God International (1,800 ministers). The Gospel Assembly (about 10,000 constituents), also known as the School of the Prophets, is a similar and related organization. These groups have a relatively small number of churches and constituents.

Most of the Latter Rain churches left their parent organizations and became independent. Some ceased to exist. For the most part, the New Order of the Latter Rain has become part of the Charismatic movement.

Doctrines of the Latter Rain Movement

As we have seen, the New Order of the Latter Rain was a Pentecostal revival movement. Although it was not primarily doctrinal in nature, it developed some distinctive approaches and practices. The classical Pentecostal denominations—including the Assemblies of God, the United Pentecostal Church International, the International Pentecostal Holiness Church, and the Pentecostal Assemblies of Canada—rejected the movement because of these characteristics, which they regarded as extreme and excessive. They also opposed it for drawing people away from existing congregations, splitting many churches, and advocating that churches should become independent. The movement was theologically diverse, and not everyone embraced all the beliefs and practices we will discuss. In general, however, the Latter Rain emphases were as follows:

1. *Spiritual gifts, including the bestowal of gifts upon others*. Pentecostals have always advocated the gifts of the Spirit, but Latter Rain people urged individuals to seek various gifts, sometimes even naming the gifts they would receive or attempting to transfer gifts to one other.

2. *Laying on of hands, including its use to bestow*

spiritual gifts. Pentecostals likewise have always advocated the laying on of hands, but this practice assumed great significance with the Latter Rain people. In many cases, they sought to obtain spiritual gifts through prophecy and laying on of hands. They advocated human initiative, citing I Timothy 4:14 and II Timothy 1:6. Classical Pentecostals asserted that the spiritual gifts were bestowed at God's initiative and according to His will. (See I Corinthians 12:11.)

3. *Prophecy, particularly personal prophecy.* Once again, Pentecostals believe in prophecy, but the Latter Rain adherents placed more emphasis on this gift and commonly employed it to give instructions to the church, the pastor, or individuals. Many people made important decisions on the basis of personal prophecies. Some promoted new teachings on the basis of direct revelations.

4. *Identification of modern-day apostles and prophets.* Latter Rain people pointed to scriptural evidence for modern-day apostles and prophets. (See I Corinthians 12:28; Ephesians 2:20; 4:11.) That concept in itself was not objectionable, but problems came when they attempted to identify who was and who was not an apostle or a prophet. Further problems developed when self-designated apostles and prophets sought to assert spiritual authority over others and to give authoritative pronouncements.

5. *Fellowship with all professing Christians.* The Latter Rain people minimized doctrinal teachings and standards of holiness, which were quite important to the entire Pentecostal movement at that time. In essence, they sought active fellowship with anyone who confessed Christianity. Issues such as the Oneness-trinitarian con-

troversy, the initial evidence doctrine, and many lifestyle choices were not important to them.

6. *The complete autonomy of the local church.* As a corollary to the preceding point, they felt that local churches should not submit to organizational decisions regarding doctrine, lifestyle, and fellowship. Essentially, each church should operate independently in theology and government.

7. *The "manifest sons of God" or "kingdom" theology.* According to this view, Latter Rain believers would achieve such a place of spirituality that they would become visibly identified as sons of God by various miracles and victories in spiritual warfare. In this way, the kingdom of God would be visibly established on the earth, characterized by a supernatural life in this world.

This last theme was vital to Latter Rain theology. As an example, J. Preston Eby, a former Pentecostal Holiness minister, said that the coming outpouring of the Spirit would bring "the fullness," which he described as follows:[281]

> The FULLNESS [will be] a company of overcoming Sons of God who have come to the measure of the stature of the fullness of Christ to actually dethrone Satan, casting him out of the heavenlies, and finally binding him in the earthlies, bringing the hope of deliverance and life to all the families of the earth. This . . . great work of the Spirit shall usher a people into full redemption—free from the curse, sin, sickness, death and carnality.

Typically, Evangelicals and Pentecostals have identified this scenario with the millennial reign of Jesus

Christ upon earth after His second coming, but in Latter Rain theology it would occur among mature believers before His coming and would actually help bring about His coming. Latter Rain believers typically expected great visible signs of power shortly before the Second Coming, such as instantaneous healings of all who were sick. Some thought the manifested sons of God would never die. Others expected them to acquire various supernatural powers, perhaps being able to appear, disappear, and transport themselves like the resurrected Christ.

In the view of classical Pentecostals, the Latter Rain movement stressed certain Pentecostal themes to the point of imbalance. Widespread excesses and abuses took place, particularly with the use of personal prophecies, and some people lost faith in God altogether. Questionable and fanciful claims were made. For example, some said that God placed dental fillings in tooth cavities as an answer to prayer. Classical Pentecostals questioned these accounts, wondering why God would not simply make the teeth whole instead.

The excesses and the disruption of local churches ultimately caused the Pentecostal denominations to turn away from the Latter Rain movement. For instance, at its general conference in 1950, the UPCI condemned the following ten teachings as its response to the New Order of the Latter Rain:[282]

1. The promiscuous laying on of hands for the bestowing of spiritual gifts.
2. The teaching that the church is based upon present-day apostles and prophets.

3. The teaching that Christians must sever themselves from all church organization.
4. The compromising of the truths of Oneness and water baptism in the name of Jesus Christ.
5. The teaching that one can receive the Holy Ghost without speaking in tongues.
6. The teaching that candidates for the Holy Ghost baptism should not praise the Lord while tarrying for this gift.
7. The sowing of discord among the assemblies and ministers.
8. The prophesying of prophets who speak out of their human spirits.
9. The fellowshipping of those whose lives are ungodly.
10. The teaching that the true church is composed of all who call themselves Christians regardless of doctrinal belief.

Not all Latter Rain people embraced all of these points, but they were significant issues among them. It is important to note that the UPCI and other classical Pentecostal groups did not reject the nine spiritual gifts of I Corinthians 12, the fivefold ministry of Ephesians 4, signs, wonders, or miracles. These beliefs had always been characteristic of Pentecostal teaching, but the feeling was that the Latter Rain movement promoted and practiced these beliefs in an unscriptural, unbalanced way while neglecting important doctrinal truths. Some classical Pentecostals did become excessively cautious in these areas, however, in reaction to the damage caused by the Latter Rain. (For further doctrinal discussion, see

Spiritual Gifts by David K. Bernard.)

Conclusions

The post-war healing evangelists brought Pentecostal concepts, such as the supernatural gifts of the Spirit, to the average American. In doing so, they prepared the way for the Charismatic movement and later helped attract many people to it. Their message and methods, often suspect by classical Pentecostal standards, became typical among Charismatics. Today, most of these evangelists or their successors identify primarily with the Charismatic movement rather than classical Pentecostalism.

The Latter Rain movement was another significant catalyst for the Charismatic movement of the late 1950s and early 1960s. Indeed, most of the characteristic innovations, beliefs, and practices of the Latter Rain have found their way into the Charismatic movement. Put another way, most of the distinctive Charismatic tenets have their roots in Latter Rain theology.

Classical Pentecostals were correct to withdraw from the New Order of the Latter Rain. While in many ways it was a sincere manifestation of spiritual hunger, and while in some cases it brought revival, most often it resulted in confusion, division, doctrinal compromise, neglect of holiness lifestyle, mysticism, and unscriptural excesses. Today, however, many classical Pentecostals, particularly trinitarians, have in essence endorsed some of the same beliefs and practices by an unreserved endorsement of the Charismatic movement.

10

The Charismatic Movement

In the late 1950s and early 1960s, an increasing number of people in mainline Protestant denominations began to receive the Holy Spirit while remaining in their traditional churches. At first called Neo-Pentecostals, they eventually became known as Charismatics, from the Greek *charismata*—the word that I Corinthians 12 uses for spiritual gifts.

The roots of the Charismatic movement go back to classical Pentecostalism itself. Most of the early Charismatic leaders received the Holy Spirit as a result of contact with classical Pentecostals. As the movement grew, many of the teachers who became prominent had previously been affiliated with classical Pentecostal churches such as the Assemblies of God (AG). In theology, methodology and lifestyle, however, the early Charismatics were greatly influenced by the healing revivals and the Latter Rain movement of the 1940s and 1950s.

Important Pentecostal Influences

Pentecostals have always witnessed to Christians of other denominations and converted many of them to the Pentecostal message and experience. Three factors made the early Charismatics different from most of the past converts: (1) They were members of mainline Protestant denominations instead of more conservative groups. (2) They stayed in their denominations instead of joining Pentecostal churches, and later some formed their own independent churches. (3) Generally they did not want to adopt the theology, lifestyle, or religious culture of the Pentecostals, but they sought to renew their churches from within.

The Pentecostal message came to mainline Protestants from several important sources in addition to the individual witness of many believers. As we discussed in chapter 9, *Demos Shakarian* (born 1913), a Pentecostal, founded the *Full Gospel Businessmen's Fellowship International* (FGBMFI) in 1951 as a nondenominational group that could bring the Pentecostal message to businessmen outside the movement. Many Protestant and Catholic businessmen first heard about and experienced the baptism of the Holy Spirit through FGBMFI and its magazine, *Voice*.

Another important witness was *David du Plessis* (1905-87), a South African Pentecostal preacher who immigrated to America and joined the Assemblies of God. In the 1950s, when there was little contact or dialogue between Pentecostals and the mainline denominations, he felt that God was leading him to witness to mainline Protestants, the World Council of Churches (WCC), and even the Roman Catholic Church. Over the years, he developed close ties to leaders in these organizations. He was received by three popes, he attended all the WCC international conferences, and he spoke at a number of mainline Protestant churches. He became known in those circles as "Mr. Pentecost."

In most cases, du Plessis gave denominational leaders their first close encounter with an authentic Pentecostal. He combined an intelligent theological presentation with Pentecostal spirituality, contradicting the stereotype of Pentecostals as poor, lower class, ignorant, and fanatic.

In 1962, du Plessis was forced to withdraw from the AG, because in effect he advocated ecumenical relations with the WCC and the Roman Catholic Church, which the AG opposed. He sometimes made controversial statements in his pursuit of ecumenism—for instance, commenting favorably on the papacy and on the supposed apparitions of Mary—and he urged Charismatics to stay in their denominational churches. The AG was concerned about compromise of Pentecostal theology and lifestyle, especially by recognizing groups that denied essentials of biblical faith by Evangelical standards. Moreover, the general superintendent of the AG, Thomas Zimmerman, was the head of the National Association of Evangelicals, which was the conservative rival to the National Council of Churches and the WCC. Eventually, however, the AG came to accept the Charismatic movement, and du Plessis was reinstated in 1980.

Another classical Pentecostal influence was *David*

Wilkerson (born 1931), an AG minister who began an effective ministry among the street gangs of New York City. He ultimately founded Teen Challenge as a nationwide deliverance ministry. His book, *The Cross and the Switchblade* (1963), recounted how God had led him into this work and how many youth were miraculously delivered from drugs, alcohol, gang violence, and promiscuity. It spoke of the baptism of the Holy Spirit as a key factor in the process. A film by the same name was also produced. Many Protestants and Catholics first learned of the baptism of the Spirit from the book or film and developed a hunger to receive this experience for themselves.

Early Charismatic Experiences

After World War II, a few Protestant ministers began receiving the Holy Spirit yet remained in their denominations. Probably the first significant case was Harald Bredesen (born 1918), a Lutheran minister who received the Holy Spirit at a Pentecostal camp in 1946. He offered to resign as a minister, but Lutheran authorities refused to accept the resignation. In 1957, Bredesen became a pastor—at Mount Vernon Dutch Reformed Church in New York City—and he soon began a charismatic prayer meeting there. Later, when the Charismatic movement blossomed, he became a prominent leader and media figure. For example, he appeared on Walter Cronkite's television program in 1963.

Another early forerunner of the Charismatic movement was Tommy Tyson (born 1922), a United Methodist pastor. He received the Holy Spirit in 1952 and became an evangelist.

A number of mainline Protestants received the Holy

Spirit at the Camps Farthest Out. As an example, Don Basham (born 1926) of the Disciples of Christ received the Holy Spirit in 1952. Although these camps were not explicitly Pentecostal, some of the speakers had received the Holy Spirit.

Robert Walker (born 1912), the editor of an Evangelical magazine called *Christian Life*, received the Holy Spirit in 1952. He did not publicly witness to this experience, but he began to write about the need for renewal. He did witness to Billy Graham, who acknowledged that his brother-in-law and sister had spoken in tongues and that he had received an experience with the Holy Spirit but without tongues.[283] *Christian Life* helped create a hunger within Protestant churches for a new move of God. In 1987 the magazine merged with *Charisma*.

Agnes Sanford (1897-1982), the wife of an Episcopalian priest, became interested in healing after she was healed of depression. She received the Holy Spirit in 1953-54 after contact with Pentecostals and became one of the foremost promoters of healing and charismatic renewal within mainline Protestant churches.

A prolific writer and teacher, she developed views beyond those of classical Pentecostalism. She emphasized positive thinking as a natural law of healing that anyone could operate. Blending psychology with religion, she also advocated the healing of memories, which she equated with forgiveness of sin. In essence, she stated that many problems are the result of past events and wrongs. When a person is healed of these negative memories, then he or she will overcome the problems.

One of the first Mennonite ministers to be baptized

with the Holy Spirit was Gerald Derstine (born 1928). He was asked to leave his church in Ogema, Minnesota, when he received this experience in 1955.

An early catalyst for charismatic experiences was the Order of St. Luke, an Episcopalian organization that promoted healing. While it did not explicitly advocate the baptism of the Holy Spirit with speaking in tongues, many people who sought divine healing also received the Holy Spirit. Richard Winkler (born 1916) was one of the early participants to receive the Holy Ghost (1956). As rector (parish pastor) of Trinity Episcopal Church in Wheaton, Illinois, he began a charismatic prayer group there in the 1950s.

A Presbyterian pastor, James H. Brown (1912-87), received the Holy Ghost in 1956 after contact with Pentecostals. He followed the advice of David du Plessis, who urged him to stay within his denomination to renew it. Brown soon instituted a charismatic service on Saturday evening at his pastorate, Upper Octorara United Presbyterian Church in Parkesburg, Pennsylvania, just outside Philadelphia. The main church services remained traditional, however.

In 1958, John Osteen (1921-99), a Southern Baptist pastor in Houston, Texas, received the Holy Spirit after being influenced by Pentecostal literature. About that time, his daughter, who was born with cerebral palsy, was healed. He was tried for heresy by the Southern Baptists in Texas and left his pastorate to form the independent Lakewood Church.

The Beginning of the Movement

The Charismatic movement became a distinct movement in the eyes of the public in 1960. As we have just seen, a number of Protestants who would become leaders in the Charismatic movement had received the Holy Spirit before this time. Most historians, however, identify the defining event with Dennis Bennett (born 1917), rector at St. Mark's Episcopal Church in Van Nuys, California. Bennett and some of his parishioners had received the Holy Spirit with tongues in November 1959, but it was not until April 1960 that he announced this news to his congregation.

The announcement proved to be quite controversial, and Bennett was soon forced to resign his pastorate. Jean Stone (born 1924), a church member who had received the Holy Spirit along with Bennett, alerted the news media to the controversy, including *Newsweek* and *Time*. Both of these national news magazines carried the story of mainline Protestants who had embraced Pentecostal experiences. It was also widely reported in the religious press and on television.

As a result of the publicity, many people began to inquire about the Pentecostal experience and to seek it. Many who had already received the Holy Spirit in mainline churches began to openly acknowledge the fact and to make contact with one another. A network of Spirit-filled Protestants grew, and the Charismatics became a distinct, identifiable movement.

Protestant Charismatics

By the early 1960s, all the major Protestant denominations had a Charismatic movement within them. *Eternity* magazine labeled it Neo-Pentecostal, but Harald Bredesen and Jean Stone proposed the name that the participants preferred: the Charismatic Renewal.

The term "Charismatic" identified the movement with the diversity of spiritual gifts of I Corinthians, rather than stressing the uniqueness of tongues in Acts 2 as the label "Pentecostal" would. Most of the early Charismatics spoke in tongues, but unlike the classical Pentecostals most of them did not accept tongues as the necessary, initial evidence of Spirit baptism.

The Charismatic movement was particularly strong among Episcopalians. Early Episcopalian leaders were Sanford, Winkler, Bennett, and Stone. After resigning his church in Van Nuys, Bennett became pastor of St. Luke's Episcopal Church in Seattle, Washington, which was at the point of closing down. He revived the church and transformed it into a powerful Charismatic center. Both Bennett and his wife, Rita (born 1934), became prominent Charismatic teachers. To promote the movement, Jean Stone (later Williams) founded the Blessed Trinity Society and *Trinity* magazine, published from 1961 to 1966.

Among Lutherans, the foremost Charismatic leader and theologian was Laurence "Larry" Christenson (born 1928). An American Lutheran pastor in San Pedro, California, he received the Holy Spirit at a Foursquare Gospel church in 1961. His church became a strong center for Lutheran Charismatics.

Among Presbyterians, key leaders were James Brown, Robert Whittaker, George "Brick" Bradford, and J. Rodman Williams (born 1918). The United Presbyterian Church sought to expel Whittaker for his Pentecostal beliefs, but after two appeals in which his case went to the highest church court, he won the right to remain in the denomination. Williams received the Holy Spirit in

1965 while a professor of systematic theology at Austin Presbyterian Theological Seminary in Austin, Texas. He became a noted theologian in the Charismatic movement.

John Sherrill (born 1923), an Episcopalian and a senior editor for *Guideposts*, and his wife, Elizabeth (born 1928), decided to investigate the Charismatic movement. In the process, they received the Holy Spirit themselves. The result was a book called *They Speak with Other Tongues* (1964). One of the first books to tell about the Charismatic movement, it had a great impact upon people of many denominations. The Sherrills also collaborated in the writing of a number of other influential books, including *The Cross and the Switchblade* (1963) with David Wilkerson, *God's Smuggler* (1967) with Brother Andrew (a Dutch missionary who smuggled Bibles into communist countries), and *The Hiding Place* (1975) with Corrie ten Boom (a Dutch Charismatic who had helped hide Jews from the Nazis in World War II).

In 1972, the Mennonite Church officially recognized the validity of the Charismatic movement in its ranks. By one estimate, perhaps as many as twenty percent of the Mennonites have received the Holy Spirit, and in some countries a majority have done so.

Initially, the Charismatics met much rejection. Some churches expelled pastors who had received the Holy Spirit, and some churches split. As time went on, however, most of the major denominations accommodated to the movement. Most merely tolerated it: as long as pastors continued to affirm traditional theology, continued to conduct traditional services on Sunday, and did not promote their views in a dogmatic or controversial manner, then they could conduct Charismatic prayer meetings or praise services also. Some denominations eventually welcomed the Charismatic movement as an antidote to the decline in membership of liberal Protestants, for it attracted new people and renewed the devotion of many who had been drifting away. Some churches even began to conduct most or all of their services in Charismatic fashion.

By century's end, the Charismatic movement no longer encountered opposition from the large Protestant denominations, with the notable exception of two conservative groups who were Evangelical in theology: the Lutheran Church–Missouri Synod and the Southern Baptist Convention. While these groups did not take an official stand nationally, on the local and district levels most Charismatics in these groups were pressured to leave. A significant number still remained, however, particularly among the Baptists. Usually, they had to hide or minimize their distinctive beliefs. Most used the term "fulness" instead of "Charismatic" to describe their experience.

James Robison (born 1945), a prominent Southern Baptist evangelist, experienced healing and deliverance in 1981. Thereafter he focused his ministry on gifts of the Spirit, but he did not explicitly accept or reject the label "Charismatic."

In sum, the more liberal Protestant denominations freely allowed the Charismatic movement within their ranks. The most vigorous opponents were Fundamentalists, Holiness churches, and some Evangelicals. For instance, the conservative Wesleyan and Holiness churches, such as the Church of the Nazarene, denied the validity of speaking in tongues.

The Catholic Charismatic Renewal

In 1967 the Charismatic Renewal swept into the Roman Catholic Church, beginning at Duquesne University in Pittsburgh, Pennsylvania. Some students there heard about the Holy Spirit through *The Cross and the Switchblade, They Speak with Other Tongues,* and testimonies of Pentecostals. They began praying for the Holy Spirit and received the experience in February 1967.

From there, the movement spread to Notre Dame University in South Bend, Indiana. Leaders who received the Pentecostal experience at Notre Dame were Kevin Ranaghan (born 1940), his wife, Dorothy (born 1942), and Edward O'Connor, a priest.

The movement went on to Michigan State University in Ann Arbor, Michigan. These three universities became great centers of the Catholic Charismatic movement, and through them it spread throughout Roman Catholicism.

For a time, Catholic Charismatics held annual national meetings at Notre Dame, but later they began to hold regional meetings. In 1976, 30,000 Catholic Charismatics gathered at Notre Dame. The next year, a regional meeting in Atlantic City, New Jersey, had an attendance of 37,000.[284]

Some Charismatics formed spiritual communities in the Catholic tradition. In some of them, all the members lived in the same community; in others, members lived in separate residences but made a covenant to meet together and submit to one another. These communities became powerful vehicles for teaching and evangelism, helping to spread the Charismatic movement throughout Catholicism. The most prominent of them were the Word of God community in Ann Arbor, Michigan, which established a network of communities under its leadership called the Sword of the Spirit; People of Praise community in South Bend, Indiana; and Mother of God community in Gaithersburg, Maryland. While they were not restricted to Catholics, most of their members were Catholic Charismatics.

For the most part, the Catholic Charismatic movement took the form of prayer groups within parishes, instead of taking over entire parishes or splitting away to form independent churches. Most Catholic Charismatics continued to attend traditional mass and participate in parish life, but they also attended Charismatic prayer groups where they could speak in tongues and worship spontaneously. In1986, there were an estimated six thousand Catholic Charismatic prayer groups in the United States.

The Roman Catholic Church's response was to accept the Catholic Charismatic Renewal as long the participants remained in the church and continued to acknowledge church authority and doctrine. Indeed, on this basis both Pope Paul VI and Pope John Paul II endorsed the movement. In 1975, Pope Paul VI appointed Léon-Joseph Cardinal Suenens (born 1904), an archbishop in Belgium, to a special position as overseer of the Catholic Charismatic Renewal. Cardinal Suenens had been one of the leaders of the Second Vatican Council, and he began to participate openly in the Charismatic movement in 1973. As a result of this recognition, Catholic Charismatics have had a significant influence in the church. One of them, Raniero Cantalamessa, was appointed as special preacher to the Vatican.

The Catholic Church recommended that each diocese establish a liaison with the Charismatic movement in its jurisdiction. To some extent, then, depending on the diocese, the Charismatic Renewal was incorporated into the structure of the Catholic Church.

Influential Catholic Charismatics were Kilian McDonnell (born 1921), Benedictine monk, theologian, and ecumenical leader; Francis MacNutt (born 1925), Dominican priest and healing preacher who later withdrew from the priesthood and married; Peter Hocken (born 1932), Anglican convert to Catholicism, historian, theologian, and ecumenist; and John Bertolucci (born 1937), priest and evangelist.

In the 1980s and 1990s, the Catholic Charismatic movement declined somewhat. Many people participated in prayer groups for a few years but then dropped out. There was a decline both in the number of prayer groups and in the number of participants.

In contrast to Roman Catholicism, Eastern Orthodoxy took a strong stand against the Charismatic movement. Despite this opposition, there are small Charismatic groups within the Orthodox churches.

Further Developments

As we have just seen, from 1960 to 1967 the Charismatic movement spread to all major branches of Christendom. This dramatic growth led to the development of a number of distinctly Charismatic institutions, including the following:

• *Christian Broadcasting Network* (CBN), founded by M. G. "Pat" Robertson (born 1930). The son of a U.S. senator, Robertson was a Southern Baptist minister who received the Holy Spirit. He began his worldwide network with the purchase of a defunct television station in 1959. The flagship program was "The 700 Club." In 1988, Robertson ran for the Republican nomination for U.S. president, but he never became a serious contender.

• *Youth with a Mission* (YWAM), a nondenominational, youth-oriented missionary movement. It was founded by Loren Cunningham, an AG minister, in 1960-61, but he left the AG in 1964 after he and AG officials could not agree on policy for YWAM.

• *Oral Roberts University* (1965). (See chapter 9.)

• *Logos International Fellowship* (1966), the first Charismatic publishing house, founded by Dan Malachuk. It became quite well known, distributing millions of books on Charismatic themes, including the prosperity message. It suffered financial difficulties, however, and finally went bankrupt. Part of its operation was taken over by *Bridge Publishing*. Other Charismatic publishers have since arisen, including *Harvest House*, *Bethany House*, and *Creation House*.

• *Women's Aglow Fellowship* (1967), a nondenominational women's fellowship similar to the Full Gospel Businessmen's Fellowship International.

• *Trinity Broadcasting Network* (TBN) (1973), founded by Paul Crouch (born 1934) and his wife, Jan. Crouch was a minister with the AG.

• *Charisma* magazine (1975), probably the most influential publication in the Charismatic movement today. It was founded by Stephen Strang (born 1951), who had his origin in the AG. Strang later acquired *Christian Life* magazine (which he merged with *Charisma*) and Creation House. He also launched other publications including *Ministries Today*.

• *Regent University* (1977), founded by Pat Robertson (originally as CBN University).

Several influential ministries arose but then fell. Examples were the media empires of Jim Bakker (based in Charlotte, North Carolina), Jimmy Swaggart (based in Baton Rouge, Louisiana), and Robert Tilton (based in Dallas, Texas). Bakker and Swaggart were prominent television evangelists in the AG who developed a nationwide following outside classical Pentecostalism. In the 1980s, both acquired lavish incomes, fell into sexual immorality, and lost their credentials with the AG. Bakker's ministry, PTL, folded, and he served time in prison for fraud. Swaggart continued his ministry but lost most of his following. Tilton's ministry likewise crashed in the 1990s after two divorces and accusations of dishonesty and financial wrongdoing.

In the late 1960s and early 1970s, many hippies and other youth who embraced street culture were converted to Christianity, especially on the U.S. West Coast. Some adopted Baptist beliefs, while others received the Pentecostal experience. They turned from drugs, promiscuity, and other sins, but many retained their countercultural hairstyles, dress, music, and informality. Charles "Chuck" Smith (born 1927), a Foursquare Gospel pastor, was able to incorporate many of these Jesus People into his church—Calvary Chapel in Costa Mesa, California— giving rise to a network of such churches.

This time period also saw the rise of Messianic Jewish congregations and organizations, including Jews for Jesus. These Jewish believers in Jesus embraced conservative Christian theology but retained Jewish culture and forms of worship. Most of the Messianic Jews were Charismatic.

The coming of age of the Charismatic movement—and perhaps its high-water mark—was signified by the first national conference in 1977 in Kansas City. It drew over 50,000 participants from many denominations—classical Pentecostals, mainline Protestants, and Roman Catholics (18,000). Officials of some classical Pentecostal denominations took part, indicating approval of the Charismatic movement and its ecumenical thrust. Demonstrative worship occurred to a degree that was quite unusual for Charismatics: "One firmly entrenched memory from Kansas City was the 'Holy Ghost breakdown' which occurred while Bob Mumford was speaking. For 10 unrestrained minutes the crowd worshipped wildly."[285]

In 1987, another conference was held in New Orleans. About 35,000 to 40,000 participated—much less than the anticipated 70,000 to 80,000.[286] In 1990, an international Charismatic conference in Indianapolis drew 23,000 people. In both conferences about one-half of the participants were Roman Catholic.

In 1994, a great revival began at the Toronto Airport Vineyard Fellowship in Toronto, Ontario, Canada, under Pastor John Arnott. People from across the world came to receive the "Toronto Blessing" and bring it back to their churches. The emphasis of this revival was on strengthening and renewing existing believers. One of the churches most affected was Holy Trinity Brompton, an Anglican church in London, England, which in turn became a revival center. In the first two years, an estimated 200,000 people visited the Toronto church, and about 4,000 churches were touched as a result.

The revival was somewhat controversial, however, because of emphasis on unusual physical manifestations such as laughter, roaring, and animal noises. Consequently, the Vineyard association severed ties with the Toronto church, which became known as the Toronto Airport Christian Fellowship. The church responded to criticism by explaining that it did not try to promote or insist on these unusual manifestations. In 1999, the church made a controversial claim, reminiscent of the Latter Rain, that God was transforming people's dental fillings into gold, although no such cases were officially documented. To promote this type of miracle, it produced a video entitled *Go for the Gold*, and it cited Psalm 81:10 as scriptural support.[287]

In 1995, a great revival broke out at Brownsville Assembly of God in Pensacola, Florida, with Evangelist Steven Hill and Pastor John Kilpatrick. Although this church was part of a Pentecostal denomination, the revival attracted people of many denominations. The emphasis was on repentance, deliverance, and inward holiness. By early 1999, over 2,300,000 people had visited the revival, and over 130,000 people had made decisions to become Christians. Some Oneness Pentecostal observers concluded that there was a genuine work of the Spirit to draw people, similar to what typically occurs in revivals and camp meetings of the UPCI.

Four Major Streams

Over time, some Charismatics left their traditional denominations and formed new congregations, networks, and organizations. They were joined by many people who had left classical Pentecostal denominations, including participants in the post-war healing revivals and the Latter Rain movement. By the 1970s, it was possible to identify four distinct streams within the Charismatic movement.

1. *Charismatic Renewal.* As we have discussed, this term refers to the Charismatic movement within the mainline denominations, Protestant and Catholic. It is particularly strong within the Episcopal Church and the Roman Catholic Church. The participants attend Charismatic prayer meetings, exhibit renewed zeal for spiritual matters, and enjoy relatively free and spontaneous worship in contrast to traditional liturgy. They believe in deliverance, healing, miracles, and gifts of the Spirit.

2. *Faith, Word, or Word of Faith Churches.* These churches developed outside preexisting denominations and emphasize positive confession, healing, health, and prosperity.

The acknowledged founder of this stream is Kenneth Hagin (born 1917), a former AG minister who developed his own unique theological system. He established Rhema Bible Training Center in 1974 in Broken Arrow, Oklahoma, near Tulsa. Since that time his influence and ministry have mushroomed. By 1988 he had written eighty-five books, and 180 stations carried his radio program. Each year, about three million of his books and a half million of his cassette tapes are distributed.[288]

Hagin's theology owes much to the influence of E. W. Kenyon (1867-1948), an independent Baptist evangelist and teacher.[289] For instance, Hagin's writings contain many quotations or paraphrases of the earlier writings of

Kenyon (but without attribution). Other prominent teachers in this camp are Kenneth Copeland, Frederick Price, Jerry Savelle, Charles Capps, Norvell Hayes, Robert Tilton, and David (formerly Paul) Yonggi Cho.

The Word of Faith teachers emphasize healing and prosperity. They typically proclaim that if a person truly has faith and makes the right confession, then he will be healthy and rich. His only limitations in these areas would be deficient faith and negative confessions. For instance, if he says, "I think I am getting sick," then he will get sick. On the other hand, if he says, "I am not sick; I am healed," then he will be healed. He should rebuke and deny any symptoms of sickness and confess his healing. His level of faith will determine whether he is sick or well, and his words will actually create the condition.

3. *Nondenominational Churches and Fellowships.* This stream consists of nondenominational, Spirit-filled churches and fellowships that sprang up in the last quarter of the twentieth century. It has become the fastest-growing segment of the Charismatic movement.

Many of the leaders were formerly in the classical Pentecostal movement but sought to operate independently of their one-time Pentecostal doctrinal formulas, ecclesiastical organization, and ministerial disciplines. Others were associated with the Charismatic Renewal in mainline churches but decided that they could be more effective by leaving their denominations and operating full-fledged Charismatic churches.

Many megachurches (churches with two thousand or more in weekly attendance), a relatively recent phenomenon, fall into this category. In addition, a number of church networks emerged that fell short of being full denominations yet fostered cooperation on many endeavors. Some have dissolved, others have remained as fellowships of independent churches, and some have evolved into the equivalent of denominations.

Examples of such networks, with founders and leaders, are as follows: National Leadership Conference (Ken Sumrall and Gerald Derstine); People of Destiny International (Larry Tomczak and C. J. Mahaney); Maranatha Christian Churches (Bob Weiner); Fellowship of Covenant Ministers and Conferences (Charles Simpson); Network of Christian Ministries (Charles Green); International Convention of Faith Ministries (Happy Caldwell); Charismatic Bible Ministries (Oral Roberts); Victory Ministry Fellowship (Billy Joe Dougherty); Church on the Rock (Larry Lea); International Communion of Charismatic Churches (John Meares and Earl Paulk); and Global Christian Network (ex-UPCI ministers).

4. *Third Wave, or Signs and Wonders Movement.* C. Peter Wagner (born 1930), a church growth specialist, coined the name "Third Wave" to refer to Evangelicals who do not want to be identified as Pentecostal (the first wave) or Charismatic (the second wave) but who seek miracles, healings, and other "power" encounters with God. Most of them do not speak in tongues. Those who do, generally do not publicize or emphasize this experience.

The Third Wave adherents seek to retain Evangelical theology. Thus they do not speak of the baptism of the Holy Spirit as a distinct experience but consider that they have had it all along as part of their conversion. They simply learned to "release" or "manifest" miraculous gifts of the Spirit. This theology prompted Dennis Bennett to reaffirm the reality of the baptism of the Holy Spirit as a distinct experience subsequent to Evangelical conversion. He asked, "Does this mean that what has happened to me and to the people at St. Luke's—and to all those other Christians over the last three decades—has been just a happy illusion?" He warned, "Don't let any wave wash away the blessing of Pentecost."[290]

The Third Wave has successfully introduced Pentecostal-Charismatic beliefs and experiences into many conservative Protestant churches, including many that were resistant both to the early Pentecostal revival and to the Charismatic Renewal. Increasingly, Evangelicals have begun to acknowledge the validity of speaking in tongues, healing, miracles, and casting out of demons, even though they are somewhat doubtful about experiencing these things personally.

Peter Wagner, a Congregationalist minister, became a proponent of the Third Wave. As an Evangelical missionary in Bolivia, he had actively opposed Pentecostalism. In 1971, however, he joined the faculty of Fuller Theological Seminary as a church growth specialist. His research documented a close association of signs and wonders with church growth. He began to advocate the pursuit of supernatural gifts for the purpose of facilitating church growth.

John Wimber (born 1934) was a Friends (Quaker) pastor who became a church growth researcher along with Wagner. Eventually he decided to implement his Third Wave views by founding a church in Anaheim, California, which he called the Vineyard Christian Fellowship. This led to the Association of Vineyard Churches, which in

1999 consisted of about 500 churches in the U.S. and 850 worldwide. Since Wimber's death it has been led by Todd Hunter. It is the most significant Third Wave organization, and it emphasizes teaching, signs and wonders, contemporary worship, and small groups.

As of 1988, David Barrett reported that there were 123 million Charismatics worldwide, excluding the Third Wave, and 28 million in the Third Wave.[291] Of the 123 million, however, he identified 80 million as post-Charismatics. They were once active in Charismatic meetings, but later stopped attending or attended rarely. It is doubtful if most of this number ever received the Holy Spirit. Thus, the net number of active Charismatics was about 43 million. As a more conservative estimate, J. I. Packer stated in *Christianity Today* that in 1989 total Charismatics numbered about 25 million.[292]

In an update of Barrett's figures, by the end of 1998 there were an estimated 92 million Catholic Charismatics and 71 million Protestant Charismatics, for a total of 163 million.[293] When we consider the percentage of post-Charismatics reported by Barrett, however, probably only about 60 million of these could be counted as active Charismatics. There were reportedly 110 million Third Wavers.

Doctrines and Practices

Peter Hocken, a Catholic Charismatic priest and a well-known scholar in the Charismatic movement, presented nine characteristics of the Charismatic movement that it shares with Pentecostalism:[294]

1. *"Focus on Jesus"*—renewed devotion, worship, praise, and proclamation of Jesus.

2. *"Praise."*

3. *"Love of the Bible"*—renewed emphasis on reading and studying the Scriptures.

4. *"God Speaks Today"*—God reveals Himself and gives direction to His people, corporately and individually. In short, people can have a personal, supernatural relationship with God.

5. *"Evangelism"*—telling others about one's experience and converting them to it.

6. *"Awareness of Evil"*—believing in the reality of sin, Satan, and demons.

7. *"Spiritual Gifts."*

8. *"Eschatological Expectation"*—looking for the second coming of Jesus.

9. *"Spiritual Power."*

Hocken also discussed seven points of contrast with classical Pentecostals:[295]

1. *The Charismatic movement began in the white middle class and has not had a significant impact among racial minorities.* By contrast, the Pentecostal movement began primarily among the lower classes and the poor, and from the beginning it was strong among blacks, Hispanics, immigrants, and other minorities.

2. *Charismatics are not as missionary oriented as Pentecostals.* Pentecostals established vigorous missionary efforts from the outset, while Charismatics have only recently begun to give significant attention to missions.

3. *Charismatics exhibit less concern for holiness of life.* The Pentecostal movement historically emphasized holiness of life, including standards of conduct and dress. Examples are abstention from alcohol and tobacco, avoiding worldly pleasures and amusements, and dress-

ing modestly. The Charismatic movement has exhibited little concern for these external issues. It is common for Charismatics to smoke, drink, attend movies, and wear makeup, jewelry, and relatively scanty clothing. In recent years, however, some voices in the Charismatic movement have called for moderation and caution in these areas, while most Trinitarian Pentecostals have relaxed their stand.

4. *Charismatics have greater fellowship across doctrinal boundaries.* Pentecostals have tended to have fellowship along major doctrinal lines, while Charismatics have generally said that love and unity should predominate over doctrine. For this reason, it is common for Charismatics of various denominations, including both Protestants and Catholics, to have close fellowship.

Historically, Pentecostals have wondered, How can we unite with Roman Catholics, when we emphasize justification by faith in Jesus Christ and the sole authority of Scripture while Roman Catholics believe in papal infallibility, venerate the virgin Mary, worship the bread and wine at mass as the actual body and blood of Jesus, confess their sins to a priest, and perform acts of penance to pay the temporal penalty for sin? How can we unite with Protestants whose churches do not proclaim the fundamentals of the Christian faith? How can we have close fellowship with people who do not adopt the beliefs, worship, and lifestyle that we believe the Bible commands? In recent years, however, Trinitarian Pentecostals have broadened their fellowship under the influence of the Charismatics.

5. *Most Charismatics are not dispensationalist premillennialists*, whereas Pentecostals are premillen-

nialists, and historically most of them have been dispensationalists. Premillennialism presupposes a literal interpretation of end-time prophecy, under which the next great event is the coming of the Lord Jesus followed by His reign of a thousand years on earth (the Millennium). Many Charismatics, however, follow the traditional view of mainline denominations—amillennialism or postmillennialism.

6. *Charismatics emphasize inner healing*—psychological healing or healing of memories. While both Pentecostals and Charismatics teach healing for the whole person—body, soul, and spirit—there is some difference of emphasis. Pentecostals speak more of physical healing. They approach spiritual problems with a greater stress on repentance, prayer, deliverance from sinful habits, and developing godly disciplines, whereas Charismatics speak more of the need to overcome personal hurts.

7. *Charismatics have a different theology concerning the baptism of the Holy Spirit and speaking in tongues.* First, most Charismatics do not believe that speaking in tongues is the initial evidence of receiving the Holy Spirit. Instead, they consider it to be merely one of the spiritual gifts that may be manifested in the life of a Spirit-filled believer. Thus, many of them call it a "prayer language"—simply an aid or accompaniment to spiritual prayer. Some regard it as an evidence, but one that can come some time after a person has received the Holy Spirit.

Some deny that one should expect any initial evidence. Instead, they say that the baptism of the Holy Spirit comes simply by asking, confessing, or claiming it—with or without a miraculous manifestation. Harald

Bredesen suggested the following prayer for receiving the Spirit:[296]

> Heavenly Father, I thank You for the promise of Your Spirit. Jesus, You are my Savior. I trust You now by grace through faith. You are the One who baptizes with the Holy Spirit. I'm not waiting for any sign or feeling to believe that You have baptized me with the Holy Spirit. I receive Your gift. Thank You that I am now a Spirit-filled child of God. Amen.

Nevertheless, many Charismatics do expect that the typical Spirit-filled person will speak in tongues. For them, speaking in tongues is still the most common manifestation if not the uniform evidence. Thus Kilian McDonnell was willing to speak of tongues and prophecy as having a "privileged place," present in the vast majority of cases.[297] David Pawson considered the sign to be "spontaneous spiritual speech"—tongues, prophecy, or ecstatic praise.[298] John Wimber said that tongues and prophecy are the "initiatory" gifts that should normally accompany the baptism of the Holy Spirit.[299]

Many Charismatics believe that they already received the Spirit when they first confessed faith or were baptized in water, and they do not consider the baptism of the Holy Spirit to be a distinct experience theologically. Instead, they speak of the "release" of the Spirit with miraculous power in their lives. Others speak of multiple comings of the Spirit in a person's life. Kilian McDonnell explained, "If the effects of the Spirit are not fully manifest [at initiation or water baptism] . . . subsequent prayer for the outpouring of the Spirit . . . is wholly appropriate."[300]

In short, when Charismatics say they have received, been filled with, or been baptized with the Holy Spirit, they may not mean that they have spoken in tongues. Instead, they may mean simply that they had some sort of spiritual encounter with God, but one that Pentecostals may not consider to be the baptism of the Holy Spirit.

Moreover, many Charismatics believe that it is possible to teach someone how to speak in tongues, or that the gift of tongues can come by imitation, practice, and human efforts. In essence, they regard it as a psychological phenomenon, while Pentecostals insist that true speaking in tongues can only come as the Spirit gives utterance (Acts 2:4). For Charismatics, tongues may simply be language-like sounds; for Pentecostals they are genuine languages.

As an example, Charles Hunter, a well-known Charismatic evangelist, gave the following instructions on how to receive the Holy Ghost:[301]

> In just a moment when I tell you to, begin loving and praising God by speaking forth a lot of different syllable sounds, but not in a language you know, and don't try to think of the sounds. At first, make the sounds rapidly so you won't try to think as you do speaking in your natural language.
>
> Continue making the sounds with long flowing sentences; don't just make a few sounds and stop and start. . . .
>
> I am going to speak in tongues talking to God in my spirit language so you can hear what my language sounds like.

With these instructions, he said that hundreds instantly receive the Holy Spirit. Pentecostals would say that many of these people may repeat, copy, or manufacture certain sounds, but they do not truly receive the baptism of the Holy Spirit, with the Spirit of God giving the prompting and the utterance.

On the *doctrine of salvation*, Charismatics typically affirm the standard theology of their parent denominations. Some Charismatic theologians teach that both water baptism and Spirit baptism are integral to Christian initiation, or the new birth. Larry Christenson (Lutheran) taught that repentance, baptism in water, and baptism of the Holy Ghost are all links in the conversion process.[302] David Pawson (former Baptist) held that repentance, water baptism, and the baptism of the Holy Spirit are all necessary for salvation, justification, and new birth.[303] Kilian McDonnell (Roman Catholic) affirmed that both water baptism and Spirit baptism are part of Christian initiation.[304] In principle, the position of such teachers is quite similar to that of the Oneness Pentecostal doctrine of the new birth, although in practice most of them do not baptize specifically in the name of Jesus Christ or expect tongues to be the initial sign in every case of Spirit baptism.

A number of Charismatics practice *baptism in Jesus' name* after the pattern of the Book of Acts. Examples are David Pawson in England, Bob Weiner in the U.S., and the churches that formerly were associated as Maranatha Christian Fellowship. Recently, a prominent Charismatic leader in the Philippines was baptized in the name of Jesus Christ, and by one report as many as 500,000 of his followers have been so baptized.[305]

Some leading Charismatic and Pentecostal ministers invoke both the Father, Son, and Holy Spirit and the Lord Jesus Christ at baptism. For instance, Peter Kuzmic, a Pentecostal Croatian and the most prominent theologian in the Balkans, usually baptizes with both formulas.[306] Larry Lea has reportedly done the same. Some say, "I baptize you in the name of the Father, and of the Son, and of the Holy Spirit, which is Jesus Christ."

There is no accurate measurement of how many Charismatics have been baptized in Jesus' name, but estimates range from ten to twenty-five percent. Most of them do not regard water baptism as essential to salvation, however, or insist that invoking the name of Jesus is the only correct way. Nor do they explicitly reject trinitarianism in favor of the Oneness doctrine. Even some classical Trinitarian Pentecostals, such as ministers in the AG, baptize in the name of Jesus Christ on this basis, although they do not rebaptize those who have already been baptized with the trinitarian formula.

The *worship* of Charismatics is free in comparison to that of their parent denominations. It is generally not as spontaneous or intense as that of classical Pentecostals, however. Charismatics tend to be more subdued. There is less emphasis on altar calls and extended prayer, and more emphasis on praise celebration and entertainment. For example, the independent churches commonly employ rock music and choreography in their worship. As *Charisma* noted, "Ecstatic 'dancing in the Spirit' has largely given way to spontaneous and choreographed 'dancing before the Lord.'"[307] The services of the megachurches often take the form of Christian shows and concerts, including dance teams and body building shows.

Huge crowds are often attracted as a result, but much of the Pentecostal spontaneity, fervor, and spirituality seem to be lost.

Charismatics are also prone to follow *new spiritual trends, doctrines, and fads*. Some such practices have little or no biblical support. Others have precedents in the Bible and in classical Pentecostalism, but Charismatics have transformed them into norms or rituals. Examples are being "slain in the Spirit" and "holy laughter." While these expressions of worship have always existed in Pentecostal ranks, they have generally been left to individual action under the unction of the Spirit. In some Charismatic circles, however, they have become norms, with leaders pressing for everyone to exhibit these manifestations. The result is often a stylized, mechanical, or psychologically induced phenomenon instead of a genuine move of the Holy Spirit.

For example, the meetings of evangelist Benny Hinn (originally from Israel) are noted for people falling down when he blows on them or waves at them. Typically, however, the people do not enter into deep prayer or a trancelike state as Pentecostals do, but they gently descend to the floor, lie there for a short while, look around to see what is happening, and then get up. Evangelist Rodney Howard-Browne (originally from South Africa) promotes mass laughter in his meetings. He often initiates this response by making funny statements and sounds, laughing infectiously, urging others to imitate him, and commanding the crowd to laugh.

There is a wide variety in *church government and leadership style* in the Charismatic movement. Many of the independent churches have strong, authoritarian leadership, and many are heavily oriented toward the leader's personality. Many institutions and ministries are named after an individual. As a result, huge churches and ministries can mushroom almost overnight but then quickly deflate when the founder is discredited or dies, or when a more exciting leader comes along.

In addition to the doctrines and practices that generally characterize the entire Charismatic movement, there have also been some doctrinal innovations and some recycling of Latter Rain doctrines. While we cannot attribute them to all Charismatics, they have become prominent, especially among the independent Charismatics, and they have also affected classical Pentecostal churches.

Positive Confession

As we have already mentioned, the Positive Confession doctrine is quite prominent among Charismatics. Its teachers proclaim, "What you say is what you get," and, "What you confess, you possess." (Detractors often call this message, "Name it, claim it.") Under this view, since humans are created in the image of God, they are actually little gods. As such, they have great creative power in their own right. Just as God created the world by speaking it into existence and allegedly by having faith in His words, so humans can speak things into existence in their own lives. Instead of merely having "faith in God," they are to have "the faith of God."

This view goes beyond the typical Pentecostal understanding of prayer. Classical Pentecostals believe in the power of prayer and expect miraculous results from prayer, but they focus their faith on God, stress the sovereignty of

God, and expect God to answer according to His will and timing, which may not always correspond to their desire or expectation. The Positive Confession doctrine, however, is essentially an abstract principle that purportedly operates by a natural power within humans. When people decide what they want and speak that desire in complete faith, then their desire will surely come to pass.

Positive Confession teachers use the Greek word *rhema* for the "word of faith." For them, *logos* is God's eternal Word, while *rhema* is an individual's spoken confession that secures a particular desire. (Actually, however, the Greek New Testament often uses these words interchangeably.) This word spoken in faith becomes anointed, powerful, and creative.

The practical effect of this teaching is to shift the focus of faith: the object of faith and the effective cause of miracles is no longer God Himself but the mental state and utterance of the individual. Instead of stressing the sovereignty of God, this teaching stresses techniques and formulas for receiving answers to prayer. Some of the writers speak of faith formulas, formulas for healing, and formulas for prosperity. Some explicitly say that faith, not God, causes the results and that even people who reject the gospel can achieve these results when they use these principles.

When the Positive Confession doctrine is taken to its ultimate conclusion, faith becomes a natural law that operates apart from the sovereignty of God, much as Christian Scientists teach. Here are some book titles that illustrate the problem: *How to Have Faith in Your Faith, The Tongue: A Creative Force, God's Will Is Prosperity, The Laws of Prosperity, Having Faith in Your Faith, How to Write Your Own Ticket with God,* and *You Can Have What You Say.* This teaching minimizes or ignores basic Christian principles such as seeking the will of God, humility, moderation, self-denial, putting the kingdom of God above personal desires, and trusting in God's plan and power instead of our own.

Presentations of the Positive Confession doctrine abound with theologically aberrant concepts such as the divinity of man, the inherent power of the tongue, and the formulaic nature of faith declarations. Here are some quotations that illustrate the problems:[308]

- Kenneth Copeland: "You don't have a god in you. You are one."
- Casey Treat: "I'm an exact duplicate of God. . . . When God looks in the mirror, He sees me! When I look in the mirror, I see God! . . . You know, sometimes people say to me . . . 'You just think you're a little god!' Thank you! Hallelujah! You got that right! 'Who d'you think you are, Jesus?' Yep!"
- Kenneth Hagin: "Every born again man is an incarnation. . . . The believer is as much an incarnation as Jesus of Nazareth. . . . That's who we are; we're Christ!"
- Earl Paulk: "Just as dogs have puppies and cats have kittens, so God has little gods. . . . Until we comprehend that we are little gods and we begin to act like little gods, we cannot manifest the kingdom of God."
- Robert Tilton: "He's given us power to create wealth."
- Kenneth Hagin: *"Having faith in your word is*

> *having faith in your faith*. . . . That's what you've got to learn to do to get things from God: *Have faith in your faith*. . . . I've not prayed one prayer in 45 years . . . without getting an answer. I always got an answer—and the answer was always yes."
> - Kenneth Copeland: "The force of faith is released by words. . . . The success formulas in the Word of God produce results when used as directed. . . . You can have what you say."
> - Larry Lea: "God exercised faith in His own word to create. And He has given us the ability to create change in our lives by the same means He used to create the world: the spoken word."

Abuses abound when the Positive Confession doctrine is taken to extremes. In one case, a board member of a Charismatic church in Texas was diagnosed with terminal cancer. Initially, the church prayed fervently for him and repeatedly confessed his healing. He did the same, but he steadily declined in health. Eventually, the leaders concluded that the problem was the sick man's lack of faith, for they knew they had faith. They condemned him for his unbelief and pressured him out of the church. Fortunately, after this point God healed him.

New Revelations

Some Charismatics believe in new revelations—receiving new doctrines by direct revelation from God apart from a study of Scripture. An advertisement in *Charisma* magazine for a study Bible promised, "This is the only complete publication of all the spiritual warfare strategies that have been given Morris Cerullo, by God, through divine revelation."[309] One leader stated:[310]

> The Bible is God's Word, but through prophets the
> Holy Spirit also brings revelation to this generation
> that is equally God's Word. The prophet is not a
> method that God uses; but in fact is the only method
> He uses to speak to this generation. . . . The message
> of a true prophet of God is not to be judged.

Some of the Positive Confession teachers speak of
rhema as a direct, personal revelation that God can give
to people. This concept has some validity when speaking
of direction that God gives individuals in daily life, which
always harmonizes with the Bible, but it become dangerous when used as the basis for establishing authority,
teaching doctrine, or directing the lives of others.

Personal Prophecy

In a similar vein, some Charismatics try to exercise
the gift of prophecy at will, teach others how to prophesy, and use personal prophecies to direct the lives of
others. These practices were introduced from the Latter
Rain movement. Here are examples from the report of a
prophecy conference:[311]

> The night was . . . highlighted by tremendous war-
> fare in the Spirit led by . . . Chief Musician, Prophet
> Robert Gray. During the warfare, many prophecies
> were given about the breaking of the enemies' spiri-
> tual strongholds and God's restoring Atlanta for His
> Glory. . . .
> As a special treat this year Bishop [Bill] Hamon

offered to minister prophetically to each graduate. . . . Dr. Hamon felt God prompting him to lay hands on the graduates and prophesy the mind of the Lord. He took time to pray and prophesy over the 7 graduates in attendance. God truly blessed each one of us with His word. . . .

The February Prophets Conference will focus on God's prophetic ministry today. . . . We will . . . have times of instruction and activation. Each attendee will be taught about how to hear and discern God's voice, how to relate what you are hearing to others, and how to receive and relate to personal prophecy from others. . . . In the afternoons, prophetic presbytery teams, groups of seasoned prophets, will be ministering to each registered attendee.

Shepherding

The Shepherding movement was an attempt to place everyone in a relationship of submission to a personal shepherd. It originated with the teaching of five men: Derek Prince, Don Basham, Charles Simpson, Bob Mumford, and Ern Baxter (of the Latter Rain). In an effort to bring greater accountability and discipleship to the Charismatic movement, these men proclaimed that every Christian should enter into a covenant relationship with a mentor.

Unfortunately, many such shepherds became quite authoritative, controlling the major decisions of their disciples. Many excesses and abuses occurred, which resulted in the discrediting of the concept. The movement disbanded, and the leaders acknowledged their errors. Some renounced the doctrine altogether, while others said the principle was right but the implementation was wrong.

Spiritual Warfare Techniques

Another area of doctrinal innovation is the teaching of certain spiritual warfare techniques. Of course, the Bible clearly teaches that the church is at war with Satan, but in a search for special keys for winning this warfare, many Charismatics embrace beliefs that the Scriptures do not support.

For instance, some teach that *Spirit-filled believers can have demons inhabiting them.* The key to victory over various attitudes and habits of sin is to cast out the demons responsible for them. Don Basham popularized this view with his book *Pigs in the Parlor.* After accepting this teaching, one assistant pastor starting trying to cast demons out of various church members. When the pastor admonished him to stop this practice, he accused the pastor of having a demon of unbelief. Scripture, however, does not support such a view. While demons can attack Christians, they cannot enter the body or spirit of someone who is filled with the Spirit. (See Luke 10:18-20; I Corinthians 6:17, 19-20; I John 4:4, 13, 18; 5:18.)

Some Charismatics teach the theory of *generational curses and generational spirits.* A person can inherit a spiritual curse or an evil spirit because of the sins of an ancestor. Again, in order for the person to have spiritual victory, the particular ancestral curse or spirit must be identified and overcome. A scriptural response, however, is to recognize that a person's sins and wrong choices can indeed affect his descendants, but God treats everyone individually, based on his own response to God. (See Ezekiel 18.)

Some Charismatics teach that Christians can *command angels* to do their bidding. For example, Gloria Copeland asserted, "When you become the voice of God in the earth by putting His Words in your mouth, you put your angels to work."[312] Scripturally, however, Christians are simply to pray to God, seeking His help. He then can dispatch angels or provide answers in other ways, according to His will. While angels do protect us and minister to us, they do so at God's bidding, not ours. An attempt by Christians to order angels seems to be presumptuous and a usurpation of God's authority. (See Psalm 8:5; 91:11; 103:20.)

Here are two additional examples of *unbiblical techniques* of spiritual warfare, taken from advertisements in *Charisma:*[313]

> Subliminal Deliverance. Bible-based subliminal messages hit controlling spirits where they live and command them to leave in Jesus' name. Then the void is filled with the Word of God! . . . Renew's 35 continuous play tapes offer freedom from: Doubt, Fear, Failure, Fear of Death, Guilt, Grief, Depression, Temper, Pride, Lust, Temptation, Pornography, Procrastination, Unforgiveness, Rejection, Drugs, Alcohol, Smoking, Anger, Rebellion, Anxiety and Panic, Judging, Homosexuality, Scars of Child Abuse & Molestation. Renew tapes speak into being: Prosperity, Weight Loss, Peace, Healing, Self-Esteem, Salvation, Marital Harmony, Surrender to God, Acceptance of God's Love, A Closer Walk with God.

On April 7, 1990, 150 prayer warriors and intercessors will be departing in Eagle Seven, Eagle International's Boeing 707 jet airliner, for Israel and the Soviet Union for a vitally significant flight. The purpose of the Exodus II Airborne Intercessor's Flight is to trigger the prophetic return of Jews to Israel as we intercede in prayer on the ground and in the heavenlies over Israel and the Soviet Union. . . . The battle is spiritual, not carnal, and it is fought in "high places" or in the heavenlies as the Bible says.

Finally, there is the practice of *binding territorial spirits*. Many Charismatics seek to identify which demons rule over certain locations and then engage in vigorous prayer against them, theorizing that there can be no revival until these controlling demons are specifically bound. It is true that the devil's kingdom is well organized, and there is some indication in Daniel that specific demons are assigned to geographic or political areas. (See Ephesians 6:12; Daniel 10:13, 20.) But the Christian should recognize that Jesus Christ has already won the victory over the devil by the Cross. (See Colossians 2:14-15; Hebrews 2:14-15.)

Prayer, fasting, and spiritual warfare are vital so that we can discipline the flesh, exercise faith in God, rebuke the devil, and personally appropriate the benefits of the Cross, but the Bible does not teach that any special techniques are necessary to bind the devil in a certain location. Daniel won the victory simply through prayer to God without even knowing about the demonic opposition until afterwards. Likewise, the early church successfully evangelized their world through faith, prayer, preaching of the Word, and the power of the Holy Spirit. They trusted in God for protection and deliverance, cast out demons when they encountered them, and enjoyed the assistance of angels, but the Book of Acts does not reveal any use of the elaborate spiritual warfare strategies that some teachers propound.

Kingdom Now

Another belief of some Charismatics is the Kingdom Now doctrine, also known as dominion theology, which is essentially the same as the "manifest sons of God" teaching of the Latter Rain. Proponents include Earl Paulk, Bob Mumford, and Bill Hamon. They proclaim that, instead of looking for a rapture, the church needs to possess the earth now, before the Lord comes, and establish His visible kingdom for Him. The church must gain control over society, including the government and the economic system, in order for the Lord to return.

This view is closely associated with Christian Reconstructionism, a movement within conservative Calvinism. It is based on a postmillennial eschatology which states that the church should take over the institutions of society and operate them according to the laws of the Old Testament. In this way the church will Christianize the world and usher in the Millennium.[314]

The Bible teaches, however, that the hope of the church is the coming of Lord and that He will personally establish His kingdom on earth. (See Luke 21:27-31; Titus 2:13; Revelation 19-20.) We are to exert a positive, godly influence upon this world, but it is not our home. Our Lord's kingdom is not of this world; we are but strangers and pilgrims here (John 18:36; I Peter 2:11).

Conclusions

The Charismatic movement began with a genuine outpouring of the Holy Spirit upon hungry hearts in the denominational world. It transformed their lives and emboldened them to bear witness of this event despite ridicule and rejection. Like the Pentecostals, the early Charismatics sought and received a distinct experience known as the baptism of the Holy Spirit, and in most cases they spoke in tongues.

Today, however, most people in the Charismatic movement do not receive the Holy Spirit with the evidence of speaking in tongues. Many do not even claim to speak in tongues, some have merely been taught to say nonsense syllables as a substitute for genuine tongues, and most do not believe that tongues is the necessary evidence of the Holy Spirit.

While God has used the Charismatics to bring the witness of the Holy Spirit to every denomination and to make speaking in tongues and other supernatural manifestations broadly acceptable, it appears that the movement as a whole has fallen short of its promise. The emphasis on entertainment, personalities, and spiritual fads, coupled with a de-emphasis on fundamental doctrine, repentance, and holiness, has often resulted in shallowness of worship, commitment, and lifestyle.

In many cases, Charismatic ministers seem more intent on building personal kingdoms than in truly advancing the cause of Christ. Many of them amass wealth, power, fame, and prestige while preaching convenient doctrines and indulging in personal pleasures. (See II Timothy 3:1-7; 4:3-4.) By their own definition of salvation, many of their churches grow primarily by attracting saved people from other churches rather than by converting the lost from a lifestyle of sin to holiness. When their megachurches mushroom, there often seems to be little concern for ministerial ethics, qualifications for spiritual leadership, and discipleship of every member.

How do the Charismatics relate to Pentecostals? Initially, Trinitarian Pentecostals had great reservations about the Charismatic movement, but today there is widespread acceptance, interaction, fellowship, mutual influence, and mutual transfer of ministers, churches, and members. In 1994, major Trinitarian Pentecostal and Charismatic organizations joined together in the Pentecostal/Charismatic Churches of North America (PCCNA), which replaced the Pentecostal Fellowship of North America (PFNA).

While we have discussed various practices and emphases that are typical of Charismatics, we must also note that many classical Pentecostals, especially trinitarians, have adopted many of them. Although Pentecostalism gave rise to the Charismatic movement, the latter is now exerting greater influence on the former. The Charismatics have generally prevailed on matters of holiness and fellowship, and they are significantly affecting forms of worship, views of end-time prophecy, and the initial evidence doctrine.

Classical Pentecostal organizations have taken clear stands against the doctrinal innovations of Charismatics, however. For example, the Assemblies of God has adopted official position papers against the Positive Confession doctrine, the Kingdom Now doctrine, the excesses of the Shepherding movement, the belief that Christians can have demons, absolutist views on divine healing, and attempts to teach or imitate speaking in tongues.[315]

Oneness Pentecostals generally oppose the distinctive doctrines and practices of Charismatics, although some have followed Charismatic trends. In return, Charismatics usually do not see the Oneness doctrine as a problem, but they object to the doctrine of salvation and holiness lifestyle of Oneness Pentecostals.

In 1997, *Charisma* published the first significant analysis of Oneness Pentecostals by Charismatics. It noted their many achievements but exhibited an agenda of trying to move them toward the Charismatic position. It based its analysis primarily upon views and reports of ex-members rather than interaction with Oneness theologians. The article accused Oneness Pentecostals of "legalism," "elitism," being "mean-spirited," "judgmentalism," "hypocrisy" and embracing "a flawed theology of salvation by works"—with no awareness of the irony of judging them so harshly based on a few disgruntled sources.[316]

From a Oneness Pentecostal perspective, there are many honest-hearted, Spirit-filled people in the Charismatic movement. Indeed, many have received the full Acts 2:38 experience of salvation. The movement has led millions of people to a more biblically based faith and a greater spiritual experience with God. Nevertheless, it has fallen short in restoring them to the full apostolic doctrine and lifestyle. It still needs a revival of the message of the almighty God in Jesus Christ and the message of scriptural holiness, both inwardly and outwardly.

In many cases, the movement has actually created significant barriers to further spiritual progress. Multitudes outside the movement have been turned away by foolish, unbiblical doctrines and practices and by the poor examples of prominent leaders. Multitudes inside the movement have been led astray by the introduction of various false doctrines, by attacks on the apostolic doctrine and lifestyle, and by the belief that since they experience some work of the Spirit then they do not need anything further. But the Bible itself warns against this attitude. (See Matthew 7:21-23; Luke 13:23-27.)

Still, the Charismatic movement has helped spread the message of the Holy Spirit throughout the world, reaching into denominations and social classes that had been practically untouched. By fostering a desire for deeper spirituality while not completely fulfilling that desire, it has helped set the stage for genuine, end-time, apostolic revival.

11

Christianity Today

Since the Protestant Reformation, it has been common to identify three major branches of world Christianity—Roman Catholicism, Eastern Orthodoxy, and Protestantism. The Pentecostal movement of the twentieth century became so significant, however, that many church historians have added it as a fourth branch.

A better classification, proposed by theologian Henry Van Dusen, is to recognize three branches as follows: Catholicism/Orthodoxy, Protestantism, and Pentecostalism. Of course, Pentecostalism arose within Protestantism and affirms the distinctive points of Protestantism in its opposition to Catholicism. Nevertheless, Pentecostalism is distinctive enough and large enough to be classified as a branch in its own right.

Statistics

Of approximately 6 billion people on earth in 1999, about 2 billion—one-third—identified themselves as Christians. As of 1999 here are two attempts at classification. (The numbers are rough estimates, and not every group is included.)[317]

Branch	Adherents
Roman Catholic	1,030,000,000
Eastern Orthodox and Other Eastern Christian	230,000,000
African Indigenous (Protestant, Pentecostal, or marginal Christian)	110,000,000
Pentecostal	85,000,000
Baptist	80,000,000
Lutheran	75,000,000
Reformed/Presbyterian	70,000,000
Anglican	67,000,000
Methodist	50,000,000

Branch	Adherents
Roman Catholic	1,030,000,000
Eastern Orthodox and Other Eastern Christian	230,000,000
Conservative Protestant	200,000,000
Liberal Protestant	170,000,000
African Indigenous (Protestant, Pentecostal, or marginal Christian)	110,000,000
Pentecostal	85,000,000
Anglican (Protestant)	67,000,000

According to Pentecostal scholar Vinson Synan, total Pentecostals and Charismatics numbered about 540 million in 1999, categorized as follows:[318]

Denominational Pentecostals	215,000,000
Chinese Pentecostals	52,000,000
Protestant Charismatics	71,000,000
Catholic Charismatics	92,000,000
Third Wavers (Protestant)	110,000,000
Total	540,000,000

As we will discuss, the two numbers for Pentecostals include various groups that have some Pentecostal characteristics, such as demonstrative worship and belief in healing, even though they may not be fully Pentecostal. The two numbers for Charismatics also include many Protestants and Catholics who once participated in the Charismatic movement but who are no longer active. The number for the Third Wave consists primarily of people in Protestant denominations who believe in miracles but do not fully embrace Pentecostal theology or identity.

Even by the most conservative measurement, Pentecostals are now larger than any other Protestant group. By the more inclusive statistics, Pentecostals are the second-largest group of Christians after the Roman Catholic Church. Taking Pentecostals and Charismatics together, in one hundred years they attained numerical equivalency to the traditional Protestant branch, which has existed for five hundred years. They now account for about 27 percent of total Christian population and about 9 percent of world population. They are increasing by 19 million per year.[319]

Based on the above statistics, we can identify the three major branches of Christianity as follows: Roman Catholics and Eastern Orthodox at about 1.3 billion, Protestants at about 450 million, and Pentecostals (excluding Charismatics) at about 250 million.

Let us look more closely at the total of 540 million for Pentecostals and Charismatics. It does not mean that 540 million people have received the Holy Spirit with the initial sign of speaking in tongues. First of all, only about 35 to 50 percent of the members of Pentecostal churches have received the Holy Ghost, and the percentage for Charismatics is even less.

Second, 540 million represents inclusive constituency, not active membership. This figure is based on the research of David Barrett, who counts children of members and people who identify themselves with the movement even though they do not attend regularly. His numbers reflect an average of about 275 constituents per church, whereas average Sunday attendance per church is less than half of that.

Third, the numbers include marginal groups who are not fully Pentecostal. For instance, Barrett estimated that there were 406 million Pentecostals and Charismatics in 1990.[320] From his notes we find that the 1990 number includes 5 million pre-Pentecostals (mostly Holiness groups), 50 million quasi-Pentecostals (not explicitly Pentecostal), 18 million in revival groups (not explicitly Pentecostal), 3 million post-Pentecostals, 25 million or more Chinese believers who are not definitely Pentecostal, 4 million radio Pentecostals (who have no connection other than listening to the radio), 2 million in the Catholic Apostolic Church (Irvingite group in which tongues has largely died out), 92 million post-Charismatics, 5 million radio Charismatics, 7 million crypto–Third Wavers (who do not confess to being in the Third Wave), and 33 million unaffiliated with any group.

The total of these groups that are not explicitly Pentecostal or Charismatic is 244 million. This leaves 162 million who are active in Pentecostal or Charismatic groups, counting children and irregular attendees. If we assume that 35 percent of the latter number has received the Holy Spirit with tongues (which is Barrett's estimate) and that 5 percent of the former number has done so, the total would be about 69 million. This number of active, Spirit-filled believers is about 17 percent of the grand total.

This figure corresponds closely to a 1979 Gallup poll, in which 29 million adult Americans (19 percent at the time) called themselves "Pentecostal or Charismatic Christians" but only 5 million (3 percent) claimed to have spoken in tongues.[321] Thus, only 17 percent of those who identified with the label said they spoke in tongues. Another Gallup poll in 1984 found that 5.8 million American adults said they spoke in tongues. A 1992 Bliss survey reported 8.7 percent claimed to have done so, and a 1993 Barna survey reported 11 to 12 percent.[322]

In short, the estimated number of active, Spirit-filled believers in early 1999 would be about 17 percent of the total of 540 million Pentecostals and Charismatics, or about 90 million.

This analysis does not mean that it is false to say there are 540 million Pentecostals and Charismatics. This number is helpful for comparison with the other religious movements, for they too count children, constituents who do not attend regularly, and constituents who do not practice the tenets of their faith. Whether we look at total Spirit-filled believers or total constituents, the numbers are still amazing.

Of further interest, Barrett estimated that by 1990, 90 percent of the world's countries had Pentecostal/ Charismatic churches, and these countries contained 99 percent of the world's population. Barrett also estimated that there were 1,474,000 churches and house groups in his inclusive Pentecostal/Charismatic categories; 11,000 Pentecostal denominations (large and small); and 3,000 Charismatic denominations. In addition, Charismatics existed in all 150 of the non-Pentecostal denominational families.[323]

In the most thorough study of Oneness Pentecostal statistics, Talmadge French documented an inclusive constituency of 13.7 million Oneness Pentecostals in 1998. After making allowances for groups he could not document, he estimated a total of 15 to 20 million Oneness Pentecostals worldwide.[324] For comparison with Barrett's figures, the highest number is the most suitable, since Barrett includes pre-, quasi-, and post-Pentecostals. Thus, about 10 percent of all denominational Pentecostals worldwide are Oneness. Moreover, since Oneness Pentecostals report a much higher percentage of people receiving the Holy Ghost, it is probable that 15 percent of all those who have been baptized with the Holy Spirit, speaking in tongues, are Oneness Pentecostal.[325]

Among Charismatics, the Oneness message is not nearly as strong as it is among Pentecostals. If we could count Charismatics who have been baptized in Jesus' name, however, we would probably find that Jesus Name Charismatics total 10 percent or more of Charismatics worldwide.

Turning to the United States, there are approximately 1,200 denominations, including non-Christian groups.[326] There are approximately 350,000 churches.[327] Thus, the

UPCI has a little over one percent of the total. About 20 to 25 percent of American Pentecostals are Oneness believers.[328]

According to Gallup polls, about 36 percent of Americans claim to be born again.[329] There are about 400 megachurches with 2,000 or more people in attendance each week.[330] Of churches that average 400 or more in weekly attendance, from 60 to 95 percent of the numerical growth comes from transfer of members.[331]

The statistics of C. Peter Wagner, the leading church growth researcher in America, are more conservative than those of David Barrett.[332] He estimated that in 1985 the total number of active, faithful Pentecostals and Charismatics in the U.S. was 9 to 10 million. That number probably doubled by 1999.

For U.S. churches, Wagner estimated an average attendance per church of 76. As of 1988, eight of the ten largest churches in the world were Pentecostal or Charismatic, and so were the largest churches in 40 American states.

Wagner provided the following information on decadal growth rates in the U.S. in the early 1980s:

Charismatics (smaller base contributed to higher rate)	457%
Pentecostals and Charismatics	173%
Classical Pentecostals	52%
Oneness Pentecostals	48%
Christian and Missionary Alliance	49%
Seventh-day Adventists	33%
Southern Baptists	14%

According to Wagner, 100 percent is a good growth rate, 50 is fair, and 25 is marginal. He further noted that

Pentecostals and Charismatics are the fastest-growing group in about 80 percent of all nations.

Church Growth Factors

Peter Wagner identified seven reasons why the Pentecostal movement has grown so rapidly:[333]

1. *"Biblical Triumphalism"*—preaching power, victory, and overcoming based on the Bible; proclaiming a message of hope, salvation, deliverance, and healing.

2. *"Targeting the Poor and Oppressed."*

3. *"Multiple Tracks to Ordination."* Instead of requiring seven years of college and seminary for ordination, Pentecostals base ordination on the call of God, spiritual qualifications, and mastery of basic Bible doctrines. As preparation, they consider self-study, experience, and on-the-job training.

4. *"High Local-Church Autonomy."* Instead of denominations controlling the local church and its finances, the local church makes its own decisions. The strength of the movement rests in the local churches and not at the top.

5. *"The Apostolic Model of Church Planting"*—using recognized leaders to plant churches in new areas, and using large churches to start daughter works.

6. *"Schism."* Over time, two churches in an area usually reach more people than just one church would. Pentecostals have proliferated from divisions over the years. The point is not that the church should encourage church splits, but if a split occurs, it is wise not to castigate those who have left. Instead, if the wounds can be healed and the wrongs can be righted, then both sides can achieve great growth. Moreover, this principle can

work in a positive way through the deliberate planting of daughter churches.

7. *"Local Institutional Factors."* Here Wagner listed eight additional factors: "conservative evangelical theology," "strong pastoral leadership," "prayer," "openness to the person and work of the Holy Spirit," "abundant financial support," "worship [as] a central feature of church life," "participation in lay ministry . . . expected of all church members," and "extensive Bible-teaching ministry . . . focused on the felt need of church members."

Wagner also warned about three factors that could stunt the growth of Pentecostals:[334]

1. *"The Dark Side of Respectability."* When churches receive wide social acceptance, they tend to minimize or abandon some of the factors that caused them to grow. Social status and cultural approval become more important to them, so they moderate their distinctive elements, which are their primary reasons for existence and growth.

2. *"St. John's Syndrome . . . losing their first love."* The initial zeal and commitment are not always passed down to subsequent generations. As children grow up in middle-class society and comfortable churches, they can become social Pentecostals, no longer fully committed to strong doctrinal preaching and teaching, godly disciplines, fervent worship, or zealous evangelism. The constant influx of new converts helps to counteract this trend, however.

3. *"Ministerial elitism"*—making the technical or academic standards for the ministry too strict. Instead, the primary goal should be to find ministers who are called of God and anointed by the Spirit. The system should fos-

ter the selection of ministers who come from the people themselves and who minister among the people.

Conclusion

The most significant story in twentieth-century Christianity is the rise of the Pentecostals. A movement that did not formally exist at the beginning of the century became one of the three major branches of Christendom by century's end.

The outpouring of the Holy Spirit in the twentieth century is amazing. The movement advanced far beyond the imagination of its founders and other early adherents. In the first half of the century, the Pentecostals were ignored, ridiculed, and persecuted. The religious leaders of the day rejected the baptism of the Holy Spirit, speaking in tongues, and Pentecostal-style worship. Today, however, Pentecostals are generally respected. Their doctrines and practices are widely accepted, imitated, and followed. They have penetrated every denomination with their message and made a significant impact on society.

Oneness Pentecostals and Revival

To this point, the Jesus Name, Oneness message has not enjoyed the same level of acceptance. Moreover, many Pentecostals have compromised the message and practice of holiness. Nevertheless, Oneness Pentecostals are the most biblical, apostolic movement in the world today. They face unprecedented opportunity. If they will continue to affirm their distinctive doctrines, they will experience increasing revival and growth. In 1900 the great twentieth-century outpouring of the Holy Spirit was inconceivable, yet it took place. Similarly, a great revival of Jesus Name and holiness seems quite possible. Indeed, such a revival has begun.

It is God's will to send a mighty revival of the full apostolic message. To a great extent it is the responsibility of Oneness Pentecostals, as they enter a new century and a new millennium, to see this revival come to pass. It will not come automatically, but if they will pray, be fervent in Spirit, remain committed doctrinally, be zealous in evangelism, and live a holy life, they can realize this goal.

God desires to give a revival of the Name to match the outpouring of the Holy Spirit. He also desires to lead everyone into a lifestyle of true holiness, inwardly and outwardly. By faith, diligence, sacrifice, and the power of the Holy Spirit, Oneness Pentecostals can participate in the greatest move of God in human history, as they await the soon coming of our Lord.

Appendixes

Appendix A

Dates in the History of Christianity
1900-2000

Secular History	Church History
1861-65 U.S. Civil War	1862-1916 G. B. Cashwell
	1865-1943 A. J. Tomlinson
	1866-1923 E. N. Bell
	1866-1961 C. H. Mason
	1867-1948 Glenn Cook
	1870-1922 William Seymour
	1873-1929 Charles Parham
	1873-1912 William Durham
	1876-1947 Frank Ewart
	1880-1931 G. T. Haywood
	1883-1964 Howard Goss
	1884-1976 Rudolf Bultmann
	1886-1968 Karl Barth
	1890-1944 Aimee Semple McPherson
	1892-1971 Reinhold Niebuhr
	1898-1963 C. S. Lewis
1901 New century begins	1901 Pentecostal movement begins, Topeka, KS
	1906-9 Azusa Street revival, Los Angeles
	1906-7 Pentecostal Assemblies of the World
	1910 Durham proclaims Finished Work doctrine
	1910 Edinburgh Missionary Conference
	1910-15 *The Fundamentals*

Secular History	Church History
	1913 Arroyo Seco camp meeting
1914 World War I begins	1914 Oneness movement begins
	1914 Assemblies of God
1917 U.S. enters World War I	1916 AG rejects Oneness doctrine
1918 World War I ends	1919 Karl Barth's *Commentary on Romans*
	1931 Conversion of C. S. Lewis
	1934 Wycliffe Bible Translators
1939 World War II begins	1941 Rudolf Bultmann's demythologizing
1941 U.S. enters World War II	1942 National Association of Evangelicals
	1945 Dietrich Bonhoeffer's prison writings
1945 World War II ends	1945 United Pentecostal Church
	1946 Post-war healing revivals
1948 Israel becomes a nation	1948 Latter Rain movement begins
	1948 World Council of Churches
	1949 Billy Graham's Los Angeles crusade
	1950 Assumption of Mary proclaimed by Pius XII
	1960 Charismatic movement begins
1963 Martin Luther King marches on Washington	1962-65 Second Vatican Council
1967 Six Day War; Israel regains Old Jerusalem	
	1972 Catholic-Pentecostal dialogue begins
	1994 Pentecostal/Charismatic Churches of North America

Appendix B

Early Pentecostal Leaders
Baptized in Jesus' Name

The following is a list of some prominent figures in the early Pentecostal movement who were baptized in Jesus' name. They were well-known leaders at the time of their baptism, or would be shortly thereafter. For documentation, see endnote 74. Charles Parham is not included here, for there is no direct evidence that he himself was baptized in Jesus' name, although his testimony implies that he was.

- *Andrew H. Argue* (1868-1959), a convert of William Durham, a pastor in Winnipeg, and an influential leader in western Canada. He did not enter the Oneness movement but was an early leader in the Pentecostal Assemblies of Canada. A grandson, Don Argue, served as president of the National Association of Evangelicals.
- *Leanore "Mother Mary" Barnes* (1854-1939), an early evangelist in the Midwest, associate of "Mother" Mary Moise in rescue mission work in St. Louis, and a charter member of the Assemblies of God.
- *Frank Bartleman* (1871-1936), historian of the Azusa Street revival and an international evangelist. Bartleman never joined a Pentecostal organization but maintained fellowship with both Oneness and trinitarian believers, although he remained committed to Oneness beliefs.
- *Eudorus N. Bell* (1866-1923), the first general chairman of the Assemblies of God (1914). He later repudiated his baptism in Jesus' name and served as chairman a second time (1920-23).
- *William Booth-Clibborn*, a grandson of William Booth (founder of the Salvation Army) and an evangelist. He was

active in early Oneness organizations but later returned to fellowship with trinitarians, although he never renounced his Oneness views. He penned the words of "Down from His Glory."

- *George A. Chambers* (1879-1957), an early Canadian leader. He was a minister in the Pentecostal Assemblies of the World in 1919. He soon repudiated the Oneness position, however, and became the first general chairman (superintendent) of the Pentecostal Assemblies of Canada.
- *Glenn A. Cook* (1867-1948), business manager of the Azusa Street Mission, evangelist who brought the Pentecostal message to Indianapolis and to the Church of God in Christ, and assistant to Frank Ewart in Los Angeles. He brought the Oneness message to St. Louis and Indianapolis, baptizing Mother Barnes, Mother Moise, and Ben Pemberton in St. Louis and L. V. Roberts and G. T. Haywood in Indianapolis.
- *Frank J. Ewart* (1876-1947), assistant pastor and successor to William Durham in Los Angeles. He was the chief proponent of the Oneness doctrine in 1914, in conjunction with Glenn Cook. At his death he was a minister in the United Pentecostal Church.
- *Elmer K. Fisher* (1866-1919), associate of William Seymour and then pastor of the Upper Room Mission in Los Angeles. He did not enter into the Oneness movement. His son-in-law, Wesley Steelburg, was a minister in the Pentecostal Assemblies of the World, but he later became general superintendent of the Assemblies of God. A grandson, Stanley Horton, became a well-known Assemblies of God theologian.
- *Howard A. Goss* (1883-1964), a convert of Charles Parham in 1903 and onetime field director of Parham's work in Texas. He and E. N. Bell were the chief organizers of the Assemblies of God in 1914, and he served as one of its first executive presbyters. He later became the general superintendent of the Pentecostal Church Incorporated and the first general superintendent of the United Pentecostal Church.

- *Lemuel C. Hall* (1867-?), a convert from Zion City and an evangelist. He later became the first chairman of the Pentecostal Ministerial Alliance (a Oneness organization). Eventually, he accepted the pastorate of a trinitarian church, but he never abandoned his Oneness beliefs.
- *Thoro Harris* (1874-1955), black gospel songwriter. His songs include "Jesus Loves the Little Children," "All That Thrills My Soul Is Jesus," and "He's Coming Soon."
- *Garfield T. Haywood* (1880-1931), black pastor of a large interracial church in Indianapolis, outstanding Bible teacher, author, songwriter, and one of the most influential leaders in the Finished Work camp. He later became the presiding bishop of the Pentecostal Assemblies of the World and served until his death. His songs include "I See a Crimson Stream of Blood," "Thank God for the Blood," "Jesus the Son of God," and "Baptized into the Body."
- *Bennett F. Lawrence* (1890-?), author of the first history of the Pentecostal movement, *The Apostolic Faith Restored* (1916), and first assistant secretary of the Assemblies of God in 1914.
- *Robert E. McAlister* (1880-1953), Canadian evangelist and pastor in Ottawa, Ontario. He helped found the Pentecostal Assemblies of Canada and became its first secretary-treasurer. He stayed with his organization when it embraced trinitarianism and denounced the Oneness belief.
- *Aimee Semple McPherson* (1890-1944), missionary and evangelist. In 1923 she founded the International Church of the Foursquare Gospel. She did not enter the Oneness movement.
- *Charles H. Mason* (1866-1961), co-founder of the Church of God in Christ and general overseer when the group was reorganized as a Pentecostal body. According to numerous sources in the black Apostolic movement, he was baptized privately in Jesus' name in Chicago in 1930. When the leaders under him did not accept the message, he did not proclaim it

but stayed with his organization. He continued to have some fellowship with black Apostolics.

- *"Mother" Mary Moise* (1850-1930), a pioneer in Pentecostal social work and operator of a rescue mission in St. Louis for social outcasts. She received a first prize at the World's Fair in St. Louis in 1904 for her work with homeless girls.
- *Daniel C. O. Opperman* (1872-1926), a founder of the Assemblies of God, one of its first executive presbyters, and its first assistant chairman. He had formerly been superintendent of the high school system in Zion City, Illinois, under Alexander Dowie. He was an early leader in Pentecostal education, conducting short-term Bible training programs. He soon became the chairman of the General Assembly of the Apostolic Assemblies, the first group to be founded as a Oneness organization.
- *L. V. Roberts*, pastor in Indianapolis and evangelist who baptized E. N. Bell in the name of Jesus. He later returned to trinitarianism.
- *H. G. Rodgers*, an early leader in the South who received the Holy Ghost under G. B. Cashwell. He briefly led a loose association of ministers called the Church of God (Dothan, Alabama) but soon merged that group with Howard Goss's white wing of the Church of God in Christ. One of the founding members of the Assemblies of God, he never withdrew. He maintained fellowship with Oneness ministers and continued to baptize in Jesus' name, however. His daughters became part of the United Pentecostal Church.
- *Franklin M. Small* (1873-1961), Canadian evangelist and one of the founders of the Pentecostal Assemblies of Canada. After it adopted trinitarian theology, he withdrew and founded the Apostolic Church of Pentecost of Canada.
- *George B. Studd* (1859-1945), younger brother of missionary C. T. Studd, an associate of Dwight Moody, and an organizer of the Worldwide Camp Meeting at Arroyo Seco in 1913. He served as Frank Ewart's assistant pastor in the Los

Angeles area for many years. He was a noted supporter of missions who gave away his inherited fortune.

- *Andrew D. Urshan* (1884-1967), immigrant from Persia and international evangelist. He brought the Oneness message to Russia and was rebaptized there in 1916. He served as foreign missions secretary of the Pentecostal Assemblies of the World and of Emmanuel's Church in Christ Jesus. At his death he was a minister in the United Pentecostal Church. His son, Nathaniel A. Urshan, became general superintendent of the United Pentecostal Church International.
- *Harry Van Loon,* associate of William Durham and Frank Ewart in Los Angeles.

Appendix C

Answering the Charge of Cultism

In recent years a small but vocal group of opponents of the Jesus Name message has sought to label the United Pentecostal Church (UPCI) as a cult. How should we respond to this charge?

1. This charge stems from a small segment of the Evangelical community inspired by "ministries" who garner their financial support by making charges of this nature and who take their cue from the late Walter Martin, founder of Christian Research Institute and self-styled "Bible Answer Man." In many cases the charge is repeated by people who have had no personal knowledge of, or contact with, the UPCI and who have an inaccurate concept of the UPCI's beliefs. It does not come from any mainline Christian organization, nor is it the official position of any Evangelical denomination. Trinitarian Pentecostal groups, who have had the most contact with us, consider our views on the Godhead to be erroneous but still regard us as saved.

The National Religious Broadcasters, an arm of the National Association of Evangelicals, has accepted Oneness individuals and groups as members. The Society for Pentecostal Studies, an interdenominational organization of Pentecostal and Charismatic scholars, also accepts Oneness believers as members, and one recently served as its president. Major Evangelical and Charismatic publishers publish and market books and music by United Pentecostals. Evangelical radio stations worldwide routinely carry programs by United Pentecostals, including Harvestime, the UPCI's official radio broadcast.

2. This labeling is an unfair tactic. It is designed to

prejudice people against us, not to open dialogue regarding scriptural truth. To the general public, the word *cult* means a group that is sociologically aberrant and even dangerous, typically characterized by authoritarian leadership, exotic beliefs, manipulative methods, financial exploitation, mind control, and rebellion against government. Our critics do not use the word in this sense, however, for sociologically and organizationally we are quite similar to most other Evangelical and Pentecostal churches. They actually mean that they differ with us theologically. To be honest and fair, they should explain their differences of biblical interpretation with us, and let people examine the issues for themselves.

An editorial by Terry Muck in the February 5, 1990, issue of *Christianity Today*, the leading Evangelical periodical, gave three reasons why Christians should not use the pejorative label of cult: (1) "The spirit of fair play suggests it is best to refer to groups of people as they refer to themselves." (2) "There is also a theological reason for avoiding" the label, for it wrongly implies that certain sinners "are the worst kind." (3) "It simply does not work well to use disparaging terms to describe the people whom we hope will come to faith in Christ. . . . In fact, we are commanded to love them as ourselves."

An editorial in the August 1993 issue of *Charisma* magazine specifically rebuked Hank Hanegraaff, Walter Martin's successor as president of Christian Research Institute and "Bible Answer Man." Editor and publisher Stephen Strang said, "The heresy hunters are still with us. Only now, instead of stakes, they use their books and radio programs to destroy those they consider heretics. . . . I'm concerned that heresy hunting may be turning into leukemia because some cult-watchers seem more intent on destroying parts of the body than healing the body. . . . Hanegraaff goes way too far [in attacking independent Charismatics]. . . . It's time he shows as much respect to fellow Christians with whom he disagrees as he does to those outside the faith."

3. The critics rely on the authority of "historic Christianity" or "orthodoxy" instead of the Bible, even though they claim that the Bible is their only authority and denounce the use of extrabiblical authority as cultic. For instance, they say we are a cult because we do not accept the doctrine of the trinity as defined by creeds developed from the fourth to eighth centuries. If by "orthodoxy" they mean anything more than the doctrines of the Bible, then they have an extrabiblical authority. If they do not mean anything else, however, why do they not simply appeal to Scripture?

Moreover, they are inconsistent and selective in their appeal to "historic orthodoxy." For example, they denounce our teaching that baptism is part of the salvation experience, even though this has always been the majority view in professing Christianity. Not only have Roman Catholics, Eastern Orthodox, and the theologians of the first five centuries consistently held this view, but the founder of Protestantism, Martin Luther, did so as well. Yet these critics, who are Protestant, do not label Luther as a cultist. The Nicene Creed, to which they often appeal for its doctrine of the trinity, also proclaims that there is "one baptism for the remission of sins," yet they reject its teaching on this subject.

When trying to prove that their doctrine of the trinity is the only orthodox view in history, the critics appeal to early writers such as Justin, Tertullian, and Origen, yet these men's definition of the trinity is considered heretical by orthodox trinitarians today because they subordinated the second and third persons of the trinity to the first. Ironically, Walter Martin was heretical according to the ancient creeds, because he denied the eternal generation of the Son. In short, our critics determine what is "orthodox" not by the Bible or even by the historic creeds, but by their personal theologies.

4. Many Christians in major denominations hold similar or the same views. Southern Baptist seminary professor Frank Stagg taught a doctrine of God that he acknowledged to be essentially the same as Oneness. W. A. Criswell, past president of the Southern Baptist Convention, stated in his commentary on Revelation that the only God we will see is Jesus, and described Father, Son, and Holy Spirit in the same terms that Oneness believers do.

Calvin Beisner, an ally of Walter Martin, conceded in his book *God in Three Persons*, "Monarchianism is represented today by the United ('Jesus Only') Pentecostals. . . . As the differences between modalism and pure trinitarianism are rather minute, it is not surprising that a great number of Christians in mainline denominations, including Roman Catholicism, hold a modalistic conception of the Trinity, at least unconsciously" (p. 18). Noted Roman Catholic theologian Karl Rahner similarly stated in *The Trinity*, "Despite their orthodox confession of the Trinity, Christians are, in their practical life, almost mere 'monotheists'" (p. 10). Many ministers and lay persons of various trinitarian denominations have similarly stated to United Pentecostals that they accept the Oneness view of the Godhead.

A number of Charismatic scholars, including Larry Christenson, Kilian McDonnell, and David Pawson, teach that water baptism and the baptism of the Holy Spirit are part of Christian initiation and not subsequent to it. Evangelical writers such as Leighton Ford and James Dunn have argued essentially the same thing, but without associating the baptism of the Holy Spirit with tongues. Many Trinitarian Pentecostals and Charismatics agree that water baptism should be performed in the name of Jesus. Many theologians and scholars, including Martin Luther and F. F. Bruce, have acknowledged that this was the formula of the apostles.

Our critics do not attack these teachers, because they belong to major denominations or use traditional theological terminology. It is not fair, however, to single us out for views that many other professing Christians also hold, just because we have formed our own group or refuse to use the nonbiblical terminology treasured by so many.

5. The attack on us is inconsistent with the critics' doctrine of salvation. They commonly say they believe in salvation "by grace alone through faith alone in Christ alone." How does this doctrine negate the salvation experience of the typical United Pentecostal convert? Most United Pentecostals do not decide to join the UPCI after an intellectual study of the Oneness doctrine. Many come to God as children. Many come from no church background, or a nominal church background. Typically they hear a simple evangelistic message about the death, burial, and resurrection of Jesus Christ, believe that Jesus is their Savior, decide to accept the offer of salvation, and come to the altar of repentance.

For example, I repented of my sins, believed on the Lord Jesus Christ, and received the Holy Spirit at age seven. At that point I could not debate Oneness versus trinitarianism, but I knew that Jesus was God manifested in the flesh to be my Savior, that He loved me, that I was trusting in Him for salvation, and that I was devoting my life to Him as my Lord.

If someone were to make the identical response in a Baptist church, our critics would not hesitate to pronounce him saved, and many would argue that he could not lose this salvation under any circumstances. How, then, could his subsequent baptism in the name of Jesus, reception of the Holy Spirit, and acceptance of the Oneness doctrine annul this genuine experience with God?

If someone professes to believe in salvation by grace through faith but denies that our converts are saved, then actually he must believe in salvation by faith plus a creed, a denomination, or intellectualism. Such a position is more exclusive than that of the UPCI, for we readily acknowledge that people of various denominations can have genuine faith in God and a genuine relationship with God, even before receiving the full Acts 2:38 experience.

On the other hand, if our critics concede that we are saved, what justification do they have for attacking us so vehemently and uncharitably?

Several years ago, Robert Bowman, one of Walter Martin's chief researchers, acknowledged to me in a telephone conversation that most UPCI converts truly have faith in Christ and receive salvation, but he maintained that when they progress in doctrinal study and consciously embrace the Oneness view then they lose salvation. It is an unusual cult indeed that leads people to salvation but then gradually takes it away from them! Would he say the same of any other group he considers cultic, such as Mormons or Jehovah's Witnesses?

Martin not only believed that some UPCI members are saved but also that once a person is saved he can never lose his salvation. This means he attacked those whom he considered to be fellow Christians and sought to destroy their churches. It would seem more appropriate to let the Lord of these people decide how to judge these churches and deal with them as He wills, rather than appointing oneself to that role. "Who art thou that judgest another man's servant? to his own master he standeth or falleth. Yea, he shall be holden up: for God is able to make him stand" (Romans 14:4).

6. The critics do not recognize that we are involved in ministry. While our critics raise money by attacking us and feel that their "ministry" is to label us, our ministers and churches are busy leading people to a saving and transforming relationship with Jesus Christ. We are restoring broken marriages and homes, strengthening families, freeing people from sinful habits and addictions, training people in morality, and helping them to become productive citizens and saints. We do not fulfill our ministry by name calling, denunciations, and anathemas, but we seek to share with the world God's great gift of salvation that He has made available in Jesus Christ.

We invite everyone to open their hearts and their Bibles, for we believe that truth is its own best defense. The Bereans exemplified the "more noble" course of action, "in that they received the word with all readiness of mind, and searched the scriptures daily, whether those things were so" (Acts 17:11).

With the apostle Paul, we say, "After the way which they call heresy, so worship I the God of my fathers, believing all things which are written in the law and in the prophets" (Acts 24:14). We remember that Jesus said, "Ye shall be hated of all men for my name's sake" (Matthew 10:22). Nevertheless, like the apostles, we can go our way "rejoicing [to be] counted worthy to suffer shame for his name" (Acts 5:41). Despite unjust opposition and unfair accusations, we "rejoice with joy unspeakable and full of glory" (I Peter 1:8).

Appendix D

Response to a Cult Hunter

Book Review of E. Calvin Beisner, *"Jesus Only" Churches* (Grand Rapids: Zondervan, 1998), 87 pages. Reviewed in 1998, citing sources available prior to publication of the book.

It is important for trinitarians and Oneness believers to communicate with each other and to develop a greater understanding of one another's beliefs. The back cover of Beisner's booklet promises to provide "essential and reliable information and insights" on Oneness Pentecostalism. Unfortunately, the booklet fails in this purpose and actually creates significant obstacles for understanding and communication. The prejudicial tone does not foster dialogue, much of the information is simply wrong, the presentation of Oneness Pentecostal doctrinal views is seriously flawed, and the presentation of "historic, orthodox understanding" is surprisingly narrow and controversial.

Strident Polemics

The title itself provides an indication of problems to come, for it uses a derogatory and misleading label to characterize the movement it seeks to understand. This branch of Pentecostalism uses the designations of Apostolic, Jesus Name, and Oneness to identify itself. The label "Jesus Only" arose as a description of its baptismal formula, but soon opponents began using it against Oneness adherents, erroneously claiming that they denied the Father and the Holy Spirit. As a result Oneness Pentecostals today do not designate themselves by the term "Jesus Only" and generally consider it misleading and offensive. Similarly, the booklet's use of three theatrical masks to symbolize the Oneness doctrine is inaccurate and inappropriate.

It is evident that the author and publisher wish to portray Oneness Pentecostals as cultists and false religionists. The booklet is one of the newest in a series by various authors entitled *Zondervan Guide to Cults and Religious Movements*. On the cover, the most prominent word in this series title is *Cults*. The introductory booklet to the series is *Unmasking the Cults*. The last booklet in the series summarizes all the movements studied, and its title is *Truth and Error: Comparative Charts of Cults and Christianity*. The other twelve titles in the series are *Jehovah's Witnesses; Masonic Lodge; Mormonism; New Age Movement; Satanism; Unification Church; Mind Sciences; Astrology and Psychic Phenomena; Buddhism, Taoism and Other Far Eastern Religions; Goddess Worship, Witchcraft and Neo-Paganism; Hinduism, TM and Hare Krishna;* and *Unitarian Universalism*.

Classifying Oneness Pentecostals with these groups implies a spiritual similarity and a common satanic origin. At the least, it seems that the author and publisher discredit all Oneness Pentecostal experiences with God. But how can they venture to make such a judgment with no indication that they have ever attended Oneness Pentecostal worship services or interacted significantly with Oneness Pentecostals on a personal level?

How can they seemingly denigrate all faith, repentance, reception of the Holy Spirit, spiritual gifts, and spiritual fruit among Oneness Pentecostals while apparently accepting the same manifestations among Trinitarian Pentecostals? Have they no concern that they could be ascribing works of the Holy Spirit to Satan, something Jesus warned strongly against in Matthew 12:22-32? In this connection, it is noteworthy that many Oneness Pentecostals first believed on the Lord, repented, or received the Holy Spirit in trinitarian churches and then continued serving the Lord in Oneness churches.

The author's willingness to excoriate Oneness Pentecostals for their doctrine of God is particularly surprising in light of views expressed in his book *God in Three Persons*:[335]

Monarchianism is represented today by the United ("Jesus Only") Pentecostals. . . . As the differences between modalism and pure trinitarianism are rather minute, it is not surprising that a great number of Christians in mainline denominations, including Roman Catholicism, hold a modalistic conception of the Trinity, at least unconsciously.

According to this passage, the Oneness doctrine is a relatively insignificant deviation from "pure trinitarianism" and amounts to nothing more than "a modalistic conception of the Trinity." Why then it is sufficient to make someone a cultist? Is the author now willing to extend this blanket condemnation to the "great number of Christians in mainline denominations" who hold essentially the same view?

Serious Factual Errors
The booklet begins with historical background and statistics. Here we find many egregious errors, such as these examples from pages 8 and 9:

- *Claim*: There have been two "recent schisms" in the United Pentecostal Church International (UPCI). First, in 1986 a "3,000-member" church left.
  Response: The church in question had about one-fifth this number at the time, and there was no schism.
- *Claim*: In 1993 "over 200 pastors" left the UPCI rather than "pledge conformity with the UPCI's 'Holiness Standard.'" The booklet repeats a 1993 prediction that "800 ministers would leave the denomination soon" and comments, "It is not yet disclosed how many defected."
  Response: In the spring of 1993, the UPCI reported that 50 pastors withdrew by missing the final deadline to sign an annual reaffirmation of two sections of the UPCI's Articles of Faith entitled "Fundamental Doctrine" and "Holiness." A total of 120 ministers did not sign the affirmation, representing 1.6 percent of the total of 7,668 in

the United States and Canada in 1992.[336]

- *Claim*: "Oneness Pentecostalism worldwide comprises about 90 denominations in 57 countries."

  Response: The UPCI by itself exists in 137 countries.[337]

- *Claim*: "Estimated affiliated [Oneness Pentecostal] church members worldwide in 1990 totaled about 1.4 million." The cited source is David Barrett (1988).

  Response: The author misread his source, because Barrett listed two categories of Oneness Pentecostals totaling 4,704,960.[338] Moreover, this estimate is over ten years old and incomplete. In June 1997, *Charisma* magazine reported 17 million Oneness believers.[339] The most thorough study of this subject, presented as a master's thesis for Wheaton College in 1998, documents 13.7 million Oneness Pentecostals and estimates a total of 15 to 20 million.[340]

- *Claim*: "About 75 percent (1.03 million) were affiliated with the UPCI."

  Response: In 1997, the UPCI published the following statistics as of midyear: In the U.S. and Canada, there were 8,091 ministers; 3,821 churches (not including daughter works); and a reported Easter attendance of 428,513. In the rest of the world, there were 14,588 ministers; 20,348 churches and preaching points; and 1,908,943 constituents.[341] If we estimate total constituency to be approximately 60 percent more than average attendance, as does the Assemblies of God, then as of 1998 the total worldwide constituency was almost 4 million.

- *Claim*: "The schism of 1993 throws membership figures in doubt from that year forward. Before the schism [1992], worldwide membership was about 1.1 million. About two years later [1994], it decreased to about 1.02 million."

  Response: The booklet provides no source for these

erroneous statistics or the mythical decrease. In 1992 reported Easter attendance in the U.S. and Canada was 384,610, and total foreign constituency was 1,050,973.[342] In 1994 Easter attendance was 400,991, and foreign constituency was 1,623,030.[343] The respective growth rates for this two-year period are 4.3 percent and 54.4 percent.

Numerous other errors exist in the booklet, but these will suffice to demonstrate the extent of the problem. The research is careless, to say the least. The booklet consistently uses outdated and false information that puts Oneness Pentecostals in an unfavorable light when accurate, current information is readily available, thereby revealing that prejudice has significantly compromised the scholarship. The seriousness of the errors calls into question the integrity and trustworthiness of the entire enterprise.

Faulty Presentation of Oneness Doctrine

The bulk of the booklet is devoted to three theological topics: the doctrines of Christ, trinity, and salvation. It contains numerous quotations from various Oneness authors, but never when it gives the "basic statement of the Oneness position" on each topic (pages 11, 25, and 51). In each case, it significantly distorts the Oneness position and thus argues against a straw man.

On *the doctrine of Christ*, it reduces the Oneness teaching concerning the relation of Jesus to the Father and Holy Spirit as follows: "Jesus is the Father and the Holy Spirit." On *the doctrine of God*, the booklet represents Oneness believers as saying "Jesus = the Father = the Holy Spirit." As they stand, these statements are simplistic, incomplete, out of context, and therefore distortions. Here are more accurate statements, the first one from the UPCI Articles of Faith:

Before the incarnation, this one true God manifested Himself in divers ways. In the incarnation, He manifests

Himself in the Son, who walked among men. As He works in the lives of believers, He manifests Himself as the Holy Spirit. . . . This one true God was manifest in the flesh, that is, in His Son Jesus Christ.[344]

The doctrine known as Oneness can be stated in two affirmations: (1) There is one God with no distinction of persons; (2) Jesus Christ is all the fullness of the Godhead incarnate. . . . Jesus is the one God incarnate. . . . Jesus is the Father incarnate. . . . The Holy Spirit is literally the Spirit that was in Jesus Christ. . . . The UPCI teaches that the one God existed as Father and Holy Spirit before His incarnation as Jesus Christ, the Son of God, and that while Jesus walked on earth as God Himself incarnate, the Spirit of God continued to be omnipresent.[345]

We do not believe that the Father *is* the Son, [but] we do believe that the Father is *in* the Son (John 14:10). Since Jesus is the name of the Son of God, both as to His deity as Father and as to His humanity as Son, it is the name of both the Father and the Son.[346]

On **the doctrine of salvation**, the booklet represents Oneness Pentecostals as believing that "water baptism is the indispensable means of regeneration." This statement is false. While Oneness Pentecostals generally agree that water baptism is for the remission of sins, part of the new birth, and part of the experience of New Testament salvation, they believe that regeneration is supremely the work of the Holy Spirit and purchased by the blood of Jesus.

The booklet says the true view is that "God, the agent of regeneration and remission, may elect to use it [baptism] or not. . . . Christ's blood, not water, washes away sins" (pages 57-58). Oneness Pentecostals accept this view. They would argue, however, that while God is sovereign in establishing a plan of salvation and then in judging an individual's fulfillment of that plan, from the human perspective water baptism is not an option but a divine command to obey and a necessary act of faith. The following statements summarize their true views:[347]

> Water baptism is not a magical act; it is without spiritual value unless accompanied by conscious faith and repentance. Baptism is important only because God has ordained it to be so. God could have chosen to remit sin without baptism, but in the New Testament church He has chosen to do so at the moment of baptism. Our actions at baptism do not provide salvation or earn it from God; God alone remits sins based on Christ's atoning death. When we submit to water baptism according to God's plan, God honors our obedient faith and remits our sin.
>
> The Bible describes water and Spirit baptism as two distinct events. . . . The New Testament particularly associates the Holy Spirit with God's work of regeneration and His dwelling in man. . . .
>
> God could have chosen to remit sins without water baptism, but we exceed our authority if we assert that He will or list circumstances under which He will. . . . We should obey the full gospel to the utmost of our understanding and capacity, encourage everyone else to do the same, and leave eternal judgment to God.

For a detailed discussion of the various doctrinal and historical points that the booklet raises, see the following books by David K. Bernard, published by Word Aflame Press: *The Oneness of God, The Oneness View of Jesus Christ, The New Birth,* and *Oneness and Trinity: A.D. 100-300.*

Narrow Presentation of "Historic Orthodoxy"

The booklet's presentation of the "historic, orthodox understanding" of Christ, the trinity, and salvation is surprising in places. Its position on a number of issues is quite controversial, and its appeal to historical authority is inconsistent. Here are some examples:

• *It relies heavily on postbiblical tradition to support the doctrine of the trinity and trinitarian baptism, when Scripture alone should be our doctrinal authority, in practice as well as in theory.* For the "basic statement of the doctrine of the Trinity" it quotes the Athanasian Creed instead of Scripture (pages 42-43). It asserts, "The proper formula for water baptism is triune," and as proof it cites the following authorities: Matthew 28:19, the *Didache*, Justin, Irenaeus, Tertullian, Cyprian, Augustine, and the church historians Sozomen and Socrates (pages 71-72).

• *Ironically, on other subjects the booklet ignores prominent and even majority teachings in church history, thereby falsely portraying its views as the only "historic, orthodox" ones.* For instance, most of the writers it cites as authorities for the baptismal formula taught that baptism effects the remission of sins and is part of the new birth. So taught Justin, Irenaeus, Tertullian, Cyprian, Augustine, and many more.[348] It vehemently denounces as cultic the teaching that baptism is part of the experience of salvation, yet it conveniently omits that throughout history and even today most professing Christians have affirmed this very doctrine, including Roman Catholics, Eastern Orthodox, and Lutherans (the first Protestants). The Nicene Creed affirms "one baptism for the remission of sins," and the framers clearly meant that in the ceremony of water baptism God washes away sins.

If the creeds and the ancient writers known as the church fathers represent so-called historic orthodoxy on the doctrine of God, why do they not equally represent historic orthodoxy on the doctrine of water baptism? The truth is that the author is highly selective in what he deems orthodoxy. To support the doctrine of the trinity he invokes the creeds and fathers and denounces anyone who would deviate from their supposed authority, yet he renounces their authority when it comes to water baptism.

Similarly, the booklet says that the holiness teachings of the UPCI "are strange and legalistic and lack biblical ground" (page 74), yet it ignores the strong teachings of ancient writers such as Tertullian and Cyprian on this very subject. While embracing John Calvin's doctrine of predestination, the booklet says nothing about Calvin's teachings on practical holiness and the laws he promulgated on this subject in Geneva, which were stricter than the voluntary disciplines that the UPCI has adopted in obedience to the Scriptures.

• *The presentation of the doctrine of the trinity suffers from the classic weaknesses of the doctrine, namely tendencies toward tritheism and subordinationism.* Many trinitarians will have problems affirming his views in this area.

For instance, the booklet argues strongly that the Godhead is a substance that subsists in three centers of consciousness. "The term *person* can properly denote self-conscious things other than human beings, such as angels, demons, imaginary self-conscious beings, and each of the three persons of God" (page 47). Interestingly, *A Handbook of Theological Terms* asserts, "No important Christian theologian has argued that there are three self-conscious beings in the godhead,"[349] but this booklet certainly comes close to doing so.

One passage of Scripture seems to give the author particular trouble: "Now the Lord is that Spirit" (II Corinthians 3:17). To avoid saying that "the Spirit" here is the Holy Spirit, he argues that there are at least two divine Spirits, "the Holy Spirit" and "the spirit that is God's substance": "There are many spirits other than the Holy Spirit, both literal (e.g., angels, demons, the spirits of men, and the spirit that is God's substance [John 4:24]) and metaphorical" (page 34).

To avoid saying that "the Lord" in II Corinthians 3:17 is Jesus, he indicates that Jesus and Jehovah are not the same being and that there is more than one divine Lord: "The word

Lord in 1 Corinthians 8:6 denotes Jesus, while in 2 Corinthians 3:17 it may instead denote Jehovah. . . . 1 Cor. 8:6 teaches only that one Lord is in special relationship to believers, not that there is only one lord at all" (page 35, text and note 91).

The author admits a certain subordination in the Godhead, using terms that one could apply to children or to subjects of an absolute monarch: "Although it affirms their equality of nature, trinitarianism acknowledges a subordination of will by the Son to the Father and of the Spirit to the Father and the Son" (p. 39).

• *When presenting the "historic, orthodox" view of salvation, the booklet advocates a strict, five-point Calvinism, including unconditional election and unconditional eternal security.* The implication is that all who do not adhere to this view—and the vast majority of professing Christians do not—are heretical. Here are some surprising statements based on this view:

> "New birth is a gift of God's sovereign grace, independent of the sinner's actions" (page 64).
> "Faith and repentance follow new birth" (page 65).
> "Acts 2:1-4 does not report the disciples' receiving the Spirit" (page 62).

Conclusion
In summary, it appears that the purpose of the booklet is not to engage in serious, respectful dialogue with the goal of ascertaining biblical truth, but to prejudice readers against Oneness Pentecostals by labeling them a cult, presenting a superficial caricature of their teachings, and leaving a false impression that many are abandoning this message while only a few are embracing it. These seem to be desperate tactics motivated by a fear that if people indeed give careful consideration to the message of Oneness Pentecostals, then many will embrace it.

When sinners on the Day of Pentecost cried out to the

apostles, "Men and brethren, what shall we do?" the apostle Peter responded, "Repent, and be baptized every one of you in the name of Jesus Christ for the remission of sins, and ye shall receive the gift of the Holy Ghost" (Acts 2:37-38).

By contrast, the author of this booklet would have responded, in effect, "You can do nothing but hope that God has already chosen you for salvation. If He has, you will be born again before you believe on Jesus Christ and before you repent of your sins. Assuming you are regenerated, then you will automatically believe and repent, and afterwards if you wish you may be baptized, although it is not necessary for the remission of sins. If you do get baptized, you do not need to use the name of Jesus, but you should invoke three divine persons—the Father, the Son, and the Holy Spirit—in accordance with the doctrine of the trinity that will be developed over the next three centuries. Finally, the Spirit will have filled you, although not according to the experience that we have just received and you have just witnessed, for after all, we already had the Spirit anyway. One day you too will realize that you already received the Spirit, and then you may wish to seek for an optional baptism of the Spirit."

The contrast is stark. Let us embrace the message and experience of the apostles.

Appendix E

Major U.S. Pentecostal Organizations[350]

Name U.S. U.S.	World Churches	Constituents[351]	Constituents[352]
Assemblies of God	11,920	2,494,574	30,000,000
Church of God (Cleveland, TN)	6,060	753,230	4,000,000
Church of God in Christ	15,300	5,499,875	6,500,000
Church of God of Prophecy	1,908	76,531	286,848
Full Gospel Fellowship of Churches & Ministers Int'l	650	195,000	195,000
International Church of the Foursquare Gospel	1,832	231,522	2,500,000
International Pentecostal Holiness Church	1,681	170,382	378,538
Pentecostal Assemblies of the World	1,760	450,000	1,000,000
Pentecostal Church of God	1,230	111,900	301,786
United Pentecostal Church International[353] Attendance	3,861	500,000	2,500,000
Inclusive constituency		800,000	4,000,000

Appendix F

Major Jesus Name Pentecostal Organizations[354]

Name	U.S. Churches	U.S. Constituents	World Churches	World Constituents[355]
Apostolic Assembly of the Faith in Christ Jesus	455	100,000	622	116,700
Apostolic Church of Pentecost of Canada			413	42,000
Apostolic Church of the Faith in Christ Jesus (Mexico)			1,723	302,200
Assemblies of the Lord Jesus Christ	339	40,000	426	48,500
Bible Way Church of Our Lord Jesus Christ Worldwide	320	80,000	470	101,000
Church of Our Lord Jesus Christ of the Apostolic Faith	430	120,000	550	140,000
International Ministerial Association	339	34,000	635	63,600
Light of the World (Mexico)			2,900	600,000
Pentecostal Assemblies of the World	1,760	450,000	4,141	1,000,000

Name	U.S. Churches	U.S. Constituents	World Churches	World Constituents[355]
Pentecostal Church of Indonesia			2,500	1,000,000
Spirit of Jesus Church (Japan)	11	2,000	776	420,000
True Jesus Church (China)	40	5,000	12,000	3,300,000
United Pentecostal Church Int'l (attendance)	3,861	500,000	25,268	2,500,000
(inclusive constituency)		800,000		4,000,000
United Pentecostal Church of Colombia	30	3,000	3,543	1,000,000
Voice in the Desert Apostolic Church (Chile)		300		70,000

Appendix G

Major United Pentecostal National Organizations[356]

Country	Churches[357]	Constituents[358]
Brazil	795	47,500
Colombia	769	16,410
Ecuador	526	14,541
El Salvador	967	76,000
Ethiopia	6,847	1,000,638
Guatemala	252	12,000
Haiti	288	24,698
India, Northeast	676	66,885
India, South	441	42,000
Indonesia	420	35,805
Jamaica	218	31,000
Kenya	334	25,164
Liberia	400	20,794
Madagascar	400	40,000
Malawi	245	10,500
Mexico	260	24,024
Myanmar (Burma)	164	13,602
Nicaragua	283	13,000
Pakistan	409	26,949
Papua New Guinea	129	52,000
Peru	317	12,063
Philippines	3,355	164,400
Venezuela	603	60,000

Notes

Chapter 1. The Pentecostal Movement

[1]Ethel E. Goss, *The Winds of God*, rev. ed. (Hazelwood, MO: Word Aflame Press, 1977), 35, 37.

[2]Ibid., 104.

[3]William Seymour, ed., *The Apostolic Faith* (Los Angeles) [hereafter *AF*] 1, no. 1 (September 1906): 1, reprinted in *The Azusa Street Papers* [hereafter *Papers*] (Foley, AL: Together in the Harvest Publications, 1997), 10.

[4]J. L. Hall, "United Pentecostal Church International," Stanley Burgess et al., eds., *Dictionary of Pentecostal and Charismatic Movements* (Grand Rapids: Zondervan, 1988), 860.

[5]Sarah E. Parham, *The Life of Charles F. Parham* (Baxter Springs, KS: Apostolic Faith Bible College, 1930), 107.

[6]Charles F. Parham, *A Voice Crying in the Wilderness*, rev. ed. (Baxter Springs, KS: Apostolic Faith Bible College, 1910), 25-38.

[7]Ibid., 64, 75.

[8]Ibid., 123.

[9]Ibid., 137-38. There is some ambiguity here as to whether those who are sanctified but not baptized with the Holy Ghost will be part of the church and inherit the new heavens. See also Charles Parham, *The Everlasting Gospel* (Baxter Springs, KS: Apostolic Faith Bible College, 1911), 50, 54-55, 62, 82, 98-99, 102, 104.

[10]Charles Parham, *Voice*, 21-24.

[11]Fred Foster, *Their Story: 20th Century Pentecostals* (Hazelwood, MO: Word Aflame Press, 1975), 98, 121.

[12]Frank J. Ewart, *The Phenomenon of Pentecost*, rev. ed. (Hazelwood, MO: Word Aflame Press, 1975), 92.

[13]Frank Bartleman, *Azusa Street* (Plainfield, NJ: Logos International, 1980) (reprint of *How "Pentecost" Came to Los Angeles*, 1925), 54.

[14]For a reproduction, see James L. Tyson, *The Early Pentecostal Revival: History of Twentieth-Century Pentecostals and The Pentecostal Assemblies of the World, 1901-30* (Hazelwood, MO: Word Aflame Press, 1992), 90.

[15]Bartleman, 55-60.

[16]*AF* 1, no. 3 (November 1906): 2, in *Papers*, 18.

[17]*AF* 1, no. 11 (October 1907 to January 1908): 4, in *Papers*, 57.

[18]*AF* 1, no. 1 (September 1906): 2, in *Papers*, 11. (Paragraphs 2-3 are almost identical to the wording of Charles Parham in *Everlasting Gospel*, 13-15.)

[19]Ibid., 1, in *Papers*, 10.

[20]*AF* 1, no. 3 (November 1906): 4, in *Papers*, 21.

[21]*AF* 2, no. 13 (May 1908): 4, in *Papers*, 65.

[22]*AF* 1, no. 5 (January 1907): 2, in *Papers*, 27. See Charles Parham, *Voice*, 123-24, for the same teaching.

[23]*Papers*, 15, 19, 21, 26.

[24]Ibid., 14, 33, 36.

[25]"Church of God in Christ History," *www.cogic.org/history.htm* (Memphis: COGIC, 1999).

[26]*AF* 1, no. 6 (February-March 1907): 7, in *Papers*, 36.

[27]*AF* 1, no. 10 (September 1907): 2, in *Papers*, 51. The text actually says "Acts 2.28" but quotes Acts 2:38.

[28]Cecil M. Robeck, Jr., "Making Sense of Pentecostalism in a Global Context" (paper presented at the annual meeting of the Society for Pentecostal Studies, Evangel University, Springfield, MO, 1999), 10-11, citing "Apostolic Church Stirred by Vision," *Los Angeles Express*, 4 March 1907, 4.

[29]See Daniel Ramirez, "Flor y Canto Apostólico: Preliminary Inquiries into Latino Pentecostal Hymnody" (paper presented at the annual meeting of the Society for Pentecostal Studies, Oakland, CA, 1997), 7; Manuel Gaxiola, "The Spanish-Speaking Oneness Churches in Latin America" (paper presented at the First Occasional Symposium on Aspects of the Oneness Pentecostal Movement, Harvard Divinity School, Cambridge,

MA, 1984), in Jeffrey Gill compilation, 125. See also Manuel Gaxiola, *La Serpiente y la Paloma: Historia, Teología Análisis de la Iglesia Apostólica de la Fe en Cristo Jesús (1914-1994)*, 2ⁿᵈ ed. (Mexico: Libros Pyros, 1994), 117.

[30]James Tinney, "The Significance of Race in the Rise and Development of the Apostolic Pentecostal Movement" (paper presented at the First Occasional Symposium on Aspects of the Oneness Pentecostal Movement, Harvard Divinity School, Cambridge, MA, 1984), in Jeffrey Gill compilation, 60.

[31]*AF* 1, no. 12 (January 1908): 4, in *Papers*, 61.

[32]*AF* 1, no. 10 (September 1907): 2, in *Papers*, 51.

[33]*AF* 2, no. 13 (May 1908): 2, in *Papers*, 63.

[34]*AF* 1, no. 1 (September 1906): 1, in *Papers*, 10.

[35]Charles Parham, "A Note of Warning," *The Apostolic Faith* (Zion City, IL), January 1907, in Sarah Parham, *Life*, 166-170.

[36]The *San Antonio Light* reported on July 24, 1907, that Parham and J. J. Jourdan were arrested for "the commission of an unnatural offense," or sodomy, but that Parham would fight the charge and that he attributed the numerous stories of his alleged immoral conduct to the anti-Pentecostal followers of Dowie in Zion City. For a reproduction of the article, see Tyson, 41.

Sarah Parham wrote, "One day I received word that he had been arrested while preaching but some of his true friends had immediately came [sic] to his release and he continued the meeting. The city attorney told him that he would not have to appear, because he (the attorney) would not even call the case for trial for he 'was satisfied it was all spite work.' I was with him in Texas, at the date set in the indictment, but the case was never called, the prosecuting attorney declaring that there was absolutely no evidence which merited any legal recognition." Sarah Parham, *Life*, 198.

Howard Goss stated about the events in 1907: "The greatest test of our whole lives came, as Satan struck our movement a terrible blow from within. One of our leading ministers fell into an awful sin, which turned out to be only a temporary affair. He repented, confessed, was forgiven, and afterward lived an exemplary life so far as I ever heard." Ethel Goss, 134. W. C. Parkey, a United Pentecostal minister, stated that Goss told him the sin was an act of homosexuality with no evidence that Parham ever became involved with it again. Personal interview, Hazelwood, MO, 8 September 1986.

[37]Ewart, *Phenomenon*, 180. G. Campbell Morgan used the first phrase.

[38]Robert Mapes Anderson, *Vision of the Disinherited: The Making of American Pentecostalism* (New York: Oxford University Press, 1979), 141.

[39]Ethel Goss, 148.

[40]Anderson, 77-78.

Chapter 2. The Finished Work Controversy

[41]William Durham, *Pentecostal Testimony* [hereafter *PT*] 2, no. 3 (August 1912): 3-4.

[42]Ibid., 14.

[43]Ibid. 2, no. 1 (January 1912): 6.

[44]Ibid. 2, no. 3 (August 1912): 6.

[45]Ibid., 10.

[46]Ibid., 5.

[47]Ibid., 12.

[48]Ibid., no. 1 (January 1912): 9; no. 3 (August 1912): 6.

[49]Edith Blumhofer, *The Assemblies of God: A Popular History* (Springfield, MO: Gospel Publishing House, 1985), 43.

[50]E. N. Bell, *Word and Witness*, August 1912, quoted in Edith Blumhofer, "Finished Work of Calvary," *Assemblies of God Heritage*, Fall 1983, 11.

[51]Durham, *PT* 2, no. 3 (August 1912): 10.

[52]Ibid., 3.

[53]Ibid., no. 1 (January 1912): 14; no. 3 (August 1912): 10.

[54]Ibid., no. 1 (January 1912): 1, 13-14.

[55]Ibid., 3, 5.

[56]Ewart, *Phenomenon*, 98.

[57]Gordon Mallory (a United Pentecostal minister), personal interview, Austin, Texas, 14 February 1999. His mother told him that her father, R. E. Sternall, one of the founders of the Pentecostal Assemblies of Canada, was baptized in Jesus' name by William Durham in Chicago.

[58]Durham, *PT* 2, no. 1 (January 1912): 13; *PT* 2, no. 3 (August 1912): 6.

[59]See, for example, James Bowers, "The Neglect and Loss of Sanctification Teaching and Experience in the Church of God" (paper presented at an overseas training conference, 1995).

Chapter 3. The Jesus Name Controversy

[60]David Reed, *Origins and Development of the Theology of Oneness Pentecostalism in the United States* (Ann Arbor, MI: University Microfilms International, 1978), 27-45.

[61]Edith Blumhofer, *The Assemblies of God: A Chapter in the Story of American Pentecostalism* (Springfield, MO: Gospel Publishing House, 1989) 1:238.

[62]Walter J. Hollenweger, *The Pentecostals* (Peabody, MA: Hendrickson Publishers, 1972), 311-12.

[63]Blumhofer, *History*, 30-31.

[64]Gary B. McGee, personal interview, Dallas, TX, 9 November 1990.

[65]Andrew Urshan, *The Life of Andrew Bar David Urshan* (Portland, OR: Apostolic Book Publishers, 1967), 91, 99-102.

[66]Ewart, *Phenomenon*, 106.

[67]Reed, *Origins*, 159.

[68]Ibid., 118.

[69]Franklin Small, *Living Waters*, quoted in Ewart, *Phenomenon*, 141-42.

[70]Ewart, *Phenomenon*, 112-13.

[71]Ibid., 127.

[72]See Anderson, 177; Talmadge L. French, "Oneness Pentecostalism in Global Perspective: The Worldwide Growth and Organizational Expansion of the Oneness Pentecostal

Movement in Historical and Theological Context" (M.A. thesis, Wheaton College Graduate School, Wheaton, IL, 1998), 39.

[73]Oliver F. Fauss, *What God Hath Wrought: The Complete Works of O. F. Fauss* (Hazelwood, MO: Word Aflame Press, 1985), 181-82.

[74]See Ewart, *Phenomenon*, 117, 142-43, 195; Hollenweger, *Pentecostals*, 32, 43 n. 21; and various articles in Burgess et al., eds., *Dictionary*. The evidence for the rebaptism of C. H. Mason is anecdotal; it is widely stated in black Apostolic circles, including the Pentecostal Assemblies of the World and the Pentecostal Churches of the Apostolic Faith. See Tinney, in Gill, 61, 66. According to Robert Spellman, historian for the Church of Our Lord Jesus Christ of the Apostolic Faith, Mason was baptized in 1930 or 1931 in Chicago. When the leaders under him did not accept the message, he did not proclaim it but stayed with his organization. Robert Spellman, telephone interview, 22 January 1999.

[75]Carl O'Guin, personal interview with J. L. Hall and David Bernard, Granite City, Illinois, 18 December 1987.

[76]*Combined Minutes of the General Council of the Assemblies of God* (1915), 7.

[77]Ibid. Interestingly, Justin Martyr advocated the same formula in the second century A.D. It appears that he endorsed a compromise that led the church away from its original baptism solely in the name of Jesus to baptism in the name of Father, Son, and Holy Ghost.

[78]O'Guin interview, 1987. He eventually joined the Pentecostal Church of God and served as pastor of Trinity Tabernacle in Madison, Illinois. He authored *Special Occasion Helps* (Grand Rapids: Baker, 1965).

[79]The 1916 minutes contain the roster roll for the meeting. It consists of 67 people who held credentials and 13 who did not hold credentials but were granted "privileges of the floor." A few Oneness ministers appear on this roster roll, but most do not, including Ewart, Goss, Haywood, and Opperman.

Apparently, those known to have withdrawn were not included. *Combined Minutes of AG* (1916), 15-16.

[80]Foster, 115.

[81]Anderson, 183-84.

[82]Ibid., 189-91.

[83]Ewart, *Phenomenon*, 192.

[84]Reed, *Origins*, 122-23, citing articles in *Weekly Evangel* and *Word and Witness*, both official Assemblies of God publications at the time.

[85]Published in Oliver F. Fauss, *Buy the Truth and Sell It Not* (1965), reprinted in Fauss, *What God Hath Wrought*, 165-74.

Chapter 4. Oneness Pentecostal Organizations

[86]*Minute Book and Ministerial Record of the General Assembly of the Pentecostal Assemblies of the World* (1919), reprinted in Tyson, 293-314.

[87]States *not* represented were Arizona, Delaware, Maine, Nebraska, Nevada, New Hampshire, New Mexico, Rhode Island, South Dakota, Utah, Vermont, and Wyoming. Provinces of Canada represented were British Columbia, Manitoba, Ontario, and Quebec.

[88]Tyson, 195.

[89]R. A. N. Kydd, "Pentecostal Assemblies of Canada," in Burgess et al., eds., *Dictionary*, 695.

[90]Thomas W. Miller, *Canadian Pentecostals: A History of the Pentecostal Assemblies of Canada* (Mississauga, Ontario, Canada: Full Gospel Publishing House, 1994), 16-17.

[91]Foster, 125-26, quoting S. C. McClain.

[92]Tyson, 192-93, 195, 247.

[93]Arthur Clanton and Charles Clanton, *United We Stand*, jubilee ed. (Hazelwood, MO: Word Aflame Press, 1995), 97.

[94]Department of Commerce, Bureau of the Census, *Religious Bodies: 1936* (Washington, D.C.: Government Printing Office, 1941) 2:1323, 1330, 1343; idem, *Religious Bodies: 1926* (1929) 2:1086.

[95]See Irvin J. Cunningham and J. L. Hall, comps., "The United Pentecostal Church North America: Growth Trends and Other Insightful Statistics" (Hazelwood, MO: General Home Missions Division, UPCI, 1996), 1. The figures most commonly quoted—900 churches and 1,838 ministers—apparently come from the first official report, in 1949.

[96]*Financial Reports, United Pentecostal Church International, Year Ending June 30, 1998* (Hazelwood, MO: United Pentecostal Church International, 1998), vi, 71.

[97]Jerry Jones (general secretary-treasurer, UPCI), personal interview, Hazelwood, MO, 16 February 1999.

[98]Gary Erickson (secretary, General Sunday School Division, UPCI), telephone interview, 18 February 1999. Reported Easter attendance for 1997 was 429,066. For 1998 there was not an actual decrease in attendance but only a decrease in reporting. For 1997 and 1998 figures broken down by district, see *Christian Educator*, Fall 1998, 12.

[99]*The Assemblies of God Current Facts* (Springfield, MO: Gospel Publishing House, 1997).

[100]Add 60 percent to estimated Easter attendance of 500,000 and foreign constituency of 2,000,000. The number reported by the Foreign Missions Division for foreign constituency "represents our regular attendance in our churches." *Financial Reports, UPCI* (1986), 77.

[101]French, 100.

[102]There were 3,543 churches in 1988 and 3,861 in 1998. Sources: *Financial Reports, UPCI* for number of churches and Sunday School Division reports for attendance.

[103]Outside the U.S. and Canada, there were 9,803 churches and 787,677 constituents in 1988, and 21,407 churches and 2,000,000 constituents in 1998. Source: *Financial Reports, UPCI* (1988, 1998).

[104]Harry Scism, "Together Winning the Lost," *Pentecostal Herald*, June 1992, 6.

[105]T. F. Tenney, "Ethiopia," *Superintendent's Communi-*

que, April 1999, 2-3. Tenney is the superintendent of the Louisiana District UPCI and had recently returned from attending the crusade.

[106]Gordon Mallory, public statement, Texas Men's Conference, Lufkin, TX, 15 May 1999. Mallory is a UPCI minister and former missionary to the Philippines.

[107]Donald Hanscom, Sr. (coordinator of multicultural ministries, General Home Missions Division, UPCI), personal interview, Hazelwood, MO, 16 February 1999.

[108]Constituency in Ethiopia and Mizoram is based on reports from the Foreign Missions Division. (Source: see Appendix G.) Constituency in New Brunwick and Louisiana is based on 1998 Easter attendance reports of over 5,000 for New Brunswick and 42,438 for Louisiana. (Source: see note 98.) I assumed reporting by 100 percent of churches but added 60 percent to obtain inclusive constituency.

[109]Cornelia Butler Flora, *Pentecostalism in Colombia: Baptism by Fire and Spirit* (Cranbury, NJ: Associated University Presses, 1974); Donald Palmer, *Explosion of People Evangelism* (Chicago: Moody Press, 1974).

[110]French, 133-37. My parents and I met leaders of the True Jesus Church in Korea in the 1970s. The church estimated actual membership in 1995 to be 1,079,000. See "True Jesus Church, Our Church," *www.tjc.org/church/index.shtml* (Los Angeles: TJC, 1999).

[111]See John Yang, *The Essential Doctrines in the Holy Bible*, trans. M. H. Tsai (Taichung City, Taiwan, Republic of China: The General Assembly of the True Jesus Church in Taiwan, 1970).

[112]"True Jesus Church, Our Basic Beliefs," *www.tjc.org/beliefs/index.shtml* (Los Angeles: TJC, 1999).

[113]French, 231. My parents and I are in contact with a group in Manchuria (northern China) founded by an independent Korean minister who was baptized by the UPC of Korea. This Chinese group has translated some of my writings to use

for evangelism and discipleship, and my parents and I have provided ministerial training. As of 1999, the group numbered about 1,500 baptized believers.

[114]French, 138-40. My parents and I met members of the Spirit of Jesus Church in Korea in the 1970s.

[115]David Reed, "The 'New Issue' of 1914: New Revelation or Historical Development?" (paper presented at the annual meeting of the Society for Pentecostal Studies, Wheaton, IL, November 1994), 19-20.

[116]Laurence W. Wood, "The Rediscovery of Pentecost in Early Methodism" (paper presented at the annual meeting of the Society for Pentecostal Studies, Church of God Theological Seminary, Cleveland, TN, March 1998), 2.

[117]John Fletcher, "An Essay on the Doctrine of the New Birth," *Asbury Theological Journal*, Spring 1998, 35-56.

[118]Frank J. Ewart, *The Name and the Book* (1936; repr. Hazelwood, MO: Word Aflame Press, 1987), 47, 55, 57.

[119]Ewart, *Phenomenon*, 114. David Gray, who was trained under Ewart, confirmed that Ewart taught Acts 2:38 as the new birth. David F. Gray, telephone interview, 29 March 1993.

[120]George Farrow, "Letter to Miss Lulu Brumwell," 11 January 1915, in UPCI Historical Center, Hazelwood, MO.

[121]G. T. Haywood, *The Birth of the Spirit in the Days of the Apostles*, 15, 24, 28-29, in *The Life and Writings of Elder G. T. Haywood*, Paul Dugas, comp., (Portland, OR: Apostolic Book Publishers, 1968).

[122]See Tyson, 180.

[123]*Sing unto the Lord* (Hazelwood, MO: Word Aflame Press, 1978), 208. For the date, see Morris Golder, *The Life and Works of Bishop Garfield Thomas Haywood (1880-1931)* (Indianapolis, IN: By the author, 1977), 24.

[124]Fauss, *What God Hath Wrought*, 182.

[125]Ethel Goss, 111-12.

[126]*Combined Minutes of AG* (1915), 9; *Combined Minutes of AG* (1916), 11.

[127]Reed, *Origins*, 170.

[128]A. D. Urshan, *Apostolic Faith Doctrine of the New Birth* (Portland, OR: Apostolic Book Publishers, n.d.), 13.

[129]Clanton, 28.

[130]*Minute Book and Ministerial Record of PAW* (1919), 2, 5, 9-10, reprinted in Tyson, 295, 299-300.

[131]Clanton, 52.

[132]Ibid., 52, 114.

[133]Ibid., 52-53.

[134]Ibid., 135-36.

[135]Stanley W. Chambers, telephone interview, 27 February 1993.

[136]E. J. McClintock, personal interview, Hazelwood, MO, 8 April 1993.

[137]Nathaniel Urshan, personal interview, Austin, TX, 24 April 1999.

[138]David Gray, youth president of the Western District of the PCI at the time of the merger and first youth president of the UPC, estimated that two-thirds of the PCI and practically all the PAJC held this view. (Telephone interview, 29 March 1993.) Since the PAJC was twice the size of the PCI, this number represent about eight-ninths of the merged body. J. L. Hall independently estimated ninety percent. E. J. McClintock said he could not give statistics but agreed that Gray's estimate is reasonable, and he pointed out that most PCI members who did not hold a firm view of the new birth were concentrated in a few districts. Ellis Scism, who served as superintendent of the Northwestern District of the PCI at the time of the merger and who was elected to the same position for the UPC immediately after the merger, stated, "A minority in the PCI did not believe that water baptism or a tongues experience was essential to salvation." Ellis Scism with Stanley Scism, *Northwest Passage: The Early Years of Ellis Scism* (Hazelwood, MO: Word Aflame Press, 1994), 227. Scism would not have called this group a "minority" unless it was clearly less than one-half of the PCI, and thus probably no more than one-third or one-fourth. His district

was a major area of concentration for this minority.

[139]See Clanton, 143-44; Foster, 143-44.

[140]David F. Gray, telephone interview, 29 March 1993.

[141]J. L. Hall, personal interview, Hazelwood, MO, 28 October 1993.

[142]*Manual* (Hazelwood, MO: United Pentecostal Church International, 1999), 22. These two paragraphs compose a section of the UPCI's Articles of Faith entitled "Fundamental Doctrine." It appears every month in the *Pentecostal Herald*, the official organ of the UPCI.

[143]David Reed, "The 'New Issue' of 1914" (paper presented at the annual meeting of the Society for Pentecostal Studies, 1994), 8. For *The Christian Evangel*, see Tyson, 165.

[144]*Combined Minutes of AG* (1914), 4-5; Miller, 116.

[145]Frederick Bruner, *A Theology of the Holy Spirit: The Pentecostal Experience and the New Testament Witness* (Grand Rapids: Eerdmans, 1970), 166; James D. G. Dunn, *Baptism in the Holy Spirit: A Re-examination of the New Testament Teaching on the Gift of the Spirit in Relation to Pentecostalism Today* (London: SCM, 1970), 91; Leighton Ford, "The 'Finger of God' in Evangelism," in J. I. Packer and Paul Fromer, eds., *The Best in Theology, Vol. 1* (Carol Stream, IL: Christianity Today, 1987), 292-93; J. David Pawson, *The Normal Christian Birth* (London: Hodder & Stoughton, 1989), 13, 143-46; Kilian McDonnell and George Montague, eds., *Fanning the Flame* (Collegeville, MN: The Liturgical Press, 1991), 14.

[146]Gordon D. Fee, *God's Empowering Presence: The Holy Spirit in the Letters of Paul* (Peabody, MA: Hendrickson, 1994), 863-64.

[147]Ewart, *Phenomenon*, 200-2.

[148]G. T. Haywood, *Birth of the Spirit*, in *Life and Writings*, 10, 12, 21. Parham said that at conversion people were conceived but at sanctification they were born again and entered the church. *Everlasting Gospel*, 10-11, 102.

[149]Urshan, *Life*, 9, 88, 116, 151-52, 175-77.

[150]Reed, *Origins*, 354.

Chapter 5. Trinitarian Pentecostal Organizations

[151]Worldwide statistics are from Preston D. Hunter, "Adherents.com," *www.adherents.com* (Dallas, 1999). U.S. statistics are from Kenneth Bedell, ed., *Yearbook of American & Canadian Churches 1998* (Nashville: Abingdon, 1998), reporting for 1996; Department of Commerce, Bureau of the Census, *Religious Bodies: 1916* (Washington, D.C.: Government Printing Office, 1919); idem, *Religious Bodies: 1926* (1929); idem, *Religious Bodies: 1936* (1941). A few figures are from Burgess et al., eds., *Dictionary*.

[152]James P. Bowers, "The Neglect and Loss of Sanctification Teaching and Experience in the Church of God" (paper presented at an overseas training conference, 1995), 21-23.

[153]C. Peter Wagner, "Church Growth," in Burgess et al., eds., *Dictionary*, 191.

[154]"Church of God in Christ Beliefs," *www.cogic/believe.htm* and "Church of God in Christ History" *www.cogic/history.htm* (Memphis: COGIC, 1999).

[155]C. P. Jones, "Church of God in Christ," Burgess et al., eds., *Dictionary*, 205.

[156]*Church of God History and Heritage*, Summer 1998, 5.

[157]Ibid., 6; Hollenweger, *Pentecostals*, 517.

[158]H. Vinson Synan, "International Pentecostal Holiness Church," in Burgess et al., eds., *Dictionary*, 467.

[159]"International Pentecostal Holiness Church Articles of Faith," *www.iphc.org/docs/artfaith.html* (Oklahoma City: IPHC, 1999).

[160]David Barrett, "Statistics, Global," in Burgess et al., eds., *Dictionary*, 824.

[161]*The Assemblies of God Current Facts* (Springfield, MO: Gospel Publishing House, 1997).

[162]*Combined Minutes of AG* (1916), 10-13.

[163]"Assemblies of God Statement of Fundamental Truths," *www.ag.org/info/16truths* (Springfield, MO: AG, 1999).

[164]"Assemblies of God Position Papers," *www.ag.org/info/ position* (Springfield, MO: AG, 1999).

[165]Vinson Synan, *The Holiness-Pentecostal Tradition: Charismatic Movements in the Twentieth Century* (Grand Rapids: Eerdmans, 1997), 203.

[166]Hunter, citing Patrick Johnstone, *The Church Is Bigger Than You Think* (Gerrards Cross, Buckinghamshire, U.K.: World Evangelism Crusade).

[167]C. E. Jones, "Hoover, Willis Collins," in Burgess et al., eds., *Dictionary*, 445.

[168]Steven J. Land, *Pentecostal Spirituality: A Passion for the Kingdom* (Sheffield, U.K.: Sheffield Academic Press, 1994), 101-4.

[169]Charles Parham, *Voice*, 42, 53-60.

[170]Ethel Goss indicated that jewelry was not a concern for the early followers of Parham until Holiness preachers joined the movement. Ethel Goss, 69. Of course, Holiness preachers and members were an integral part from the beginning.

[171]Edith Blumhofer, "Apostolic Faith Mission (Portland, Ore.)," in Burgess et al., eds., *Dictionary*, 18.

[172]"Church of God Relaxes Rules, OKs Makeup, Jewelry," *Houston Chronicle*, August 1988.

[173]See Harold D. Hunter, "Church of God of Prophecy, The," in Burgess et al., eds., *Dictionary*, 209.

[174]Blumhofer, *History*, 133-35.

[175]Carl O'Guin, personal interview, Granite City, IL, 18 December 1987.

[176]*Call to Holiness* 1, no. 1 (November 1961): 4; no. 4 (October 1963): 1.

[177]*Manual* (Hazelwood, MO: United Pentecostal Church International, 1999), 23-24, 132-50.

[178]Hollenweger, *Pentecostals*, 402.

[179]*Combined Minutes of AG* (1915), 11-12; Department of

Commerce, *Statistics: 1926* 2:1090; *Manual* (UPCI, 1999), 24-25.

[180]Early Pentecostal organizations reported almost twice as many women members as men. In 1936, for instance, the PAJC reported 5,777 males and 10,030 females; the PCI reported 3,566 males and 6,093 females; and the PAW had 1,901 males and 3,537 females. Department of Commerce, *Statistics: 1936* 2:1323, 1330, 1343.

[181]See Bartley J. Linder, *The "Godhead," How Many?* (Illumination Press: Kerrville, TX, 1997).

[182]Land, 47.

[183]David Barrett, "Statistics, Global," Burgess et al., eds., *Dictionary*, 820. AG officials say the number for their group is 50 percent. *Charisma*, October 1993.

[184]See Daniel Butler, *The Last Generation of Truth* (Hazelwood, MO: Word Aflame Press, 1989).

[185]See Anderson.

[186]Ibid., 149.

[187]Walter J. Hollenweger, *Pentecostalism: Origins and Development Worldwide* (Peabody, MA: Hendrickson, 1997), 192-93.

[188]Wayne E. Warner, "Pentecostal Fellowship of North America," Burgess et al., eds., *Dictionary*, 704.

[189]Land, 29.

[190]No general survey has been taken. This statistic was valid for New Life United Pentecostal Church of Austin, Texas, in January 1999, when it had about 250 people ages ten or older in regular attendance. The ten percent (or less) who had not spoken in tongues were mostly newcomers or people who did not seek the Spirit. Conversations with other pastors around the country indicated that this statistic corresponded closely to their situation also.

[191]AG membership (not constituency) is about 1,400,000, and if 35 percent have received the Holy Ghost, then the Spirit-filled number is about 490,000. UPCI attendance is about

500,000. Assuming 70 percent are ages 10 or older (for New Life United Pentecostal Church of Austin, Texas, the percentage is 75), and assuming 90 percent of these have spoken in tongues, then the Spirit-filled number would be about 315,000.

[192]Both statistics are from Manuel J. Gaxiola, public statement at the annual meeting of the Society for Pentecostal Studies, Springfield, MO, 13 March 1999.

[193]Vinson Synan, personal conversation, Cleveland, TN, March 1998. Synan is dean of the School of Divinity at Regent University and a former assistant general superintendent of the International Pentecostal Holiness Church. He also made similar comments at the Louisiana District UPCI camp meeting, Tioga, LA, July 1997.

[194]Raymond Cox, personal conversation, Springfield, MO, 12 March 1999. Cox is a Foursquare Gospel minister who was converted under Aimee Semple McPherson in 1936 and attended Angelus Temple for many years.

[195]Paul Elbert, personal conversation, Springfield, MO, 11 March 1999. Elbert is a professor at Lee University, a Church of God liberal arts university in Cleveland, Tennessee.

Chapter 6. Liberalism and Neo-Orthodoxy

[196]See David K. Bernard, *God's Infallible Word* (Hazelwood, MO: Word Aflame Press, 1992), 42-46.

[197]James Buswell, Jr., *A Systematic Theology of the Christian Religion* (Grand Rapids: Zondervan, 1980) 1:123.

[198]Tony Lane, *Harper's Concise Book of Christian Faith* (New York: Harper & Row, 1984), 188.

[199]Karl Barth, *Church Dogmatics*, trans. G. W. Bromiley (Edinburgh: T. & T. Clark, 1969) 3:4:479-80; 2:2:52-53; 2:1:261; 4:2:50-51, 128.

[200]Ibid. 2:1:26

[201]Ibid. 4:4:85-86.

[202]Ibid., 75, 91-94.

[203]Ibid., 96-99.

[204]Lane, 200.

[205]Tim Dowley et al., eds., *Eerdmans' Handbook to the History of the Church* (Grand Rapids: Eerdmans, 1977), 598.

[206]Dietrich Bonhoeffer, *The Cost of Discipleship*, rev. ed. (New York: Macmillan, 1959), 47.

[207]Ibid., 61, 69, 72, emphasis in original.

[208]See, for example, Emil Brunner, *The Christian Doctrine of God* (Philadelphia: Westminster Press, 1949).

[209]Victoria Combe, "Methodists to Worship 'God the Mother,'" *London Daily Telegraph*, 18 February 1999.

[210]Sandy Gess, "Worship and Rituals in a Feminist Key," *www.hooked.net/~sgess/rituals.html* (San Francisco: Weave of Faith, 1999).

[211]"World Council of Churches, Who Are We?," *wcc-coe.org/wcc/who/cuv-e.html#self-understanding* (Geneva, Switzerland: WCC, 1999).

[212]Kenneth S. Kantzer and V. Gilbert Beers, "Winds of Change in the World Council?" *Christianity Today*, 20 April 1984, 10.

[213]Ibid., 11-12, emphasis in original.

[214]Ibid., 15.

[215]Tom Finger, "Orthodox, Evangelicals Push for WCC Reforms," *Christianity Today*, 11 January 1999, 22.

[216]Max Thurian, ed., *Churches Respond to BEM: Official Responses to the "Baptism, Eucharist and Ministry" Text*, vol 2., Faith and Order Paper 132 (Geneva: World Council of Churches, 1986).

[217]Ibid., Faith and Order Paper 143 (1988).

[218]Finger, *Christianity Today*, 11 January 1999, 22.

[219]"National Council of Churches, NCC Member Communions," *ncccusa.org/members/index.html* (New York: NCCC, 1999).

[220]Leonard Ravenhill, *Revival God's Way* (Minneapolis: Bethany House, 1983), 145-46, citing *Christ for the Nations*, May 1982.

[221]*Christianity Today*, 1988.

[222]*St. Louis Post-Dispatch*, 17 December 1989.

[223]*Time*, 12 February 1990.

[224]*Christianity Today*, 7 October 1988.

[225]*Christianity Today*, 19 February 1990.

[226]Bill Lindelof, "Lesbian 'Blessing' Rekindles Tensions," *Christianity Today*, 1 March 1999, 17.

[227]Richard Ostling, "Those Mainline Blues," *Time*, 22 May 1989, 94.

Chapter 7. Fundamentalism and Evangelicalism

[228]C. M. Robeck, Jr. "National Association of Evangelicals," Burgess et al., eds., *Dictionary*, 634.

[229]Mark A. Noll, "Scopes Trial," in Walter A. Elwell, ed., *Evangelical Dictionary of Theology* (Grand Rapids: Baker, 1984), 989.

[230]For a thorough discussion of inspiration, inerrancy, transmission, and text of Scripture, see David K. Bernard, *God's Infallible Word* (Hazelwood, MO: Word Aflame Press, 1992).

[231]"American Council of Christian Churches, Introduction," *www.amcouncilcc.org/introduc.htm* (Bethlehem, PA: ACCC, 1999).

[232]"American Council of Christian Churches, Constitution" *www.amcouncilcc.org/constitu.htm* (Bethlehem, PA: ACCC, 1999).

[233]Ewart, *Phenomenon*, 98, 180.

[234]Reuben A. Torrey, *The Baptism with the Holy Spirit* (New York: Fleming H. Revell, 1895), 18.

[235]Ewart, *Phenomenon*, 180, 182.

[236]See David K. Bernard, "Dispensationalism and Oneness Pentecostal Theology," in *Symposium on Oneness Pentecostalism 1988 and 1990* (Hazelwood, MO: Word Aflame Press, 1990).

[237]See, for example, Frank Boyd, *Ages and Dispensations*

(Springfield, MO: Gospel Publishing House, 1955). Boyd, an Assemblies of God teacher, used Scofield's definition of "dispensation" and his seven ages but rejected his definition of the kingdom of heaven and the postponed-kingdom theory.

[238]R. V. Pierard, "Evangelicalism," in Elwell, ed., *Evangelical Dictionary*, 379.

[239]"The National Association of Evangelicals, About NAE," *www.nae.net/about.htm* (Carol Stream, IL: NAE, 1999).

[240]Christine Gardner, "Hungry for God," *Christianity Today*, 5 April 1999, 33.

[241]"The National Association of Evangelicals, Ministry, Statement of Faith," *www.nae.net/ministry-statement.html* (Carol Stream, IL: NAE, 1999).

[242]Frank Stagg, *The Holy Spirit Today* (Nashville: Broadman, 1973), 11-18. In a telephone conversation with J. L. Hall, Stagg explained that as a New Testament professor, he derived his views on the Godhead from the New Testament instead of the creeds. He further acknowledged that his views were the same as those of T. F. Tenney, United Pentecostal district superintendent of Louisiana. Interestingly, Stagg had baptized Tenney as a boy in the Baptist church, before he converted to the United Pentecostal Church.

[243]See James D. G. Dunn, *Christology*, vol. 1 of *The Christ and The Spirit* (Grand Rapids: Eerdmans, 1998), 367, 371; Oscar Cullmann, *The Christology of the New Testament* (London: SCM Press, 1963), 265-66.

[244]W. A. Criswell, *Expository Sermons on Revelation* (Grand Rapids: Zondervan, 1961-66) 1:145-46.

[245]*Christianity Today*, 17 March 1989.

[246]Charles C. Ryrie, *So Great Salvation: What It Means to Believe in Jesus Christ* (1989), emphasis in original.

[247]Zane Hodges, *Absolutely Free!* (1989).

[248]*Christianity Today*, 18 March 1988.

[249]*Christianity Today*, 5 March 1990.

[250]See J. L. Hall, *The United Pentecostal Church and the*

Evangelical Movement (Hazelwood, MO: Word Aflame Press, 1990).

[251]Irving Hexham, "Cults," in Elwell, ed., 289.

Chapter 8. Roman Catholicism and Eastern Orthodoxy

[252]Lane, 213.

[253]Ibid., 213-14.

[254]Kenneth Woodward, "Hail, Mary," *Newsweek*, 25 August 1997, 49.

[255]Pope Paul VI, promulgator, *Dogmatic Constitution on the Church (Lumen Gentium)*, 21 November 1964, 2:15, in "The Holy See, Archive, Documents of the Vatican II Council, Constitutions" [hereafter "Holy See"], *www.vatican.va/archive/par_en.htm* (Vatican City: Roman Catholic Church, 1999).

[256]Ibid., 2:14, 16.

[257]Idem, *Dogmatic Constitution on Divine Revelation (Dei Verbum)*, 18 November 1965, 2:10, in "Holy See."

[258]Lane, 218.

[259]Ibid., 219.

[260]Anastasia Toufexis, "What to Do When Priests Stray," *Time*, 24 September 1990, 79.

[261]See, for example, *Church Law & Tax Report*, 13, no. 2 (March-April 1999): 18-29. In this issue, of nine reported cases of sexual misconduct by clergy, eight involved Roman Catholic priests.

[262]"Healer's Trials," *Time*, 25 October 1982.

[263]*Jackson Daily News*, 7 August 1983.

[264]"Pope attacks pardon 'directly from God,'" *Jackson Daily News*, 11 December 1984.

[265]"Christmas Gift," *Time*, 30 December 1985, 71.

[266]Richard Ostling, "Blueprint for Union," *Time*, 22 March 1982, 60.

[267]Religious News Service, "Joint Commission Agrees on Meaning of Salvation," *Christianity Today*, 20 March 1987, 61.

[268]"Lutherans and Catholics Reach Some Surprising

Agreements," *Christianity Today*, 16 December 1983, 11.

[269]"Perspectives on Koinonia: Final Report of the International Roman Catholic/Pentecostal Dialogue (1985-1989)," *Pneuma: The Journal of the Society for Pentecostal Studies* 12, no. 2 (Fall 1990): 128.

[270]Demetrios J. Constantelos, *An Old Faith for Modern Man*, 2nd ed. (New York: Greek Orthodox Diocese, 1964), 17-20.

Chapter 9. The Healing Revival and the Latter Rain Movement

[271]See David K. Bernard, *Spiritual Gifts* (Hazelwood, MO: Word Aflame Press, 1997), chapters 9-11.

[272]He rejected the idea of three persons in the Godhead and the idea of an eternal Son. He held that Jesus is the fullness of the Godhead incarnate. However, he believed that the humanity of Jesus was a special divine creation, with Mary serving as the "incubator" only and not the biological mother.

[273]Hollenweger, *Pentecostals*, 354-55.

[274]Nathaniel Urshan, personal interview, Austin, TX, 24 April 1999.

[275]"The William Branham Memorial Service," *www.biblebelievers.org/wbmtos.htm* (Mt. Pearl, Newfoundland, Canada: Bible Believers Association, 1999), emphasis in original.

[276]French, 222.

[277]P. G. Chappell, "Roberts, Granville Oral," in Burgess et al., eds., *Dictionary*, 760.

[278]Steven Lawson, "Charismatics Rally Behind Roberts," *Charisma*, September 1987, 64.

[279]D. J. Wilson, "Kuhlman, Kathryn," in Burgess et al., eds., *Dictionary*, 530, citing Jamie Buckingham, *Daughter of Destiny: Kathryn Kuhlman . . . Her Story* (1976), 247.

[280]Nathaniel Urshan (UPCI general superintendent), personal interview, Austin, TX, 24 April 1999. At the merger of the PCI and PAJC to form the UPC, PCI ministers believed that

the organization owned a publishing house and that it would now belong to the UPC. They soon discovered, however, that the publishing house was held in the name of Kidson, who was PCI secretary, and he did not allow the UPC to take possession.

[281]Quoted in R. M. Riss, "Latter Rain Movement," in Burgess et al., eds., *Dictionary*, 534, emphasis in original.

[282]Clanton, 189.

10. The Charismatic Movement

[283]Steven Lawson, "Robert Walker Reflects upon 50 Years of Christian Life" (interview), *Charisma*, July 1989.

[284]F. A. Sullivan, "Catholic Charismatic Renewal," in Burgess et al., eds., *Dictionary*, 112.

[285]Steven Lawson, "The Big Charismatic Get-Together," *Charisma*, September 1987, 56.

[286]Julia Duin, "The Holy Spirit and World Evangelization," *Christianity Today*, 4 September 1987, 44.

[287]James Beverley, "Dental Miracle Reports Draw Criticism," *Christianity Today*, 24 May 1999, 17.

[288]R. M. Riss, "Hagin, Kenneth E.," in Burgess et al., eds., *Dictionary*, 345.

[289]See D. R. McConnell, *A Different Gospel: A Historical and Biblical Analysis of the Modern Faith Movement* (Peabody, MA: Hendrickson, 1988), 3-14.

[290]Dennis Bennett, "A Second Look at the Third Wave," *Ministries Today*, July/August 1989, 8.

[291]David Barrett, "Statistics, Global," in Burgess et al., eds., *Dictionary*, 816.

[292]J. I. Packer, "Piety on Fire," *Christianity Today*, 12 May 1989, 18.

[293]Stephen Strang, "Pentecostals at a Crossroads," *Charisma*, November 1998, 130.

[294]Peter Hocken, "Charismatic Movement," in Burgess et al, eds., *Dictionary*, 155-56.

[295]Ibid., 156-58.

[296]Harald Bredesen, *Charisma*, August 1994.

[297]Kilian McDonnell and George Montague, *Christian Initiation and Baptism in the Holy Spirit: Evidence from the First Eight Centuries* (Collegeville, MN: Liturgical Press, 1991), 40.

[298]J. David Pawson, *The Normal Christian Birth* (London: Hodder & Stoughton, 1989), 73-76.

[299]John Wimber, "John Wimber Calls It Power Evangelism," *Charisma*, September 1985, 35.

[300]McDonnell and Montague, *Christian Initiation*, 41.

[301]Charles Hunter, "Receiving the Baptism with the Holy Spirit," *Charisma*, July 1989, 54.

[302]Larry Christenson, *The Charismatic Renewal among Lutherans* (Minneapolis: International Lutheran Renewal Center, 1976).

[303]Pawson, 4-5, 187-88, 294-98.

[304]McDonnell and Montague, *Christian Initiation*, 30, 35.

[305]The leader is Mike Velarde of the El Shaddai movement, a Charismatic group that began in the Roman Catholic Church. Gordon Mallory, public statement, Lufkin, TX, 15 May 1999. Mallory is a United Pentecostal minister and former missionary to the Philippines.

[306]Peter Kuzmic, personal interview, Dallas, TX, 8 November 1990.

[307]Paul Thigpen, "Praise Him with the Dance," *Charisma*, March 1989, 52.

[308]See Dave Hunt and T. A. McMahon, *The Seduction of Christianity: Spiritual Discernment in the Last Days* (Eugene, OR: Harvest House Publishers, 1985); McConnell, *A Different Gospel*. Sources of specific quotes are as follows: Copeland 1—Hunt, 84; Treat—Hunt, 83; Hagin 1—McConnell, 122; Paulk—Hunt, 219; Tilton—Hunt, 220; Hagin 2—McConnell, 134, 142; Copeland 2—McConnell, 141, 171, 173; Lea—Larry Lea, *Charisma*, October 1989. Emphasis is original.

[309]*Charisma*, April 1990.

[310]Earl Paulk.

[311]*Prophetic Ministries News* 3, no. 3 (Fall 1989): 2, 6-7, 15.

[312]Hunt, 101.

[313]*Charisma*, February 1990.

[314]See H. Wayne House and Thomas D. Ice, *Dominion Theology, Blessing or Curse? An Analysis of Christian Reconstructionism* (Portland, OR: Multnomah, 1988).

[315]See "Assemblies of God Position Papers," *www.ag.org/info/position* (Springfield, MO: AG, 1999).

[316]Lee Grady, "The Other Pentecostals," *Charisma*, June 1997, 62-68.

Chapter 11. Christianity Today

[317]Preston D. Hunter, *www.adherents.com* (Dallas, 1999).

[318]"Pentecostals Celebrate the Future," *Advance*, November 1998, 10. See also Stephen Strang, "Pentecostals at a Crossroads," *Charisma*, November 1998, 130.

[319]"Pentecostals: World Growth at 19 Million a Year," *Christianity Today*, 16 November 1998.

[320]David Barrett, "Statistics, Global," in Burgess et al., eds., *Dictionary*, 810-30.

[321]Grant Wacker, "America's Pentecostals: Who They Are," *Christianity Today*, 16 October 1987, 16.

[322]C. Peter Wagner, "Church Growth," in Burgess et al., eds., *Dictionary*, 193; Peter Hocken, "The Charismatic Movement in the United States," *Pneuma: The Journal of the Society for Pentecostal Studies* 16, no. 2 (Fall 1994): 192-93.

[323]Barrett, in Burgess et al., eds., *Dictionary*, 810-30.

[324]French, 79.

[325]If two-thirds of the inclusive constituency of 20 million Oneness Pentecostals are Spirit-filled, then that total is over 13 million, or about 15 percent of the 90 million people whom we estimated have received the Holy Ghost.

[326]J. Gordon Melton, *The Encyclopedia of American Religions* (Wilmington, NC: McGrath, 1978).

[327]Barna Research Group. In 1994, a U.S. Congressional committee estimated that there were 340,000 churches. *Church Law & Tax Report*, September-October 1994.

[328]Dowley, 619, says it is 25 percent.

[329]*Charisma*, December 1993.

[330]Tim Ferguson with Josephine Lee, "Spiritual Reality," *Forbes*, 27 January 1997.

[331]Charisma, *December* 1993, citing Carl George.

[332]C. Peter Wagner, in Burgess et al., eds., *Dictionary*, 193.

[333]Ibid., 193-94.

[334]Ibid., 194-95.

Appendix D. Response to a Cult Hunter

[335]E. Calvin Beisner, *God in Three Persons* (Wheaton, IL: Tyndale House Publishers, 1984), 18.

[336]"Ministers Who Have Not Signed Affirmation," unpublished list compiled by UPCI Church Administration, 20 May 1993. See also *Financial Reports, UPCI, June 30, 1992*, vi.

[337]U.S., Canada, and 135 mission fields. *See Financial Reports, UPCI, June 30, 1997*, 71.

[338]David Barrett, "Statistics, Global," in Burgess et al., eds., *Dictionary*, 813.

[339]J. Lee Grady, "The Other Pentecostals," *Charisma*, June 1997, 63.

[340]French, 79.

[341]*Financial Reports, UPCI, June 30, 1997*, vi, 71, 84.

[342]*Financial Reports, UPCI, June 30, 1992*, 75, 90.

[343]*Financial Reports, UPCI, June 30, 1994*, 77, 93.

[344]*Manual* (UPCI, 1999), 20.

[345]David K. Bernard, *The Oneness View of Jesus Christ* (Hazelwood, MO: Word Aflame Press, 1994), 9, 12-13, 141.

[346]David K. Bernard, *The Oneness of God* (Hazelwood, MO: Word Aflame Press, 1983), 127.

[347]David K. Bernard, *The New Birth* (Hazelwood, MO: Word Aflame Press, 1984), 131, 152, 187, 307.

[348]For documentation, see Bernard, *New Birth*, 261-64.

[349]Van Harvey, *A Handbook of Theological Terms* (New York: Macmillan, 1964), 246.

Appendix E. Major U.S. Pentecostal Organizations

[350']This list consists of all groups that teach the baptism of the Holy Spirit with the sign of speaking in tongues and that report at least 500 churches and 50,000 constituents in the U.S., using the latest available statistics, mostly from 1997.

[351]Source: Eileen Lindner, ed., *Yearbook of American & Canadian Churches 1999.* (Nashville: Abingdon, 1999), 337-51. Constituency is typically more inclusive than membership or regular attendance. It includes all who identify with the church. These numbers are the best for comparing with mainline denominations, who typically count all who have ever been baptized. They are estimates, however, and in some cases they may be unrealistically high. The most accurate gauge of an organization's strength is probably the number of churches. One can evaluate and compare the reliability of the number reported for constituents by calculating the number of constituents per church. For example, the numbers for the Church of God in Christ seem overstated, while the numbers for the Church of God of Prophecy seem understated.

[352]Source: Preston D. Hunter, *www.adherents.com* (Dallas, 1999).

[353]See pages 99-100.

Appendix F. Major Jesus Name Pentecostal Organizations

[354']This list consists of all groups that teach water baptism in the name of Jesus Christ and that report at least 300 churches and 40,000 constituents. We should note that the International Ministerial Association is a Latter Rain group; the Light of the World has an aberrant and exclusive doctrine of the church and a vague doctrine of God; and the Pentecostal Church of Indonesia is predominantly trinitarian in its doctrine of God. Source for statistics: Talmadge French, "Oneness Pentecostalism in Global Perspective," M.A. thesis, Wheaton College Graduate School, Wheaton, IL, 1998. For the United Pentecostal Church International, see pages 99-100.

[355]Constituency is typically more inclusive than membership or regular attendance. It includes all who identify with the church. These numbers are the best for comparing with mainline denominations, who typically count all who have ever been baptized. They are estimates, however, and in some cases they may be unrealistically high. The most accurate gauge of an organization's strength is probably the number of churches. One can evaluate and compare the reliability of the number reported for constituents by calculating the number of constituents per church.

Appendix G. Major United Pentecostal National Organizations

[356]This list consists of all national churches and mission fields reporting over 10,000 constituents. Source: "1998 Annual Field Report" (Hazelwood, MO: Foreign Missions Division, United Pentecostal Church International), 17 September 1998. For El Salvador and Mexico, see *Pentecostal Herald*, June 1999, 8.

[357]Number of churches and preaching points.

[358]In most cases, this number represents actual attendance. Add 60 percent to obtain estimated inclusive constituency. (See page 100.) In Ethiopia, however, it represents all who have been baptized. Teklemariam Gezahagne (superintendent), personal interview, Addis Ababa, Ethiopia, April 1997.

Select Bibliography

1. Primary Sources: Pentecostal History and Theology

Azusa Street Papers, The. Foley, AL: Together in the Harvest Publications, 1997.

Bartleman, Frank. *Azusa Street*. Plainfield, NJ: Logos International, 1980. Reprint of *How "Pentecost" Came to Los Angeles*, 1925.

Booth-Clibborn, William E., comp. *A Call to the Dust and Ashes*. St. Paul, MN: By the compiler, 1922.

Combined Minutes of the General Council of the Assemblies of God in the United States of America, Canada and Foreign Lands. Springfield, MO: Assemblies of God, 1914-1917.

Dayton, Donald, et al., eds. *"The Higher Christian Life": Sources for the Study of the Holiness, Pentecostal and Keswick Movements*. 50 vols. New York: Garland, 1984– .

Durham, William. *Pentecostal Testimony*. January and August 1912 issues.

Ewart, Frank J. *The Name and the Book*. 1936. Reprint, Hazelwood, MO: Word Aflame Press, 1986.

———. *The Phenomenon of Pentecost*. 1947. Rev. ed. Hazelwood, MO: Word Aflame Press, 1975.

Fauss, Oliver F. *What God Hath Wrought: The Complete Works of O. F. Fauss*. Hazelwood, MO: Word Aflame Press, 1985.

Financial Reports, United Pentecostal Church International. Hazelwood, MO: United Pentecostal Church International, 1981-1998.

Goss, Ethel. *The Winds of God*. Rev. ed. Hazelwood, MO: Word Aflame Press, 1977.

Hall, J. L., and David K. Bernard, eds. *Doctrines of the Bible*. Hazelwood, MO: Word Aflame Press, 1993.

Haywood, G. T. *The Life and Writings of Elder G. T. Haywood*. Compiled by Paul Dugas. Portland, OR:

Apostolic Book Publishers, 1968.

Horton, Stanley M., ed. *Systematic Theology: A Pentecostal Perspective*. Springfield, MO: Gospel Publishing House, 1994.

McDonnell, Kilian, and George Montague. *Christian Initiation and Baptism in the Holy Spirit: Evidence from the First Eight Centuries*. Collegeville, MN: Liturgical Press, 1991.

Menzies, William M., and Stanley M. Horton. *Bible Doctrines: A Pentecostal Perspective*. Springfield, MO: Gospel Publishing House, 1993.

Minute Book and Ministerial Record of the General Assembly of the Pentecostal Assemblies of the World. Indianapolis: Pentecostal Assemblies of the World, 1919.

Parham, Charles F. *A Voice Crying in the Wilderness*. 1902. Rev. ed. Baxter Springs, KS: Apostolic Faith Bible College, 1910.

————. *The Everlasting Gospel*. Baxter Springs, KS: Apostolic Faith Bible College, 1911.

Parham, Sarah E. *The Life of Charles F. Parham*. Baxter Springs, KS: Apostolic Faith Bible College, 1930.

Urshan, Andrew D. *Apostolic Faith Doctrine of the New Birth*. Portland, OR: Apostolic Book Publishers, n.d.

————. *The Life of Andrew Bar David Urshan*. Portland, OR: Apostolic Book Publishers, 1967.

Yang, John. *The Essential Doctrines in the Holy Bible*. Translated by M. H. Tsai. Taichung City, Taiwan, Republic of China: The General Assembly of the True Jesus Church in Taiwan, 1970.

2. Primary Sources: General History and Theology

Barth, Karl. *Church Dogmatics*. Translated by G. W. Bromiley. Edinburgh: T. & T. Clark, 1969. (See also edition of selected readings. New York: Harper and Row, 1971.)

Berkhof, Louis. *Systematic Theology*. 4th ed. Grand Rapids: Eerdmans, 1941.

Bloesch, Donald. *Essentials of Evangelical Theology.* San Francisco: Harper and Row, 1978.

Bonhoeffer, Dietrich. *The Cost of Discipleship.* Rev. ed. Translated by R. H. Fuller. New York: Macmillan, 1959.

Documents of the Vatican II Council. "The Holy See, Archive, Constitutions," *www.vatican.va/archive/par_en.htm.* Vatican City: Roman Catholic Church, 1999.

Evans, William. *The Great Doctrines of the Bible.* 1912. Enlarged ed. with additions by S. Maxwell Coder. Chicago: Moody Press, 1974.

Fletcher, John. "An Essay on the Doctrine of the New Birth." *Asbury Theological Journal.* Spring 1998.

Feinberg, Charles L., ed. *The Fundamentals for Today.* Grand Rapids: Kregel Publications, 1958.

Harnack, Adolf. *What Is Christianity?* Translated by Thomas Bailey Saunders. Introduction by Rudolf Bultmann. New York: Harper and Row, 1957.

Hodge, Charles. *Systematic Theology.* 3 vols. 1892. Reprint, Grand Rapids: Eerdmans, 1986.

Rahner, Karl. *Foundations of Christian Faith: An Introduction to the Idea of Christianity.* Translated by William Dych. New York: Seabury Press, 1978.

Strong, Augustus. *Systematic Theology.* Old Tappan, NJ: Revell, 1907.

Theissen, Henry C. *Lectures in Systematic Theology.* 1949. Revised by Vernon D. Doerksen. Grand Rapids: Eerdmans, 1979.

3. Secondary Sources: Pentecostal History and Theology

Anderson, Robert Mapes. *Vision of the Disinherited: The Making of American Pentecostalism.* New York: Oxford University Press, 1979.

Bernard, David. *Understanding the Articles of Faith: An Examination of United Pentecostal Beliefs.* Hazelwood,

MO: Word Aflame Press, 1998.

Blumhofer, Edith W. *The Assemblies of God: A Chapter in the Story of American Pentecostalism.* 2 vols. Springfield, MO: Gospel Publishing House, 1989.

————. *The Assemblies of God: A Popular History.* Springfield, MO: Gospel Publishing House, 1985.

Bonner, William L. *My Father in the Gospel: Bishop R. C. Lawson.* By the author, n.d.

Burgess, Stanley M., Gary B. McGee, and Patrick H. Alexander, eds. *Dictionary of Pentecostal and Charismatic Movements.* Grand Rapids: Zondervan, 1988.

Clanton, Arthur L., and Charles E. Clanton. *United We Stand.* Jubilee ed. Hazelwood, MO: Word Aflame Press, 1995.

Cox, Harvey. *Fire from Heaven: The Rise of Pentecostal Spirituality and the Reshaping of Religion in the Twenty-first Century.* New York: Addison-Wesley, 1995.

Crane, Richard. *Pentecostal Handbook.* Rev. ed. By the author, 1989.

Dayton, Donald. *Theological Roots of Pentecostalism.* Peabody, MA: Hendrickson, 1987.

Foster, Fred J. *Their Story: 20th Century Pentecostals.* Rev. ed. Hazelwood, MO: Word Aflame Press, 1981.

French, Talmadge L. "Oneness Pentecostalism in Global Perspective: The Worldwide Growth and Organizational Expansion of the Oneness Pentecostal Movement in Historical and Theological Context." M.A. thesis, Wheaton College Graduate School, Wheaton, IL, 1998.

Gaxiola, Manuel J. *La Serpiente y la Paloma: Historia, Teología Análisis de la Iglesia Apostólica de la Fe en Cristo Jesús (1914-1994)* [*The Serpent and the Dove: Historical, Theological Analysis of the Apostolic Church of the Faith in Christ Jesus (1914-1994)*]. 2nd ed. Mexico: Libros Pyros, 1994.

Gill, Jeffrey, comp. *Papers Presented to the First Occasional Symposium on Aspects of the Oneness Pentecostal Move-*

ment. Harvard Divinity School, Cambridge, MA, 1984.

Goff, James R., Jr. *Fields White unto Harvest: Charles F. Parham and the Missionary Origins of Pentecostalism*. Fayetteville, AR: University of Arkansas Press, 1988.

Golder, Morris E. *History of the Pentecostal Assemblies of the World*. Indianapolis, IN: By the author, 1973.

————. *The Life and Works of Bishop Garfield Thomas Haywood (1880-1931)*. Indianapolis, IN: By the author, 1977.

Hall, J. L. "Contending for the Faith, Parts 1-9," *Pentecostal Herald*. November 1996 to September 1998. (To be published in book form. Hazelwood, MO: Word Aflame Press.)

Hamilton, Michael, ed. *The Charismatic Movement*. Grand Rapids: Eerdmans, 1977.

Harrell, David, Jr. *All Things Are Possible: The Healing and Charismatic Revivals in Modern America*. Bloomington, IN: Indiana University Press, 1975.

Hollenweger, Walter J. *The Pentecostals*. 3rd ed. Peabody, MA: Hendrickson, 1988.

————. *Pentecostalism: Origins and Developments Worldwide*. Peabody, MA: Hendrickson, 1997.

Hunt, Dave, and T. A. McMahon, *The Seduction of Christianity: Spiritual Discernment in the Last Days*. Eugene, OR: Harvest House Publishers, 1985.

Jones, Charles Edwin. *Black Holiness: A Guide to the Study of Black Participation in Wesleyan Perfectionistic and Glossolalic Pentecostal Movements*. Metuchen, NJ: Scarecrow Press, 1987.

————. *A Guide to the Study of the Pentecostal Movement*. American Theological Librarians Association Bibliography Series, no. 6. Metuchen, NJ: Scarecrow Press, 1983.

Land, Steven J. *Pentecostal Spirituality: A Passion for the Kingdom*. Sheffield, England: Sheffield Academic Press, 1994.

McConnell, D. R. *A Different Gospel: A Historical and*

Biblical Analysis of the Modern Faith Movement. Peabody, MA: Hendrickson, 1988.

Menzies, William. *Anointed to Serve: The Story of the Assemblies of God.* Springfield, MO: Gospel Publishing House, 1971.

Miller, Thomas William. *Canadian Pentecostals: A History of the Pentecostal Assemblies of Canada.* Mississauga, Ontario, Canada: Full Gospel Publishing House, 1994.

Quebedeaux, Richard. *The Charismatics: The Origins, Development and Significance of Neo-Pentecostalism.* New York: Doubleday, 1976.

Reed, David A. *Origins and Development of the Theology of Oneness Pentecostalism in the United States.* Ann Arbor, MI: University Microfilms International, 1978.

Sherrill, John L. *They Speak with Other Tongues.* New York: McGraw-Hill, 1964.

Smith, Harold B., ed. *Pentecostals from the Inside Out.* Wheaton, IL: Victor Books, 1990.

Society for Pentecostal Studies. *Affirming Diversity.* Papers presented at the 24th meeting of the Society for Pentecostal Studies, Wheaton College, Wheaton, IL, 1994.

———. *The Fivefold Gospel.* Papers presented at the 26th meeting of the Society for Pentecostal Studies, Patten College, Oakland, CA, 1997.

———. *Purity and Power: Revisioning the Holiness and Pentecostal/Charismatic Movements for the Twenty-First Century.* Papers presented at the 27th meeting of the Society for Pentecostal Studies in special session with the Wesleyan Theological Society, Church of God Theological Seminary, Cleveland, TN, 1998.

———. *Toward Healing Our Divisions: Reflecting on Pentecostal Diversity and Common Witness.* Papers presented at the 28th meeting of the Society for Pentecostal Studies, Evangel University, Springfield, MO, 1999.

Spellman, Robert C., ed. *Pentecostal Apostolic Fellowship*

Crusade Journal. June 1989.

Synan, Vinson. *The Holiness-Pentecostal Tradition.* Rev. ed. Grand Rapids: Eerdmans, 1997.

———. *In the Latter Days: The Outpouring of the Holy Spirit in the Twentieth Century.* Ann Arbor, MI: Servant Books, 1984.

———. *The Twentieth-Century Pentecostal Explosion: The Exciting Growth of Pentecostal Churches and Charismatic Renewal Movements.* Altamonte Springs, FL: Creation House, 1987.

———, ed. *Aspects of Pentecostal-Charismatic Origins.* Plainfield, NJ: Logos International, 1975.

Tyson, James L. *Before I Sleep: A Narrative and Photographic Biography of Bishop Garfield Thomas Haywood.* Indianapolis, IN: Pentecostal Publications, 1976.

———. *The Early Pentecostal Revival: History of Twentieth-Century Pentecostals and the Pentecostal Assemblies of the World, 1901-30.* Hazelwood, MO: Word Aflame Press, 1992.

4. Secondary Sources: General History and Theology

Barrett, David B. *World Christian Encyclopedia.* New York: Oxford University Press, 1982.

Boettner, Loraine. *Roman Catholicism.* Philadelphia: Presbyterian and Reformed, 1962.

Christian History. Volume 9, number 4. Issue 28: "The 100 Most Important Events in Church History."

Constantelos, Demetrios. *An Old Faith for Modern Man: The Greek Orthodox Church, Its History and Teachings.* 2nd ed. New York: Greek Orthodox Archdiocese, 1964.

Department of Commerce, Bureau of Census. *Religious Bodies: 1916.* Washington, D.C.: U.S. Government Printing Office, 1919.

———. *Religious Bodies: 1926.* Washington, D.C.: U.S.

Government Printing Office, 1929.

———. *Religious Bodies: 1936*. Washington, D.C.: U.S. Government Printing Office, 1941.

Dowley, Tim, et al., eds. *Eerdmans' Handbook to the History of the Church*. Grand Rapids: Eerdmans, 1977.

Elwell, Walter, ed. *Dictionary of Evangelical Theology*. Grand Rapids: Baker, 1984.

Gonzalez, Justo. *A History of Christian Thought*. 3 vols. Nashville: Abingdon, 1975.

Harvey, Van. *A Handbook of Theological Terms*. New York: Macmillan, 1964.

Heick, Otto. *A History of Christian Thought*. Philadelphia: Fortress, 1965.

Hunter, Preston D. *www.adherents.com*. Dallas, 1999.

Klotsche, E. H. *The History of Christian Doctrine*. Rev. ed. Grand Rapids: Baker, 1979.

Lane, Tony. *Harper's Concise Book of Christian Faith*. San Francisco: Harper and Row, 1984.

Latourette, Kenneth Scott. *A History of Christianity*. 2 vols. Rev. ed. San Francisco: Harper and Row, 1975.

Lindner, Eileen, ed., *Yearbook of American & Canadian Churches 1999*. Nashville: Abingdon, 1999.

Mead, Frank. *Handbook of Denominations in the United States*. 9th ed. Revised by Samuel Hill. Nashville: Abingdon, 1990.

Melton, J. Gordon. *The Encyclopedia of American Religions*. Wilmington, NC: McGrath, 1978.

Pelikan, Jaroslav. *The Christian Tradition: A History of the Development of Doctrine*. 5 vols. Chicago: University of Chicago Press, 1971-89.

Piepkorn, Arthur. *Profiles in Belief: The Religious Bodies of the United States and Canada*. 3 vols. San Francisco: Harper and Row, 1979.

Sweet, William. *The Story of Religion in America*. Grand Rapids: Baker, 1950.

Index

113-14, 122, 132, 140, 146, 160, 251, 335-37, 364-65
Paul, Jonathan, 141
Paul VI, Pope, 231, 286
Paulk, Earl, 294, 307, 309, 314
Pawson, David, 121, 300, 302, 343
Pemberton, Ben, 70, 90-91, 336
Penance, 240
Pentecostal Assemblies of Canada, 87-88, 92-93, 121, 142, 243, 266, 269, 335-39
Pentecostal Assemblies of Jesus Christ, 96, 98, 118-20
Pentecostal Assemblies of Newfoundland, 142
Pentecostal Assemblies of the World, 53, 65, 70, 90-91, 93-98, 104-5, 117-18, 150-51, 337, 339, 358-59
Pentecostal Church Incorporated, 96, 98, 118-20, 268, 337
Pentecostal Church of God, 139, 358
Pentecostal Church of Indonesia, 109, 359
Pentecostal Churches of the Apostolic Faith Association, 104
Pentecostal Evangel, 149
Pentecostal Fellowship of North America, 140, 159, 316
Pentecostal Free Will Baptist Church, 40

Pentecostal Holiness Church. *See* International Pentecostal Holiness Church
Pentecostal Methodist Church of Chile, 132, 143, 162
Pentecostal Ministerial Alliance, 96, 118, 337
Pentecostal Publishing House, 99
Pentecostal Testimony, 47, 50
Pentecostal/Charismatic Churches of North America, 140, 190, 316
Pentecostals, 9-163, 166, 189, 319-29, 198, 207-13, 217, 239, 242-44, 259-60, 269-79, 293, 296-99, 305, 315-17, 358-61
People of Destiny International, 294
People of Praise community, 286
Perfectionism, 10, 12, 113
Persecution, 36, 69-70, 101, 110, 239
Persia, 62, 91
Pethrus, Lewi, 141, 267
Philippines, 101, 109, 194, 303
Phillips, William T., 54, 106
Picton, Ontario, 92
Pietists, 155, 166
Pinson, M. M., 41, 72-73, 78, 80
Piux IX, Pope, 227
Piux XII, Pope, 228-29
Portland, OR, 35, 70
Positive Confession doctrine,

Rosa, Adolph, 31
Rowe, G. B., 91, 106
Rowe, Worthy, 106
Russia, 110, 246
Russian Orthodox Church, 246
Ryrie, Charles, 219-20

Sabbatarians, 106, 108, 109,
  268
Sabellianism, 77
Sacred name groups, 106
Salvation Army, 75, 336
Salvation, 15, 28-32, 48-53, 68,
  75, 105, 111-23, 127, 145,
  152, 160-61, 192-93, 207,
  217-18, 223-24, 232, 235,
  241, 302, 343-44, 352-53,
  356-57
San Antonio, TX, 14-15, 34, 268
Sanctification, 10-11, 16, 28, 35,
  39, 43-48, 55-56, 113, 125-
  31, 135-36. *See also* Holiness
Sanford, Agnes, 279, 282
Savelle, Jerry, 293
Schaeffer, Francis, 247
Schaeffer, Franky, 247
Schaepe, John, 65, 87, 90-91
Schell, William, 76
Schleiermacher, Friedrich, 167
School of the Prophets, 269
Schooler, A. R., 91
Schweitzer, Albert, 169
Scism, Ellis, 268, 372
Scofield, C. I., 205
Scopes Monkey Trial, 201-2

Scott, R. J., 63, 75
Scripture. *See* Bible
Seattle, WA, 109
Second Coming, 15-16, 111,
  152-53, 180, 204, 217, 297
Second Work groups, 53-54,
  105-6, 125-32, 147, 154-56
Secular theology, 187
Semple, Robert, 137
Serpent seed doctrine, 256
Seventh-day Adventists, 325
Sexuality, 136, 150, 189, 194,
  196-98, 222-23, 237-38
Seymour, William, 21-26, 29-35,
  38, 39, 46-47, 53, 66, 86-87,
  113-14, 146, 160, 336
Shakarian, Demos, 255, 276
Sharon Orphanage and Schools,
  266
Shearer, Harvey, 74, 75, 91
Shearer Schoolhouse, 41
Sheng, Chang Ling, 108
Shepherding movement, 254,
  310-11, 317
Sherrill, John and Elizabeth, 283
Shiloh United Church of Church
  Apostolic (Worldwide), 110
Simpson, A. B., 11, 138
Simpson, Charles, 294, 310
Sinclair, John C., 73, 139
Sinful nature, 10-11, 111, 168,
  172-73, 192, 207
Sipe, A. W. Richard, 238
Situation ethics, 187
Small, Frank, 65, 66-68, 74, 75,

Works by David K. Bernard:

Pentecostal Theology Series

Vol. 1: The Oneness of God*
Vol. 2: The New Birth*
Vol. 3: In Search of Holiness (with Loretta
    Bernard)*
Vol. 4: Practical Holiness
A Study Guide for The Oneness of God
A Study Guide for The New Birth
A Study Guide for In Search of Holiness
A Study Guide for Practical Holiness
    (Each volume can be purchased in hardback
    with Study Guide included)

Biblical Theology (Other)

A Handbook of Basic Doctrines*
Doctrines of the Bible (ed. with J. L. Hall)
In the Name of Jesus
Justification and the Holy Spirit
On Being Pentecostal (with Robin Johnston)
The Oneness View of Jesus Christ
Spiritual Gifts*
God's Infallible Word
Understanding God's Word

Practical Theology

The Apostolic Church in the Twenty-first Century
The Apostolic Life
Growing a Church
The Pentecostal Minister (ed. with J. L. Hall)

Commentaries

The Message of Colossians and Philemon
The Message of Romans

Booklets

Essential Doctrines of the Bible*
Essentials of Oneness Theology
Essentials of the New Birth*
Essentials of Holiness
Understanding the Articles of Faith
Bible Doctrines and Study Guide

Church History

A History of Christian Doctrine, Vol. 1:
    The Post-Apostolic Age to the Middle Ages
A History of Christian Doctrine, Vol. 2:
    The Reformation to the Holiness Movement
A History of Christian Doctrine, Vol. 3:
    The Twentieth Century
Oneness and Trinity, AD 100-300
The Trinitarian Controversy in the Fourth Century

CD

Pentecostal Digital Library, Vol. 1:
    Complete Works by David K. Bernard
Preaching the Apostolic Faith
Teaching the Apostolic Faith
Pentecostal Pulpit Series, Vol. 3:
    David K. Bernard (with audiovisual CD)
An Introduction to Apostolic Pentecostal
    Theology (4 books)

*Available in Spanish

Order from:
Pentecostal Publishing House
Call: 866.819.7667
E-mail: *pphsales@upci.org*
Or Visit: *www.pentecostalpublishinghouse.com*